THE CRIMINALIZATION OF ADDICTION

The US vs Gary Scott Hancock Case

**Written by G.D. Hancock, Ph.D.
Emerita Professor of Finance**

This case was heard in the *US Eastern District Court of Missouri*

AUTHOR BIOGRAPHY

G. D'Anne Hancock earned four degrees in finance and economics, including a Ph.D., and began her academic career at the *University of Missouri* in 1988. She earned tenure in 1994 and spent over three decades teaching and publishing in financial economics.

Her professional success was upended when her son, Scott, became addicted to opioids following a legitimate prescription at age 16. In 2019, he was arrested under *drug-induced homicide* laws and sentenced to 20 years in federal prison. Hancock retired early to investigate how the U.S. justice system handles addiction, leading to this book her deeply personal account of a system that punishes the vulnerable and silences the truth.

In 2019, Scott was arrested on a *Drug-Induced Homicide* (DIH) charge for sharing fentanyl with a co-addict who subsequently died from an overdose.

Traumatized and unable to perform the duties required by her position, she retired early from the *University* and began studying criminal drug law, the US judicial system, DIH cases, and medical evidence. This book summarizes what she learned about the criminalization of addiction in the U.S justice system.

*"Everything I thought I knew, and everything I was taught, about the US justice system is **false**; the truth is truly unbelievable."*

BOOK SYNOPSIS

The Story of G. Scott Hancock is a gut-wrenching, deeply personal account of a young man's descent into opioid dependence after a legitimate medical prescription and the shocking legal nightmare that followed. Scott, raised in a stable, successful family and armed with a degree in finance, was just 29 when he was arrested and sentenced to 20 years in federal prison under a Reagan-era law meant for drug dealers. His real "crime"? Sharing fentanyl with a friend who tragically overdosed.

Written by his parent, this book is more than a memoir. It's an urgent indictment of a system that punishes the sick and ignores the truth. You'll come away questioning everything you thought you knew about addiction, justice, and what it means to be guilty in America.

If you think it could never happen to someone in your family think again.

Chapters 1 and 2 provide a summary of Scott's childhood and the details of his opioid addiction, respectively. Chapter 3 discloses the record of the Department of Justice in combating drugs as well as the laws that underlie the charge of drug-induced homicide. Chapter 4 introduces medical evidence that demonstrates advanced opioid addicts cannot be dealers, even if they want to. Chapter 5 focuses on the culpability of the deceased and death by misadventure. Chapter 6 examines the consequences of denying the accused the right to due process and the implications of mandatory minimum sentencing. Chapter 7 discusses Scott's prosecution and the prevalence of prosecutorial misconduct. Finally, Scott authored Chapter 8 on prison life, except the *Prison Life for Family* section.

Chpt	Topics	Pg
1	Growing up in St. Louis, Grade School, Family	3
2	**The Making of a Fentanyl Addict**	**11**
	Family Changes	12
	Codependency	15
	The Arrest	17
	Sentencing Day	26
	Federal Prison	28
3	**The US Department of Justice (DOJ)**	**49**
	Department of Justice Structure	52
	Sources of Fentanyl	53
	Department of Justice Goals	55
	Legal Points at Issue	75
	Retribution vs Restorative Justice	80
4	**Opioid Addicts *Can't* be Dealers**...*even if they want to*	**88**
	Advanced Opioid Addiction	91
	Consequences of Advanced Opioid Addiction	96
	Medical Evidence	101
	Relapse	108
	A Drug Dealer's Life	110
5	**Culpability Matters**	**124**
	Self-Harm vs. Suicide	124
	US vs. Hancock	128
	Overdose Death is not Murder	132
	Levels of Culpability	133
6	**Motive & Mandatory Minimum Sentences**	**141**
	Motive Matters	142
	Mandatory Minimum Sentences	147
	Fifty DIH Convictions	167
7	**Prosecutorial Misconduct**	**177**
	Prosecutorial Power	178
	Regulation	188
	Scott's Prosecution	191
	Plea Deals	197
	The Criminalization of Addiction	202
8	**Prison Life**	**214**
	County Jail	216
	FCI Coleman-Medium	221
	USP Atlanta-Low	232
	Prison Life for Family	248

CHAPTER 1: INTRODUCTION

Drug addiction is a progressive *medical* disease that cannot be cured by punishing the sufferer. By criminalizing drugs, we have moved the person with a substance use disorder from the medical arena to the legal one. Rather than regulating drugs, instituting fines, or making misuse a misdemeanor punishable by going to a rehabilitation facility, the US imprisons addicts, sometimes for decades, in a maximum stress environment. Without treatment, the addict will continue their drug use in prison and when released, resume a life of drugs. The harsh US policies around drugs mark users as criminals and, thus, contribute to the overwhelming stigma against people contending with a debilitating and often fatal medical disorder. The criminalization of addiction has led to increased overdose deaths, increased rates of addiction, and reduced use of 911 calls to save lives.[1]

This book focuses on opioids and opioid derivatives, other illicit drugs were not studied or researched. Even so, much of the medical evidence is true for advanced addiction to methamphetamines.

Introduction
This is the story of my son, Gary *Scott* Hancock, who was raised in an upper-middle-class family and became addicted to opioids at age 16 or 17 after being prescribed OxyContin for painful kidney stones. By the time Scott graduated from college, he was hopelessly addicted to heroin and within a few years was actively seeking fentanyl as his drug of choice. On February 11th, 2019, Scott was arrested for *fentanyl distribution resulting in death,* and is serving a *mandatory minimum* sentence of 20 years in federal prison. This book is about Scott's struggles with addiction to opioids, his imprisonment by the US criminal justice system for sharing drugs with a friend who subsequently died of an accidental overdose, and what our family has learned about this country's treatment of addicts.

---

[1] Jakubowski, Andrea MD, Kunins, Hillary V. MD, Huxley-Reicher, Zina and Siegler, Anne (2018). Knowledge of the 911 Good Samaritan Law and 911-calling behavior of overdose witnesses. *Substance Abuse*, 39:2, 233, 238, DOI: 10.1080/08897077.2017.1387213

Throughout this book, issues surrounding motive, addiction, mandatory minimum sentencing, and prosecutorial misconduct are described as experienced by Scott, and his family. This book shows that critical constitutional rights are regularly violated or ignored in prosecuting *Drug-Induced Homicide* (DIH) cases (sometimes called *Drug Delivery Resulting in Death*).[2] One of the criteria for a DIH charge is the accused must be a dealer. Unfortunately, it was physically and mentally impossible for Scott to be a dealer, but that did not stop the prosecutor.

The harsh sentences imposed by Congress have triggered the academic, scientific, and health communities to question the cruelty of the judicial motive of a mandatory minimum sentence of 20 years, or more, for an accident. In the US vs. Gary *Scott* Hancock case, the right to a fair trial was skillfully denied, and additional charges were applied to force a guilty plea. More importantly, due process was denied by ignoring the *intent* of the defendant, as expressed by Scott regarding opioid withdrawal: *"I could not separate the physical pain from the world around me, and I lived, and I suffered. How could trying to help someone avoid this be so wrong? I really believed it* [giving drugs to a friend] *was an act of kindness."*

The purpose of this book is to bring attention to my son's case and to contribute to the voices calling for criminal justice reform. Scott is not alone; in 2020, 185,664 people were charged with a DIH crime, and 3,793,911 others were arrested for other drug crimes. My ultimate dream is that my son will be recognized as a person with an opioid addiction and *treated* for his addiction, rather than locked away as a criminal for a crime he was not capable of committing. He needs rehabilitation, not prison. Prison provides an environment of maximum stress; it is not natural for humans to live in cages and be separated from all friends, family, and companionship. A high-stress environment is the exact opposite of what the addict needs to learn to cope in a healthy, drug-free manner.

Since 2019, I have studied numerous aspects of opioid addiction and the US criminal justice system. What I have learned frightens me to my core, and my heart goes out to all inmates and their families who are needlessly caught in the US judicial web. The US justice system, starting with the police and ending with the judges, is not concerned with guilt or

---

[2] Throughout this book, DIH is used rather than DDRD because it is more commonly used in academic research.

innocence. As one attorney told us: *"No one cares about your son's guilt or innocence; that is not relevant to the procedure."* The police care about closing a case, prosecutors care about convicting someone, and the judge's role is perfunctory in cases involving mandatory minimum sentences. The real power in the criminal justice system lies with prosecutors, who enjoy *absolute immunity* for their actions, even illegal actions. Prosecutors can use lies, scams, and fraud without worry about recourse because there is none. Prosecutors have been known to feed information to news reporters to sway public opinion before jury selection, to lie in court about their evidence, and to coerce guilty pleas from the innocent. That is why the US, like Russia, has more than a 99% conviction rate in criminal drug cases.[3]

Chapters 1 and 2 provide a summary of Scott's childhood and the details of his opioid addiction, respectively. Chapter 3 discloses the record of the *Department of Justice* in combating addiction as well as the laws that underlie charges of *drug-induced homicide*. Chapter 4 introduces medical evidence that demonstrates advanced opioid addicts *cannot* be dealers. Chapter 5 focuses on the culpability of the deceased and *death by misadventure*. Chapter 6 examines the consequences of denying the accused the right to *due process* and the implications of mandatory minimum sentencing. Chapter 7 discusses Scott's prosecution and the prevalence of prosecutorial misconduct. Finally, Scott authored Chapter 8 on prison life.

Growing up in St. Louis

Gary *Scott* Hancock was born on December 9th, 1989, in St. Louis, MO, to parents aged 30 and 37. He was a full-term, healthy baby, weighing 7lbs 11oz and 21.5 inches long. His father's name is Gary, so we called our son

---

[3] Gramlich, John (2019, June 11). Only 2% of federal criminal defendants go to trial, and most who do are found guilty. *Pew Research Center.* https://www.pewresearch.org/fact-tank/2019/06/11/only-2-of-federal-criminal-defendants-go-to-trial-and-most-who-do-are-found-guilty/.

Scott to avoid confusion. I fell in love with Scott the instant he was born. He was such a sweet, good baby. He smiled, laughed, and played. He was not a baby who fussed or cried; he was perfect. He developed allergies and asthma as a toddler that plagued him throughout his childhood, but otherwise, he was healthy and active. When Scott was 2, his father and I divorced, I took custody of Scott, and Gary remained active in Scott's life. **Figure 1.1** below shows Scott playing in the sink on the left at 18 months old. In the center picture, he is running down the hall in our home with a visual of his dad working in the background. Scott is collecting Easter eggs at 2 years old in the image on the right, with me standing by.

Figure 1.1.   **Scott at 18 Months – 2 Years**

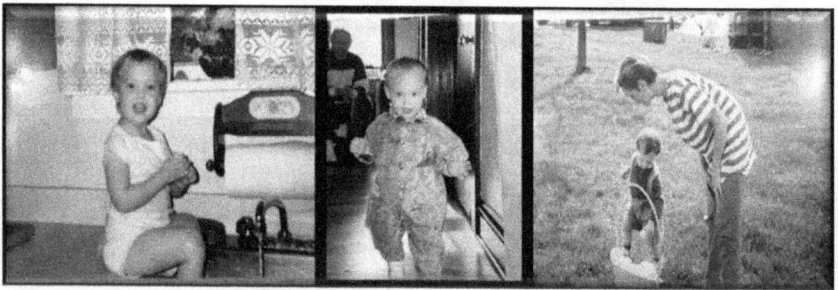

Since I had primary physical custody, I bought a home with a big backyard so we could begin our lives together. Gary was a good dad, spending lots of time with Scott, including playing sports and going fishing.

When Scott was 5, I married my current husband, Paul, and within 3 months, I was pregnant with Scott's sister, Valerie. It was time to move again; the house I bought for two would not work for four. We moved into a beautiful upper-middle-income neighborhood that I had always dreamed of for my kids! The house was large and spacious, with 5 bedrooms, 3½ bathrooms, a play area, and a finished basement that provided extra sleeping, dining, and TV options.

We soon settled into a familiar pattern for a dual-career family: nanny care for the baby and school for Scott. My position as a tenured finance professor allowed me the flexibility to be with my children during illnesses, medical appointments, sporting events, choir performances, etc. Scott and his dad enjoyed taking Tae Kwon Do together, fishing, and playing soccer during this time. There were rarely any quarrels about Scott seeing Gary because we all agreed to put Scott's needs first.

Grade School
Scott was six years old when his sister was born, and he wanted to take her to school for *show-n-tell*! How cute! So, when his sister was about six weeks old, we brought her to school, and Scott told stories about her to his teacher and classmates. There were many questions from the other kids, and Scott handled them well. I read a funny book to the kids, and we laughed together.

Figure 1.2 shows a school picture of Scott when he was 10 years old in 1999.

During the summers, we almost always traveled to Florida to visit with my father, brother, niece, and nephew. We all enjoyed the beach. We would walk along the coast, collect shells, and sometimes hermit crabs, too!

Like most families, we enjoyed celebrating all the major holidays together and tried to make each special. For example, July 4th celebrations were always fun because the weather was warm, and our neighborhood celebrated together. There were lots of hamburgers, hot dogs, ice cream, and soda! The kids and I would spend July 3rd decorating their bikes for the parade and picking out red, white, and blue outfits.

Figure 1.2. Scott (Age 10)

Figure 1.3 shows Scott at age 12 with his sister and our dog. Scott's early relationship with his sister was one of fascination and curiosity. Scott wanted to be a good big brother, so he spent time reading to her and playing with her. But he had been an only child for six years and was unsure how he felt about her intrusion into his life. Scott felt the shift in parental focus away from what had been 100% of our attention. Still, their relationship worked well until Scott was about 12 or 13 when sibling rivalry got the best of him. He began to compare himself to her and brag about his superiority, embarrassing her to make himself feel better.

Scott spent much of his boyhood with neighborhood friends—riding bikes, skateboarding, attending birthday parties, and ball games. He had plenty of friends and was a happy, amiable child. Scott continued his pattern of being a delightful child until he entered eighth grade. I do not know what happened, but my happy child was suddenly gone, and my once easy-going son was nowhere to be found. I never felt I could get a handle on everything going on in Scott's life because the time he spent with his father was a black hole. Communication with Gary was more than challenging; it was downright impossible. For example, as an explanation for being late to pick up Scott one day, he said there was a 50-car pile-up on the route, and he saw decapitated people. None of that was on the local news stations. These types of explanations for almost any question asked were the norm, making it difficult to know what was really going on.

Figure 1.3.   **Scott (Age 12)**

Regrettably, Paul, Gary, and I were all functioning alcoholics, meaning we all had demanding careers that we were able to maintain while drinking every night. My alcoholism progressed much more rapidly than either Paul's or Gary's, but thankfully, Paul and I were able to find the necessary help to stay sober. We wanted to be part of the solution for our kids, not part of the problem.

Alcoholism runs in the bloodlines on both sides of Scott's family, so I was hyper-aware that he (or my daughter) could develop alcoholism. Stupidly, the idea that he would become a drug addict never entered my mind because I was so focused on alcohol as the main family problem.

When Scott was in 8th grade, he transformed into a moody, quiet boy who wanted to live in the basement and play video games. At first, it was not too bad because Scott respected the time limits for video games. However, by the time he was in the 10th or 11th grade, video games had become an obsession, limits were ignored, and alcohol entered the scene.

By the time Scott was 15, he had started drinking despite all our warnings and his observations of the troubles caused by alcoholism. Interestingly, my daughter processed her exposure to alcoholism by staying as far away from drugs, and alcohol as possible, even as an adult. Paul and I put Scott in a youth program that helps young people get sober and set them on a better path. For more than a year, Scott did not drink, but he also did not interact much with friends. For the first time in his life, Scott was a recluse. He became more withdrawn than ever after the youth rehabilitation program and refused to speak about the program. I still do not know what to think about this experience.

Figure 1.4 shows two pictures of Scott at age 15.

Figure 1.4.   **Scott (Age 15)**

About a year after the *Cross-Roads* rehabilitation program, Scott started to drink again, HEAVILY. Unlike most alcoholics, Scott knew he had a problem, he just did not care. He said on more than one occasion, *"...so what if I am an alcoholic?"* The most crucial ingredient to sobriety and rehabilitation is the *desire* to stop drinking or using drugs. No rehabilitation program can help someone who does not want aid. It simply will not work. Scott did not want help. Period.

Family

On my side of the family, Scott has a grandfather[4] and an uncle who both live in Florida; his grandmother died before his birth. Close relationships never developed because of geography.

On Gary's side of the family, Scott's grandfather died when he was 3, and his grandmother remained in Colorado until her dog died four years later. Gary was an only child, so Scott had no aunts or uncles. After the dog died, *"Nana"* moved to St. Louis to be closer to her son and grandson. Sadly, her arrival had a substantial negative impact on the entire family dynamics. Growing up, she had a stepfather whom she hated. From that experience, she firmly believed that *all* stepparents were evil, and she freely shared her opinion with Scott, which damaged his relationship with his stepfather, Paul. Not long after her arrival, Nana began a campaign to discredit Paul and me in Scott's eyes because *she* wanted to raise Scott, with Gary's help, and wanted Paul and me to disappear.

Still blaming herself for losing a child during infancy, Nana was determined to make the most of her chance to 'raise' Scott. Every time Scott sneezed, she wanted him taken to the hospital. She would scream at Gary and tell Scott what a horrible mother I was for neglecting his health. Her tendency toward hovering over every little thing made Scott anxious about every change in his body. Nana was inclined to over-medicate Scott; she felt she knew more than the doctors. She attended doctors' appointments with Scott and Gary and would talk the doctors into prescribing what she believed he should have.

Not surprisingly, her refusal to respect our boundaries for Scott created endless problems. I went to visit her in hospice the day before she died. She only wanted to talk about Scott, and we did until I left. I thought how sad it was that she never mentioned her son, Gary.

Altogether, Scott's childhood was like most other children in our neighborhood, with good and bad times. We made mistakes as parents;

---

[4] Born 1932 and still going!

none of us were perfect, but we loved Scott with all our hearts and did our best to help him succeed.

A Word from Scott
My memory is not what it once was, but I still have many childhood memories. I remember our family trips to the beach and swimming with the dolphins. I remember getting chased by a barracuda and stepping on a stingray's tailbone. I also remember my uncle keeping me on a boat forever, and I got super seasick.

I used to love going on trips with my dad to fish for steelhead or salmon in Indiana. We always wore waders and would stand in the middle of the river with fly rods. I remember one time when I was young, the steelhead must have just spawned because they were so thick in the river they would run into our legs. I remember hooking one, and it jumped out of the water doing summersaults! I dropped my fly rod, ran to pick it up out of the mud, and it covered me in mud, jumping around so much! It bounced back into the river and took my fly rod with him...my dad was so pissed.

As for the bad stuff, there was that too. The bottom line is that my mom drank too much when I was young, my dad lied too much about everything, and my stepfather was always angry. Everyone in prison can point to bad stuff in their life and say, "That person fucked me up," but the reality is I am responsible for the decisions I made after I was an adult. That's on me.

I hope that this book will inform the public about the experience of an addict's life and the reality of the US criminal justice system. I hope you enjoy the book and learn something that will be helpful.

Summary
There is no definition for a 'normal' childhood, but we know that no one among us is a perfect parent because we are all human. We do not get to have perfect children; they are also human. Being human means making mistakes, sometimes mistakes that cut deep and last a lifetime.

Only the exceptionally strong can be honest about their mistakes, make amends, and move forward. If you are a parent, forgive yourself for your mistakes. Forgive your child for their mistakes and try to build a better future forged in close family ties.

CHAPTER 2: THE MAKING OF A FENTANYL ADDICT

Introduction
At age 16, and then again at 17, Scott had painful kidney stones and was prescribed OxyContin (an opioid), which soon became an addiction that plagued him throughout college and beyond. My ignorance about opioids meant that I missed the crucial early signs. I honestly thought he was doing better because his behavior on opioids in the early years was much better than his behavior on alcohol. I could tell he was not drinking, or at least not much; I remember feeling so pleased about that. Maybe my son would not let alcohol ruin his life!

Throughout high school, Scott gravitated toward the crowd drinking and smoking. No matter how hard we tried to create circumstances for him to befriend more stable young people, it did not work. He did not like the stable, confident kids; he wanted the party people. Scott decided to move in with his father halfway through his senior year of high school; he was tired of Paul, me, and our rules. Each time I walked into Scott's room at Gary's house to visit, it was stuffed full of empty beer cans under the bed and stacked all over every inch of furniture. I saw plenty of evidence of alcohol abuse, but I did not ever see any signs of drug abuse.

Figure 2.1 shows Scott at 18, holding his high school graduation diploma.

Figure 2.1.   **Scott (Age 18)**

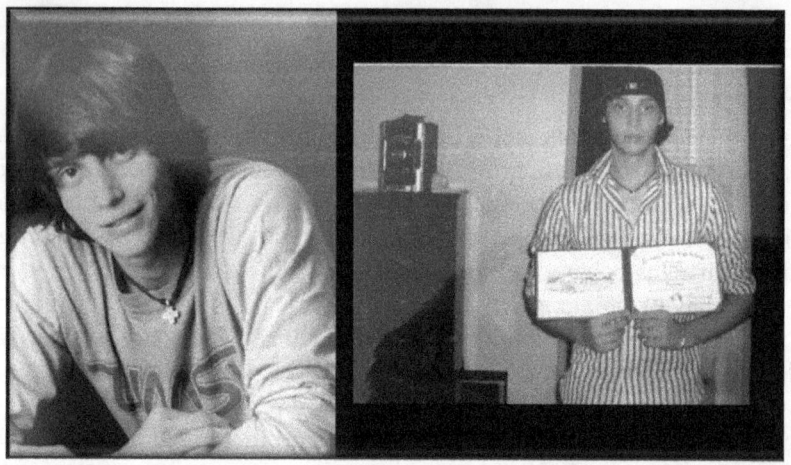

Despite my misgivings, upon graduating from high school at 18, Scott enrolled in the *University of Missouri* in 2008, majoring in business finance. We promised housing, food, tuition, and a car while he was in school, with the understanding that he would maintain passing grades throughout. He had to work for gas and any other spending money he needed. I did not believe Scott would finish his bachelor's degree, but I could not deny him the opportunity.

Family Changes
When Scott was about 19 years old, his beloved Nana died, and he was heartbroken. Scott was driving his car when his dad called and told him Nana had passed; it was the first time he had cried in many years. He had visited her just a few days earlier in hospice and couldn't believe she was now gone.

Scott would soon face several other significant changes. Gary remarried a year after his mother's death and moved to Albuquerque, NM. Scott moved back in with us so that he could complete his education. The geographical distance from his dad made it impossible for Scott to have the same kind of relationship with his dad. Gary grew embarrassed by Scott's lack of control and lack of ambition or success. His wife's three adult children were thriving, independent, interesting adults; what could Gary say about his son?

We tried to continue 'normal' family activities during the holidays and vacations. **Figure 2.2** shows Scott at age 23 on the left in a London pub near our rented apartment during a 2013 vacation. We were tourists for about a week and crammed in as much as possible. The middle picture shows Scott and Valerie eating at a pub during a long day of sightseeing. On the right, Scott is in one of the carriages of the *Eye of London*.

Figure 2.2.   **Scott (2013) London**

About a year later, on December 20th, 2014, Scott graduated from the *University of Missouri* with a bachelor's degree in business finance. It had been a 6.5-year, exhausting, expensive struggle, but he completed the program despite his growing dependence on opioids. **Figure 2.3** shows Scott in his college graduation picture just after he turned 25. Scott landed his post-graduation dream job with Paul's help. We were excited and hoped this would be his chance to succeed and turn his life around. Based on his new salary, Scott moved out of our home, rented a respectable apartment, and bought a new car. After only a few weeks, Scott lost the job due to 'lack of performance.' After this blow, Scott deteriorated rapidly; nothing seemed to slow his slide. He lost his apartment, totaled his car, and now had nothing. Scott finally agreed to enter a second 'sort of' rehab program. It was 'sort of'' rehab because it allowed the participants to stay home and go to the rehab facility every day. Since he no longer lived in our house, we never knew the extent of Scott's dedication to the program. With hindsight, I realized he was going to an outpatient medication facility to obtain *suboxone*.

At the time, I was hounding Scott about what he had learned that day at the facility, who he met, etc. I was utterly wrong about the program. *Suboxone* is a medication that combines buprenorphine and naloxone to treat opioid addiction. It lowers the risk of fatal overdoses by approximately 50%. It also reduces the risk of nonfatal overdoses, which are traumatic and medically dangerous. Suboxone works by tightly binding to the same receptors in the brain as other opiates, such as heroin, morphine, and fentanyl. By doing so, it blunts intoxication from opioids, prevents cravings, and allows many people to transition from a life of addiction to a life of normalcy and safety.[5] Health professionals often prescribe suboxone for advanced opioid addicts for the remainder of their lives.

After losing his apartment, Scott asked to move home, but we declined as his behavior had become so offensive that we could not take it anymore, or so we thought. There was no helping Scott to recover because *he did not want to*. Scott stayed with various friends until he had exhausted his welcome due to his advanced opioid addiction and lack of money. Within a year of moving out, Scott was homeless and had begun to surround himself with other addicts to reduce the risk of facing the dreaded withdrawal. Advanced opioid addicts fear nothing more than withdrawal. It is an *excruciatingly* painful experience that lasts for months and terrifies those who have an opioid addiction. For people with an addiction, forming a *safe group* is a reliable strategy for reducing the risk of withdrawal. The way it works is that when one addict is out of heroin or fentanyl, another addict in the safe group will sell to them, with the expectation that the favor will be returned when the need arises; and it always does.

---

[5] Grinspoon, Peter MD (2021). Five Myths about how to Treat Opiate Addiction. *Harvard Health Publishing, Harvard Medical School*, Oct. 7.
https://www.health.harvard.edu/blog/5-myths-about-using-suboxone-to-treat-opiate-addiction-2018032014496

Figure 2.3.   Graduation

University of Missouri-2014

This type of sharing among a group of opioid addicts is common because it reduces the high risk of withdrawal.

Codependency

I do not know where Scott lived then; he moved around quite a bit. Plus, communication was at an all-time low because Scott was still furious with me for not letting him move back home. Scott broke into our home by smashing a basement window to steal money and any marketable drugs. For about nine months, we refused to speak to each other; I had no desire to talk to him, and he had no desire to speak to me. Still, I was heartbroken and missed him every day, but I could not take it anymore. I slowly realized I did not miss the Scott of 'today'; I missed my sweet little guy…the person he once was. Then, out of the blue, he called me in desperation while I was driving home after visiting family in Florida. I heard his voice and listened to his story, which touched my heart. He had nowhere to go; he was hungry and tired, with no place to sleep--the shelters would not take him since he had no wife or children. It would take several years to recognize this event as a significant trigger for my *codependent* behavior.

Codependency is learned behavior passed down from one generation to the next. It is an emotional and behavioral condition that affects an individual's ability to have a healthy, mutually satisfying relationship. It is also known as *relationship addiction* because people with codependency often form or maintain relationships that are one-sided, emotionally destructive, and abusive. My relationship with Scott was all those things. I gave, Scott took, and he would get angry if he could not get more and then more. It was a mistake to rescue him from homelessness or buy groceries for him, pay his bills, etc. He threatened to withhold his love if I did not play the game. The best response would have been to do what was best for both of us: let Scott go his own way regardless of the consequences or emotional blackmail. I should have said, *"So be it."* Instead of doing what was best for him (and me), I was hurting him by not teaching him healthy boundaries and not allowing him to experience the consequences of his actions. *Mental Health America* says codependent behavior is learned by watching and imitating other family members who display this type of behavior.

Instead of walking away, Paul and I discussed Scott's dilemma for the remainder of the trip home. We debated whether we *should* help Scott and, if so, how. We knew we did not want him living with us, but we simply could not bear him being homeless. Too many dangerous things could happen that may result in his death. If anything had happened to him, the guilt would be unbearable. I believed I *had* to find a way to help him. Even so, it would be intolerable to have Scott living with us because he was completely unmanageable, rash, and self-absorbed. In addition, Scott took zero responsibility for his actions (or lack of actions); everything was always someone else's fault, never his. He would not work, would not help around the house, and focused only on what he could get from our relationship while simultaneously blaming me for his problems.

We bought an inexpensive house in a low-income neighborhood to 'fix' the terrible situation. He could live there for three months without rent or utility bills while searching for a job. He found a job waiting tables that he could easily travel to by bus. The job lasted for a while, but Scott never paid for rent or utilities, not once. Scott spent all his money on drugs and alcohol. He always seemed to have enough for those but never for anything else.

The 'mild' stage of Scott's opioid addiction began to disappear as he progressed from prescription pills to heroin. He said, *"I first tried heroin by snorting or taking pills and graduated to injecting about a year after that at age 27. Not long after that, I started injecting fentanyl. Sadly, my good friend CP did the injection for me, and less than a year later, he died of an overdose."*

Scott floated from job to job, rarely working at one place for more than a few months. This pattern continued until the day he was arrested. One could tell by looking at Scott that he was close to death at the time the DEA arrested him. I had spent the past year lying awake at night, waiting for the dreaded overdose call. We got at least four such calls that year-- dashing to the emergency room each time, hoping for the best. And each time, my son survived, barely. After the first emergency room experience, I could no longer deny that Scott had a major drug problem well beyond alcohol. His arms and legs had needle punctures all over, bruises surrounded the needle marks, and his bones showed through his emaciated body. Ignoring what I saw was not a choice because it was in full color. My son was dying, and I was helpless to save him.

The Arrest
On February 11th, 2019, Scott, now 29 years old, had lunch with me, and then we went to the grocery store to buy food for his house. It was a miserable day for me. Scott was not in his right mind, and I suspected he was on multiple drugs. His life was a total mess. He couldn't keep a job, and he still had no car. He never had the money for bills or rent. I was excited about a long-term treatment program in Colorado called *Stout Street* and was looking forward to talking to him about voluntarily going. Scott was long past the age we could force him into a rehab facility, but maybe he would be open to the *Stout Street* program. As soon as he walked through the door, it was painfully obvious that talking would be pointless.

The Criminalization of Addiction

Scott was talking nonsense when he told me he thought he might have a solution for getting rid of his undesirable roommate, JA. Scott said the 'police' had been calling him, but he didn't answer because he thought they were calling about a neighbor's complaint against JA.[6] Scott said the police detectives might be at the house waiting when he got home, and sure enough, two black cars were parked in front of the house. I hugged my son, and he got out of the vehicle. I did not know that would be our last hug for almost three long years. After sitting a moment, I exited the car because the situation made me uneasy. There were two men in each vehicle, and they introduced themselves to me as *Drug Enforcement Agency* (DEA) agents. Fear and dread struck immediately because, at this point, I knew my son was on all kinds of drugs.

One of the DEA officers spoke with me while Scott talked with the other officers. The officer who spoke to me was very polite, and we chatted about nothing in particular. There were no raised voices, no handcuffs, no guns, and no reason for concern, but I was still very uneasy and scared for my son. After about 10 minutes, Scott said he had to leave with them to give them some information about JA. I watched Scott get in the first black car and noted nothing *seemed* wrong, but the whole scene left me troubled. At about 6:30 pm, someone from the DEA called and asked me to pick up Scott's personal items. I was confused.

Me: *"Why can't Scott pick up his items?"*
Agent: *"He is not here."*
Me: *"Did he leave some things when he left earlier?"*
Agent: *"Your son is under arrest."*

My heart dropped as my fears were confirmed. Even though I was 99% certain the charge would be possession of some drug. I still needed confirmation.

Me: *"What was my son charged with?"*
Agent: *"I'm sorry we can't tell you the charge."*
Me: *"Why not? I'm his mother. Has he been charged with possession?"*

---

[6] As it turned out, the 'police' were DEA agents.

The Criminalization of Addiction

Agent: *"Ma'am, I'm sorry, but I cannot tell you the charge. Call back tomorrow, and maybe we can tell you. But if not, don't worry. The charge must be made public within three days."*

Click.

Three days can seem like forever when your child is facing a potentially severe unknown criminal charge. Not knowing what the sentence would be for possession of whatever drugs they found; I was sure it would mean more than a year behind bars. I called back the very next morning, hoping to hear something different from someone different. It was different, but not what I imagined. This time, the agent said my son had *requested* they not tell me the charge because he wanted to divulge the information himself – except he was not allowed to call me, and I was not allowed to contact him. Finally, after waiting three agonizing days, I was told Scott was charged under a 1986 law for the *distribution of fentanyl, resulting in death*; the common name for the charge is *Drug-Induced Homicide* (DIH). I was frozen, unable to think or move; I couldn't even ask questions, but the agent told me Scott would be going away for a long time. What did they just say? A Death? What does that mean? Weeks later, after crying my heart out, closed in my closet, I began to *try* to grasp what was happening: *What did he do? What is a DIH,* and *which 1986 law are they referencing?*

What did he do?
Scott shared fentanyl with another person with a fentanyl addiction, TG, in his safe group, who subsequently died from an overdose.

Scott knew TG through a new friend of his, KT, whom he met during his third rehab stay. KT was a fentanyl addict and introduced Scott to the drug while he was in rehab for alcohol and heroin abuse. I do not blame KT or the rehab facility for Scott's fentanyl addiction because I have learned that no outside force, including prison, can stop an addict unless or until the addict wants to get better. Scott still showed no signs or indications of wanting help—just the opposite. It was only a matter of time before Scott built additional *tolerance* to heroin, which would have necessitated graduating to fentanyl at some point anyway. *Tolerance* is the development of resistance to a drug through consistent use, which creates the need for more and stronger doses to achieve the same high.

In the summer of 2018, KT's parents sent her to a long-term treatment facility. Before leaving, she asked Scott to "take care" of her friend, TG, while she was away. At first, Scott was okay with it: TG called, but not very often, to ask for a small quantity of fentanyl pills. He would ask his group if they had any for her; usually, someone did. Other times, Scott went outside the group to find a dealer. As her addiction progressed, her requests became more frequent and demanding, and he grew tired of getting drugs for her. Scott had started dating someone else and had lost interest in keeping his word to KT. He eventually told TG to find someone else because there was nothing in it for him, and it was a hassle. She said she feared other people because KT told her to be very careful about meeting someone she did not know. After a few weeks, Scott told TG he didn't want to do this anymore and asked her to find someone else. Scott relented when she called again but began to build resentment about *"having"* to do this for her. He planned to talk to her again about finding someone who is a dealer, but that conversation did not happen before TG snorted two capsules of fentanyl and died of an overdose at age 19. What a tragic loss; her family will likely never stop grieving her death. TG was one of 67,367 people who died of a drug overdose in 2018—all heartbreaking losses. When you expand the number who died by adding the number of friends, family, coworkers, and others whose lives have been affected, there were at least 1 million people directly impacted by overdose deaths in 2018.

TG texted Scott the day before her death on October 19th, 2018, to request five *beans* of fentanyl. 'Bean' is the word used to describe a capsule, ideally filled with fentanyl and dormant material. The street names for fentanyl include Apache, China Girl, Dance Fever, Murder 8, and King Ivory, to name a few. Regardless of the name, the beans can be filled with almost anything and present the initial risk of death for unsuspecting addicts.

Scott called his usual drug dealer, BZ, who arrived shortly and made the fentanyl capsules at Scott's house. BZ gave Scott 3 pills to try—he *injected* himself with three beans of fentanyl to test its strength. It was stronger than expected, and he texted TG a warning. When TG arrived, BZ gave Scott 5 pills, which he took to her car and received $20 in return. He gave the $20 to BZ and bought another 25 pills for himself.

Injecting three beans of fentanyl and surviving indicates that Scott had an extremely high tolerance level.

DO NOT TRY THIS. Scott only survived because he had an abnormally high tolerance to opioids from extended use. That amount of fentanyl *is lethal* for anyone with no or low tolerance to opioids. **Figure 2.4** shows a fatal dose of heroin on the left versus fentanyl on the right. Notice that it takes only a few salt-sized grains of fentanyl to kill a 200-pound adult male, according to the *New Hampshire State Police*. Any measuring error can be deadly.

Figure 2.4.   Deadly Doses of Heroin and Fentanyl

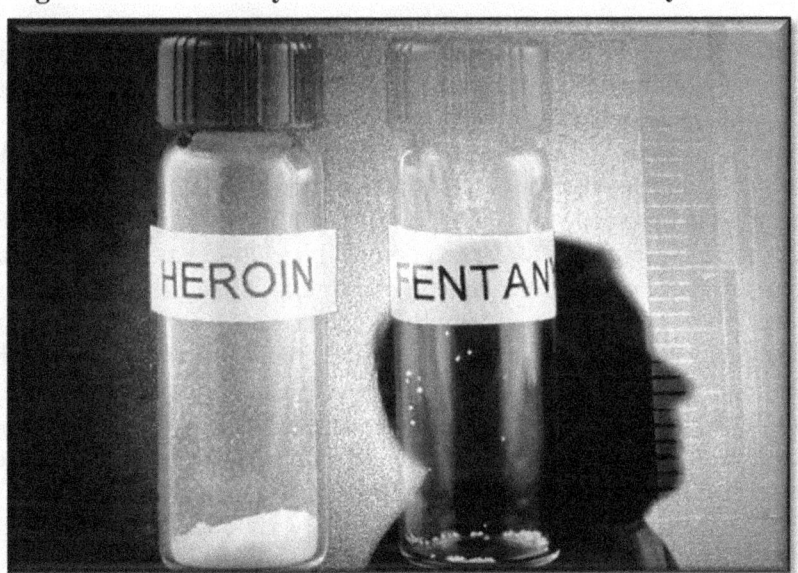

<u>Source</u>: *New Hampshire State Police Forensic Lab*

Scott warned TG again, in person, that the fentanyl was more potent than usual. TG feared going through withdrawal and was desperate for her family not to see her that way because then they would know she had not been drug-free. Thus motivated, TG insisted on the fentanyl and drove 25 miles to Scott's house to pick up the five beans in exchange for $20, which Scott gave to his dealer, BZ. According to police records, TG returned home and *snorted two* beans of fentanyl. Her Aunt found TG deceased the following day, and the coroner ruled she died from a fentanyl overdose.

TG's father called the DEA and shared relevant text messages he had stumbled across in her iCloud. The DEA responded by supposedly launching an investigation. The 'investigation,' however, only centered on Scott because TG's family blamed him for their daughter's death. Neither the DEA nor the prosecutor made any attempt to find BZ, who sold the pills to Scott, even though text messages made clear that Scott had contacted him for the fentanyl. It is clear TG had a much lower tolerance to fentanyl than Scott; TG snorted two pills, and Scott injected three pills. Snorting is a less dangerous route of experiencing fentanyl than injection, yet Scott survived, and TG did not. She was one of the thousands of young lives that are destroyed every year by advanced opioids such as heroin and fentanyl, as are their families.

After arresting him for TG's death, the DEA expressed their presumption of Scott's guilt by telling him that he would not be seeing the light of day for a long, long time. He was subjected to hours and hours of interrogation while he was still high on a combination of fentanyl, clonazepam, marijuana, methamphetamine, and crack cocaine. The video recording of the interrogation made clear that Scott was on mind-altering substances. According to the prosecutor, Scott admitted his guilt on tape. However, the tape's audio did not reveal an admission of guilt. Instead, the tape showed a strung-out, exhausted man who had no idea what he was saying to the group of agents badgering him in loud voices, putting words in his mouth; their interest was in coercing a confession. The goal was *not* to learn the truth of the crime; the goal was to extract a confession. No one makes an *honest* effort to extract information by talking to someone who is strung out on multiple drugs. The DEA did this because they can. They did this because there were no consequences. They did this to justify their extensive resources.

Scott asked for a drug test, and the agents denied his request. Then he was put in jail, where he began the long, painful process of withdrawal from fentanyl. The psychological withdrawal takes much longer than the tortuous physical withdrawal; it can last a lifetime. While my son was in physical withdrawal, he was denied medical care, was coerced to sign a *Plea Deal* admitting his guilt and was expected to understand a wide array of complex legal terms. Coercing plea deals is so obviously wrong that it speaks for itself. It seems like it should be illegal; maybe it is. The bottom line is that coercing guilty pleas by bullying those unable to defend themselves is standard practice.

What are DIH Laws?

I was mostly ignorant of the US criminal justice system beyond what I was taught in my freshman year (*common knowledge*) or heard about in the news – the topic was not particularly interesting, so those courses were never taken. It took almost a year to recover from the shock of what was happening to my son; I simply could **not** accept or believe it. A tragedy of this magnitude only happens to others; how could this be happening to us?

Eventually, there was no choice but to accept my son's dire situation. I started studying the law and medical evidence regarding opioid addiction. The research revealed some terrifying things about DIH laws:

1) *Strict liability* applies. Strict liability exists when a defendant is liable for committing an action, regardless of their intent or mental state when committing the act. Strict liability means motive, an essential part of *Due Process*, does not matter.

2) The charge only applies to *dealers,* not users.

3) The DOJ would impose a *mandatory minimum* sentence of 20 years to life if convicted.

Clinging to the provision that "*...the charge is only applied to dealers*" allowed hope because I knew it would be impossible to prove that Scott was a dealer; he didn't even have a car for transportation. I later learned the DEA and prosecutor knew Scott was not a dealer. After TG's death, the DEA put Scott under surveillance for four months to build a case against him as a dealer. They never succeeded in catching him acting as a dealer, so they arrested him without evidence.

One of the many things I learned while enduring this trauma with my son is that no one in the judicial apparatus cares about guilt or innocence—not Scott's lawyer, not the prosecutor, and not the judge. Not one person *ever* asked Scott for his side of the story; he was automatically assumed guilty upon arrest. It was the strangest feeling to finally realize that *it does not matter* that a loved one is innocent of the crime charged because *no one cares*. How do you fight that?

My son is certainly not innocent of *all* wrongdoing, but he *is* innocent of being a dealer. It is common for loved ones to hang onto any shred of hope, no matter how small. Our family, including Scott, was inexperienced with the legal system. We thought guilt or innocence mattered to everyone, from the DEA to the prosecutor to the judge and the defense. We also considered the judge to be the ultimate authority. Being uninformed about the system's power structure, we made many mistakes. Until the gavel came down, I did not *really* believe that Scott would be sentenced to 20 years for an accidental overdose, particularly given the culpability of the deceased and the fact he was not a dealer. Plus, Scott had no previous record of wrongdoing, and no weapons were involved in the crime. I knew in my heart that these things would mitigate the sentence. They didn't. Mitigating the sentence is impossible when the crime has a *mandatory minimum;* not even the judge can change that reality—only the prosecutor can. The judge sentenced Scott on April 28th, 2021, to the required minimum sentence of 20 years in federal prison. His time in the county jail counted towards his 20-year sentence, so Scott had 17½ years remaining, possibly serving only 14½ more years with good behavior.[7]

The reality of the US criminal justice system is so far removed from what is taught in schools that the only word for the lessons is *propaganda*. The US does not come close to honoring the *Constitution* when it comes to criminal drug cases. I have only studied criminal drug cases, so this observation may or may not be true of *all* criminal cases. For example, in my son's case:

1) He was **assumed *guilty***, until proven ***guiltier***. It is a cardinal principle of our justice system that every person accused of a crime is presumed innocent unless and until their guilt is established beyond a reasonable doubt. The principle of 'innocent until proven guilty' was formally established in 1894 by the *US vs. Coffin* case. If you were to ask, most Americans would automatically say that the accused is presumed innocent until

---

[7] In the Federal prison system there is no parole, but with good behavior the inmate can serve 85% of their sentence. A 20-year sentence means 17 years in prison if you have zero shots the entire time.

proven guilty. Nothing could be further from the truth. Upon arrest, you are assumed guilty; otherwise, why would they arrest you? This attitude follows through the entire judicial community *and to the public*. The day after Scott's arrest, the local papers had already assumed his guilt and passed that information along to the public as fact.

There was **no right to a trial**, fair or otherwise. Instead, the prosecution skillfully denied a trial by creating two *additional* felony charges out of thin air, with each charge subject to a mandatory minimum of 20 years. The prosecutor did this to force Scott to plead guilty to the initial charge, even though he was now under duress and still incompetent to understand everything happening to him. If he did not agree to plead guilty, he would be facing THREE felony counts, each with a mandatory minimum sentence of 20 years, for a total of 60 years in prison! According to *Pew Research Foundation*, only 2% of federal defendants go to trial, and most who do are found guilty.[8] Plea deals cover the remaining 98% of defendants and are considered *golden* wins by the prosecutors because they avoid costly trials. Clearly, Scott is not alone in being forced to take a plea deal.

Of the 2% of defendants that go to trial, only 1% (or 0.02%) win their cases. The statistics imply that prosecutors win federal drug cases **99.98%** of the time! It is a travesty, proof beyond a reasonable doubt that the US system of so-called justice is not.

By subverting a defendant's right to a trial, prosecutors adeptly avoid the *competency* issue that often arises with drug users. Theoretically, defendants cannot be convicted of a crime if they are not mentally competent to stand trial, as this would violate constitutional protections for defendants by denying them the right to a fair trial. *Competent to stand trial* means the defendant understands the proceedings and can play a role in their defense.

---

[8]Gramlich, John (2019, June 11). Only 2% of federal criminal defendants go to trial, and most who do are found guilty. *Pew Research Center*. https://www.pewresearch.org/fact-tank/2019/06/11/only-2-of-federal-criminal-defendants-go-to-trial-and-most-who-do-are-found-guilty/.

However, those protections are irrelevant when only 2% of defendants go to trial.

I struggled with how to advise my son. Should I recommend he plead *guilty* to the initial charge to avoid going to trial for the two newly created charges? What were the chances Scott would win two federal trials with three felony charges? Statistically speaking, his chances were insignificantly different from zero.

2) **Motive does not matter** in strict liability cases, such as DIHs. Motive and due process are ignored. The US Constitution *guarantees* due process under the Fifth and Fourteenth Amendments. Yet Congress decided to eliminate those 'guaranteed' rights for those charged with certain drug crimes. Scott was (is) an addict who knew the pain of withdrawal. As such, he was motivated by empathy towards TG and his word to KT, not by cruel, negligent, or murderous intentions. An accidental overdose is not murder, and the primary culprit is the deceased.

3) **Prosecutors do not have to follow the law,** and Scott's prosecutor did not. One might think it is illegal to create two additional felonies out of thin air. It may be, but it does not matter because there are no checks on prosecutorial ethics or power.

Sentencing Day

While Scott awaited sentencing, the *Federal Bureau of Prisons* (BOP) housed him in a local county jail in Illinois, about 90 miles from our home in St. Louis. I visited Scott every week until COVID-19 hit. Inside the jail were only five visitation stalls, each with a thick pane of glass separating the inmate from the visitor. Each side was equipped with a 'telephone' that we used to communicate. The phone cords were barely long enough to bring the phone to your ear and mouth. Inmates were never allowed to hug or touch their visitors. I was so nervous on my first visit, having no idea what to expect. The officer in charge that day announced a long list of items that were not permitted. Even visitors' clothing would be examined to ensure it met the guidelines. After arriving at the jail, visitors gathered in a waiting room to get in line for their turn to enter. There were only five visitation booths, so the number of families able to visit was limited. If you were number 6, you would have to wait until the second group of 5 was called, usually about 30-40 minutes later. I always got there early to be in the first group.

Then COVID-19 hit, and jails and prisons nationwide began closing their doors to visitors. The sheriff discontinued visits to the county jail in March 2020, and I had no idea when I would see my son again. It was three months before visits were allowed again. I was so grateful we could still talk on the phone and by email. We were finally allowed to visit again, which only lasted a few weeks before another COVID-19 shutdown. For over two years, prisons and jails continued to shut down and reopen in response to each outbreak. Visitation with Scott was sporadic at best. I learned to call before I left to visit to make sure they were accepting visitors. **Figure 2.5** shows Scott after 18 months in county jail.

Figure 2.5.   Scott (Age 30)

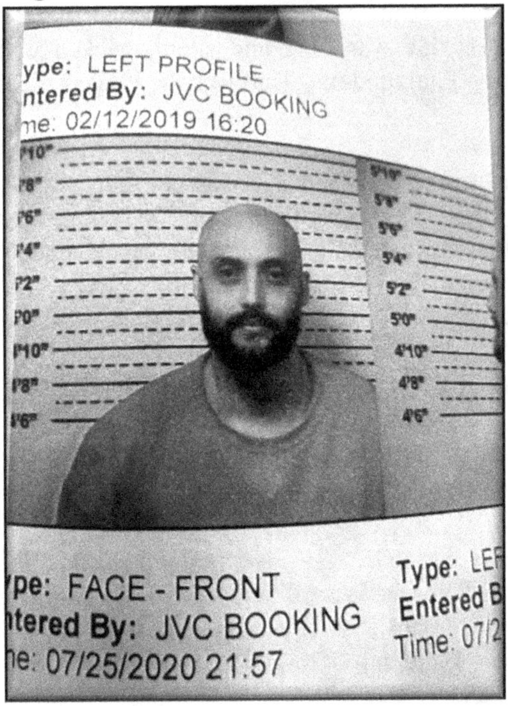

County Jail, Illinois (7/25/2020)

Scott was finally sentenced on April 28th, 2021, after two years, two months, and 17 days of waiting in jail. Through Scott's attorney, the prosecutor strongly discouraged me and Paul from attending the sentencing, but we went anyway; Scott had no one else. I refused to let the prosecutor bully us into leaving my son all by himself at such a critical time. Walking into the courtroom, Paul and I were shaken to see a room packed with the deceased's family and friends. The court attendant asked us to sit in the jury box since there was nowhere else to sit or stand. Both the deceased's mother and father were allowed to speak on their daughter's behalf; it was beyond heart-wrenching. Paul and I were prohibited from saying anything on our son's behalf. We sat alone with our thoughts, holding hands tightly. Throughout the entire time, a woman in the back of the courtroom stared daggers through us as if we had murdered TG with our bare hands. The prosecutor spoke after TG's mother and father, and the judge said, *"20 years in federal prison,"* and the gavel came down. We sat there knowing parole does not exist in the federal prison system.[9] We were all on the 13th floor of the courthouse and needed to get to the lobby to exit. The elevator ride was long and silent, packed with some of the deceased's family, Paul, and me. That was the longest elevator ride of my entire life!

Before we went to the courthouse, I was painfully aware that a 20-year sentence was most likely coming. Still, my hopes and heart were irreparably shattered when the gavel came down and made it an undeniable reality. I felt a great injustice had been done, and I felt, and still feel, helpless to stop it.

Federal Prison
Approximately five weeks passed before Scott was moved from the jail to a federal holding facility. About the move, he said, *"I was taken to Scott AFB* (Air Force Base), *then transported by bus to Kentucky. Then, I was brought back to Scott AFB and transported by plane to Oklahoma for processing. Then the BOP sent me to FCI Coleman Medium security prison in Florida."* For the second time since Scott was arrested, we could not communicate. Instead of three days, it lasted more than four long weeks this time. I did not know where my son was being held, his

---

[9] Federal inmates serve 85% of their sentence unless their behavior is unacceptable while incarcerated. Guards give 'shots' when behavior is unacceptable and severe shots can result in the inmate serving his full sentence.

condition, or how he was being treated...only that it was not good. He was not allowed to make phone calls, and it seemed I was in a frozen stasis for eternity, waiting until he could call. Unbelievably, I longed for my son to be in that county jail with known rules and procedures.

I finally received a phone call from my son and sank to my knees in relief. I have never been so happy to hear anyone's voice and clung to every word. He told me he was in a *medium-security* federal prison in Coleman, Florida, and we could only talk for 10 minutes. It seemed like 10 seconds, but I was grateful for the time we had.

The BOP houses inmates at five prison security levels. These include *minimum* (also called *camp*), *low*, *medium*, *high*, and *administrative* (also called *supermax*). A scoring system determines an inmate's security level. Approximately 21 factors are scored, and prisoners hope for the lowest possible score. The BOP factors include the current crime, age, education, previous criminal history, severity of offense(s), history of escapes, etc. Each offense or indicator is assigned a point value. After the BOP evaluates all factors, the numerical values are summed to determine the inmate's placement in a camp, low, medium, or high-security prison. Inmates who score 0-11 points will start in a minimum (camp) security prison unless they have more than ten years remaining on their sentence. Scores between 12 and 15 earn a low-security prison, while those between 16 and 23 are sent to a medium-security prison.[10]

Scott received 14 points for his crime, 4 for his age (29), and 0 for all other factors. With 18 points, Scott was sent to a medium-security prison. Any wrongdoing in prison can add more points to the total and may result in being moved to a higher security level prison.

Visiting the Coleman *Federal Correctional Complex* (FCC) was much different than visiting the county jail. First, there was the culture shock. Instead of a small county jailhouse, FCC Coleman consisted of a large compound housing all levels of security inmates, as shown in **Figure 2.6.A**. The medium-security prison was to the right of the main entrance road, with low security on the left. The high security and administrative prisoners were held near the back of the compound. The Coleman

---

[10] The point system is different for males and females as are the cutoff points for the various security levels.

Complex even had a camp. **Figure 2.6.A.** provides an aerial view of FCC-Coleman, FL, and **2.6.B.** provides a front view of Coleman Medium.

Figure 2.6.A. Aerial View of FCC Coleman   B. Front View of FCI Coleman-Medium

Paul and I arranged to visit as soon as we obtained clearance. By now, I had retired from the University, and we had sold our home in St. Louis to be closer to Scott and near family. The drive to Coleman, FL, took about 6 hours when traffic moved smoothly, but that was rarely the case. The only reasonable path between Coleman and Pensacola included I-75 South, which was always packed with vacationers to Disney and Tampa. The traffic made the excursion to the prison more like a 7- or 8-hour trip. We stayed in a hotel about 40 minutes from the prison and left early to be in line when the doors opened at 8:30 am. This trip became my once-a-month routine; sometimes, Paul accompanied me, but I often traveled alone by choice.

Upon entering the prison, we had to complete a form with many questions and provide two forms of ID, which the guards kept until we exited the prison. One of the guards told us we could not bring anything into the prison, including purses, key fobs, cell phones, sunglasses, hats, etc. A strict dress code listed the colors you could not wear and the unacceptable styles; there was even a list of prohibited shoes.[11] After completing the form and surrendering two forms of ID, we were told to walk through a metal detector shoeless, after which we were scanned with a detector wand. Next, the guard called the names of the first ten visitors' and told them to line up against a wall. The guards randomly chose a few people to search more thoroughly behind a screen. After the first ten visitors were cleared, a guard would stamp each person's arm with invisible ink to pass

---

[11] There were two single spaced pages of detailed clothing instructions.

through scanners placed at various points on the path to the visitation room. Visitors must walk in a single file along the path without talking. We followed the guard through a courtyard into a cafeteria area to be scanned. There were nonfunctional vending machines around the room that stayed empty through the two years of COVID-19.

Then. It. Happened. For the first time in almost three years, I *finally* got to hug my son! It was so bitter-sweet to hold and feel him again, knowing I would have to let go and dreading how long it would be until we could hug again. The prisons were still under COVID watch, and visitation was not guaranteed. I was not allowed to visit for many months because of an outbreak in the Coleman Complex. Even worse, many programs designed for prisoner wellness and education had been 'temporarily' suspended. Scott was in desperate need of the *Medically Assisted Treatment* (MAT) program, which provides suboxone to advanced opioid addicts to help them cope with the depleted dopamine in their brains.[12] The BOP never accepted Scott into the MAT program while he was at Coleman prison because he *"had too much time remaining on his sentence."*

One of the many challenges of overcoming opioid addiction is resisting the long-lasting cravings that can persist for many years. Small things such as a familiar smell, sight, or sound can trigger the cravings. The risk of death is greatest when an opioid addict has been drug-free for some time and then reintroduces the drug. During the period an addict is drug-free, tolerance to the drug declines, thereby increasing the risk of overdose death when use begins again. Suboxone blunts intoxication from opioid drugs, prevents cravings, and allows many people to transition from a life of addiction to a life of normalcy and safety. Suboxone works by tightly binding to the same brain receptors as opiates do, such as heroin, morphine, and fentanyl. For many advanced opioid addicts, suboxone may be needed for the remainder of their lives.

In December 2022, Scott was moved from *FCI Coleman Medium Security* prison to *USP Atlanta Low-Security* prison because his points had decreased to 35--enough to qualify for a low-security prison.[13] Prisoners can reduce the points against them by:

---

[12] There are many other medically prescribed opioid substitutes, but the federal BOP only uses suboxone.

[13] The name USP Atlanta was changed to FCI Atlanta in mid-2024.

1) **Completing programs**.

2) **Remaining '*shot*' free**. A 'shot' is the BOP name for an infraction; the shot level determines the punishment. Points differ from shots. Points are determined while in transition to prison, and shots are levied against those already in prison. Both points and shots can determine the prison security level (i.e., low, medium, or high) and the comfort level inside the prison. For serious shots, guards will throw the prisoner in solitary confinement for an indeterminate amount of time.

The BOP defines four broad categories for code infractions (shots) using a four-series scale:

    100 series: Greatest Severity (e.g., murder, rape, and drugs)
    200 series: High Severity (e.g., fighting)
    300 series: Moderate severity (e.g., indecent exposure)
    400 series: Low Severity (e.g., unauthorized physical contact)

Within each series are multiple possible violations. For example, there are 20 different infractions which can receive a 100-series shot. See **Appendix 2A** for a list of possible infractions and **Appendix 2B** for a list of potential consequences.

3) **Aging**. Each year of age eliminates 1 point because criminals typically age out of crime.

We had hoped Scott would soon transfer to a low-security prison, and now it was happening! As an added benefit, the drive to Atlanta from Pensacola is 100 miles shorter than the drive to Coleman! I was so grateful for the positive changes this would make in our lives. What could be better? Answer: *Coleman*.

Coleman was better. Experiencing USP Atlanta has been an interesting lesson in '*be careful what you wish for*.' During the four weeks it took Scott to receive his belongings from Coleman, I researched the Atlanta prison. It had an alarming history, but I was hopeful the reforms would make this a better experience than Coleman's. USP Atlanta was built in 1903 as a *high-security* prison, as shown in **Figure 2.7** below. It is an intimidating compound. The picture on the left is an aerial view of the compound; the middle is a close-up of the front of the main building. Although it is not visible from this distance, double rows of razor wire surround the entire facility, including all rooftops and gated areas (as shown on the right). There are at least four guard towers, which are not visible in the pictures. Guard towers and razor wire are not supposed to be part of a 'normal' low-security prison environment. The guard towers are no longer used today, but the entire facility screams high security.

Figure 2.7.   **USP Atlanta**

In 2021, the BOP closed the Atlanta prison due to widespread drug abuse, substandard medical and mental health care, out-of-control violence, and horrific sanitary conditions. [14] *"The problems plaguing the medium-security prison, which holds around 1,400 people, are so notorious within the federal government that its culture of indifference and mismanagement is derisively known among bureau employees as 'the Atlanta way.'"* [15] But whistle-blowers, including two top prison officials, documented the depth of dysfunction at USP Atlanta during a Senate subcommittee hearing, describing dozens of violent episodes — and the systematic effort to downplay and conceal the crisis — over the past few years.

The BOP terminated the staff and dispersed the Atlanta inmates to various prisons around the country. All staff and prisoners (including Scott) were new when the penitentiary reopened as a low-security prison. All eyes are now on the 'reformed' Atlanta prison. There have been a few visits from the BOP, including one from the director, Colette S. Peters, to assess the progress of USP Atlanta. Additionally, Georgia's Senator Jon Ossoff has

---

[14] USP Atlanta was designated a medium-security prison at the time.
[15] NYT (2022). Prison Personnel Describe Horrific Conditions and Cover Up at USP Atlanta. *The New York Times*, July 26.
https://www.nytimes.com/2022/07/26/us/politics/atlanta-federal-prisons-corruption.html

made multiple visits to the prison and believes he is watching everything. It is unknown how Peters or Ossoff felt about their visits, but the issues have not been resolved from the inmates' perspectives. Visits to prisons by the director should never be planned. The prison staff threatens inmates with the SHU if they dare to say anything wrong or if they ask a question. Scott knew of at least one inmate who had to go to the SHU for attempting to ask Director Peters a question. Unplanned visits and private talks with random inmates would reveal more information.

On our first visit to USP Atlanta, we had no problem finding the prison, but the reality of it took our breath away. Coleman did not have such an abundance of razor wire or guard towers in the medium or low-security prison areas.[16] I knew the Atlanta prison was old, but I did not realize that the BOP had not updated the buildings. It was raining hard while we waited to get into the cramped waiting room. Once inside, there was nowhere to sit and only enough room in the small space to process six people. Yet, 15 people crammed in there trying to fill out the usual paperwork, give IDs, and go through a security check while many more were waiting outside for their turn. The security check procedures were similar to Coleman's, except Atlanta did not pat down visitors. The staff was understandably disorganized and confused because our first visit coincided with the first day the prison had reopened to visitors as a low security. With all the chaos, processing the first group of visitors took more than an hour.

As we stood in a corner waiting for others to go through the check-in process, I noticed the inside walls were bleeding water from the rain. I quickly stepped away from the walls and looked up at the ceiling to see drips coming from there; it was raining inside, too. When it was finally time to go to the visiting room, we walked through the first set of locked iron doors and then a second set. We walked through other locked iron gates that required communication between our escort and central control, so there was a minute wait at each door. Then, we took an elevator to another floor and walked to a cafeteria to wait for Scott to arrive. The

---

[16] The Coleman campus houses all levels of security: camp, low, medium, and high plus prisoners held in administrative facilities. Administrative facilities are institutions with special missions, such as the detention of pretrial offenders; the treatment of inmates with serious or chronic medical problems; or the containment of extremely dangerous, violent, or escape-prone inmates.

vending machines were empty, and there was nothing to drink, not even water, which made it difficult to enjoy the allowed 5-hour visit. Even so, I would not have traded that time for anything. Hugging my son and seeing his face was worth everything…and more.

Over time, we have noticed that, on some days, inmates are already waiting in the visitation room; other times, we must wait until Scott arrives. After the first six months, the vending machines were stocked and operational, but within three months, the machines were understocked, and some were nonfunctional. Once seated, the inmates cannot move from their seats without permission—this makes getting your loved one a snack a humorous game of signaling and yelling the machine's contents. One hug is allowed at the beginning of the visit and another at the end, which translates to *two* hugs per month when everything goes as planned…a rare occurrence.

Figure 2.8 shows a picture of Scott at Coleman-Medium on the left and Atlanta-Low on the right. Notice he looks healthier in the first picture but is deteriorating under the harsher conditions in Atlanta.

Figure 2.8.   Scott (Ages 32 and 33)

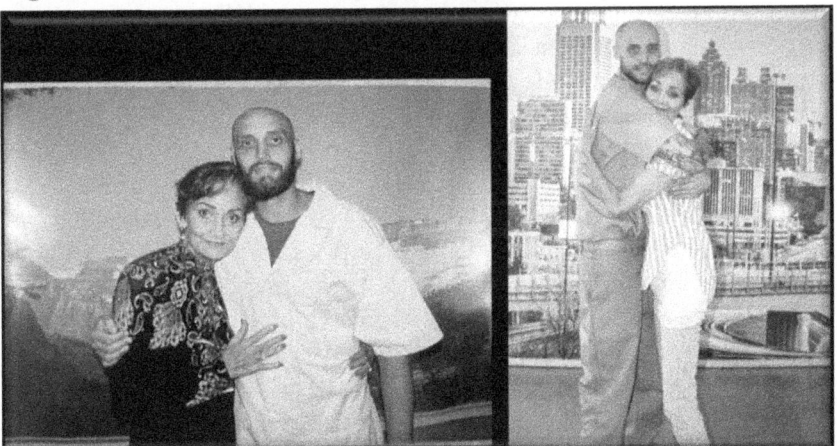

2022 FCI Coleman-Medium   2023 USP Atlanta

Scott applied to the MAT program again and was told he was getting very close to being admitted; this was welcome news. Scott had been able to obtain suboxone from inmates in the program since he was first held in county jail. At Coleman, the guards looked the other way when the drug under investigation was suboxone—but not in Atlanta.

Long after the fact, we learned that Scott was randomly drug-tested four months after he arrived in Atlanta, and the results showed suboxone in his system. The guards took him directly to the 'hole' and left him there for four weeks. Scott received a 100 series shot, the worst level offense equal to murder and rape, for violation of item #112: *Use of any narcotics, marijuana, drugs, alcohol, intoxicants, or related paraphernalia not prescribed for the individual by the medical staff.*

In prison, isolation is not called the 'hole' like on TV; it is called the **SHU** *("shoo")*, which stands for *Special Housing Unit*. Typically, Scott can call or email through the prison phone and email systems every day. Our standard communication is once a day via email and phone calls once a week. In the SHU, one phone call *per month* and no emails are allowed. We learned that 'snail' mail would be delivered to the SHU, so we wrote to each other, which helped enormously. The main problem with snail mail is the slow delivery; I was always 6-8 days behind. Initially, I did not know *how long* my son would be in the SHU (neither did he), I did not know *why* he was in the SHU, and I did not understand what to do to help. After about one week into it, a letter from Scott arrived telling us he was okay, just very hungry. For what seemed like the millionth time, I wished I could send food to the prison. He asked me to send him some books to read and some word games. I was glad to have something to do to help, no matter how small.

I visited Scott shortly after he left the SHU and was shocked by his appearance because he had lost about 40 lbs. in one month. There never seems to be enough food for everyone at the prison. Later, Scott learned that the kitchen staff regularly steals from SHU inmates' plates because the guards do not care. Also, Scott acted differently during the visit; it is hard to explain precisely how. He was fidgety, his eyes were furtive, and he had trouble focusing on our conversation. These are some of the many symptoms of *isolation stress*. According to an article in the *Journal of the American Academy of Psychiatry and the Law,* isolation can be as distressing as physical torture.[17] Humans require social contact. Over time, the stress of being isolated can cause a range of mental health problems.[18]

Barely three weeks later, and two days before the BOP approved Scott for the MAT program, the guards searched his cell and found suboxone in his locker. This time for offense number 113: *Possession of any narcotics, marijuana, drugs, alcohol, intoxicants, or related paraphernalia not prescribed for the individual by the medical staff.*

Ironically, Scott was approved to use suboxone under the MAT program while in the SHU for having self-obtained suboxone. A month in the SHU seems like such a severe punishment for having a drug they are now administering to him. Learning to leave logic at the door when dealing with the criminal justice apparatus takes a long time. There is no real answer to any question other than to accept that *"it is what it is."* There is no choice but to accept whatever it is and move forward positively, one day at a time.

Two more trips to the SHU have occurred since then, and Scott details each in Chapter 8. Suffice it to say that prison is not rehabilitation; it is maximum stress 24 hours a day, 7 days a week.

A Word from Scott

I come from an upper-middle-class family... I never grew up around guns or violence or even danger, for that matter. I grew up in the suburbs of West St. Louis County, graduating from a good high school and a good university (although it took six years). My real problem was my drug addiction. When I was both 16 and 17, I had kidney stones back-to-back. I was put on heavy painkillers, and this was my introduction to the world of opioids. After I got rid of my last kidney stones at 17 and my painkillers ran out, I started seeking them on the street. During the final semester at the University, two destructive things coincided: my connection to illegal painkillers died, and I got into a very toxic relationship with a new girlfriend. We started out using heroin; it was much easier to obtain than OxyContin and cheaper, too. As our relationship regressed, we started

---

[17] Jeffrey L. Metzner and Jamie Fellner (2010). Solitary Confinement and Mental Illness in US Prisons: A Challenge for Medical Ethics. *The Journal of the American Academy of Psychiatry and the Law*, March, 38(1), pp. 104-108.

[18] For more information see: Shalev, Sharon (2008). A Sourcebook on Solitary Confinement. *Mannhein Centre for Criminology*, Oct.

using more potent doses of heroin. We experimented with meth and other drugs, but heroin was the drug of choice. Eventually, the heroin became more of a need than a want, and I began using it more and more until I went to rehab at the end of 2017. When I got out of rehab, I got kicked out of the sober living house and went straight back to living on the street, except this time, I had a new addiction: fentanyl. Fentanyl is an opioid that is 50X-100X more potent than heroin. By the time I was about one year into my fentanyl addiction, I knew three people who had died from the drug.

This fentanyl addiction familiarized me with death like no other experience in my life. Within four months of being kicked out of the halfway house, one of my childhood friends, whom I had known for 15 years, died. Before that, a friend I met in rehab, who was trying hard to stay clean, relapsed and died. Three months after that, my girlfriend's friend TG died. I didn't know it then, but I found out the hard way four months later.

I was arrested on February 11th, 2019, and formally charged with fentanyl distribution, with TG's death resulting. At the time, I couldn't understand how I could be accused of that crime because I thought it was a crime for high-level drug offenders or murderers; that couldn't be me. I wasn't even there. I traded drugs with other addicts in my circle, a common practice among addicts, but that was it. I was the lowest of the low when it came to drug offenders. I was a bottom-of-the-barrel dope fiend with a very high tolerance level.

My advice is that if you find yourself in need of opioids due to surgery or whatever, put yourself in rehab as soon as you have finished the prescription. It only took a very short period for me to become addicted to opioids, and I did not even know I had a problem for years. A brief stay in a good rehab program won't hurt you if you are not addicted, but it might save your life if you are.

Summary

Opioids have saved millions from unbearable pain but have enslaved many others to a lifetime of addiction. It was 2022 when I first learned that some people could become addicted to opioids in as little as two days. This piece of information helped me understand how my son's addiction formed so quickly. For many years, Scott was able to function as an opioid addict until he graduated to heroin at the end of college. Scott's personality and appearance began to change dramatically. He became so self-absorbed that he could not even listen to what someone else had to say. He would interrupt and change the subject to something he wanted to discuss, even though no one else did. He never noticed.

Watching a drug steal your child's life right in front of your eyes is a particular type of hell reserved for parents of addicts. It is like watching someone alive who is already dead. There was no spark in his eyes, no genuine joy on his face, just death. My once beautiful, happy baby did not care whether he lived or died, and there was absolutely nothing I could do about it. This feeling of powerlessness and helplessness is compounded when entering the justice system. Loved ones have no control over anything—not the lawyer, the prosecutor, the jury, or the judge.

Our lives had changed forever. I was now retired because I could not handle the demands of my position and the trauma of losing my son. Having a child in prison for 20 years is like he is half dead and half alive. The alive part of him is tortured every day. We now live in a different state and house, and we feel like we live in a different country than the one we lived in before 2019. From the arrest to the sentencing, nothing proceeded as it should, with the initial assumption of guilt to the framing of Scott as a dealer.

If I could wave a magic wand, I would not free my son. Not right now. I would have him taken out of the criminal justice system and put in the best long-term rehabilitation facility that we could find. Scott needs rehabilitation desperately. Prison results in the opposite of rehabilitation; the unpredictable punishments and fear of isolation increase the compulsion to use. If Scott were to get out of prison now, with no rehabilitation, he would likely soon die from an overdose.

I add my voice to the chorus of others who want an overhaul of the US justice system as it relates to the treatment of those with the medical condition of addiction. More of Scott's story comes to light later, but Chapter 3 is devoted entirely to the history, goals, and results of the DOJ's war on drugs.

APPENDIX 2A. PROHIBITED ACTS (SHOTS)

	Maximum Level Offenses
100	Killing.
101	Assaulting any person, or an armed assault on the institution's secure perimeter (a charge for assaulting any person at this level is to be used only when serious physical injury has been attempted or accomplished).
102	Escape from escort; escape from any secure or non-secure institution, including community confinement; escape from unescorted community program or activity; escape from outside a secure institution.
103	Setting a fire (charged with this act in this category only when found to pose a threat to life or a threat of serious bodily harm or in furtherance of a prohibited act of Greatest Severity, e.g., in furtherance of a riot or escape; otherwise, the charge is properly classified Code 218 or 329).
104	Possession, manufacture, or introduction of a gun, firearm, weapon, sharpened instrument, knife, dangerous chemical, explosive, ammunition, or any instrument used as a weapon.
105	Rioting.
106	Encouraging others to riot.
107	Taking hostage(s).
108	Possession, manufacture, introduction, or loss of a hazardous tool (tools most likely to be used in an escape or escape attempt or to serve as weapons capable of doing serious bodily harm to others; or those hazardous to institutional security or personal safety, e.g., hack-saw blade, body armor, maps, handmade rope, or other escape paraphernalia, portable telephone, pager, or other electronic device).
109	(Not to be used).
110	Refusing to provide a urine sample; refusing to breathe into a Breathalyzer; and refusing to take part in other drug-abuse testing.
111	Introduction or making of any narcotics, marijuana, drugs, alcohol, intoxicants, or related paraphernalia, not prescribed for the individual by the medical staff.
112	Use of any narcotics, marijuana, drugs, alcohol, intoxicants, or related paraphernalia, not prescribed for the individual by the medical staff.
113	Possession of any narcotics, marijuana, drugs, alcohol, intoxicants, or related paraphernalia, not prescribed for the individual by the medical staff.
114	Sexual assault of any person, involving non-consensual touching by force or threat of force.
115	Destroying and/or disposing of any item during a search or attempt to search.
196	Use of the mail for an illegal purpose or to commit or further a Greatest category prohibited act.

	Maximum Level Offenses (cont.)
197	Use of the telephone for an illegal purpose or to commit or further a Greatest category prohibited act.
198	Interfering with a staff member in the performance of duties is most like another Greatest severity prohibited act. This charge is to be used only when another charge of Greatest severity is not accurate. The offending conduct must be charged as "most like" one of the listed Greatest severity prohibited acts.
199	Conduct which disrupts or interferes with the security or orderly running of the institution or the Bureau of Prisons is most like another Greatest severity prohibited act. This charge is to be used only when another charge of Greatest severity is not accurate. The offending conduct must be charged as "most like" one of the listed Greatest severity prohibited acts.
	High-Level Offenses
200	Escape from a work detail, non-secure institution, or other non-secure confinement, including community confinement, with subsequent voluntary return to Bureau of Prisons custody within four hours.
201	Fighting with another person.
203	Threatening another with bodily harm or any other offense.
204	Extortion; blackmail; protection; demanding or receiving money or anything of value in return for protection against others, to avoid bodily harm, or under threat of informing.
205	Engaging in sexual acts.
206	Making sexual proposals or threats to another.
207	Wearing a disguise or a mask.
208	Possession of any unauthorized locking device, or lock pick, tampering with or blocking any lock device (includes keys), or
209	Adulteration of any food or drink.
211	Possessing any officer's clothing.
212	Engaging in or encouraging a group demonstration.
213	Encouraging others to refuse to work, or to participate in a work stoppage.
216	Giving or offering an official or staff member a bribe, or anything of value.
217	Giving money to, or receiving money from, any person for the purpose of introducing contraband or any other illegal or prohibited purpose.
218	Destroying, altering, or damaging government property, or the property of another person, having a value in excess of $100, or destroying, altering, damaging life-safety devices (e.g., fire alarm) regardless of financial value.

High Level Offenses (cont.)	
219	Stealing; theft (including data obtained through the unauthorized use of a communications device, or through unauthorized access to disks, tapes, computer printouts, or other automated equipment on which data is stored).
220	Demonstrating, practicing, or using martial arts, boxing (except for the use of a punching bag), wrestling, or other forms of physical encounter, or military exercises or drill (except for drill authorized by staff).
221	Being in an unauthorized area with a person of the opposite sex without staff permission.
224	Assaulting any person (a charge at this level is used when less serious physical injury or contact has been attempted or accomplished by an inmate).
225	Stalking another person through repeated behavior that harasses, alarms, or annoys the person, after having been previously warned to stop such conduct.
226	Possession of stolen property.
227	Refusing to participate in a required physical test or examination unrelated to testing for drug abuse (e.g., DNA, HIV, tuberculosis).
228	Tattooing or self-mutilation.
229	Sexual assault of any person, involving non-consensual touching without force or threat of force.
231	Requesting, demanding, pressuring, or otherwise intentionally creating a situation, which causes an inmate to produce or display his/her own court documents for any unauthorized purpose to another inmate.
296	Use of the mail for abuses other than criminal activity which circumvents mail monitoring procedures
297	Use of the telephone for abuses other than illegal activity which circumvent the ability of staff to monitor frequency of telephone use, content of the call, or the number called; or to commit or further a High category prohibited act.
298	Interfering with a staff member in the performance of duties most like another High severity prohibited act. This charge is to be used only when another charge of High severity is not accurate. The offending conduct must be charged as "most like" one of the listed High severity prohibited acts.
299	Conduct which disrupts or interferes with the security or orderly running of the institution or the Bureau of Prisons most like another High severity prohibited act. This charge is to be used only when another charge of High severity is not accurate. The offending conduct must be charged as "most like" on

	Medium Level Offenses
300	Indecent Exposure.
302	Misuse of authorized medication.
303	Possession of money or currency, unless specifically authorized, or in excess of the amount authorized.
304	Loaning of property or anything of value for profit or increased return.
305	Possession of anything not authorized for retention or receipt by the inmate, and not issued to him through regular channels.
306	Refusing to work or to accept a program assignment.
307	Refusing to obey an order of any staff member (may be categorized and charged in terms of greater severity, according to the nature of the order being disobeyed, e.g., failure to obey an order which furthers a riot would be charged as 105, Rioting; refusing to obey an order which furthers a fight would be charged as 201, Fighting; refusing to provide a urine sample when ordered as part of a drug-abuse test would be charged as 110).
308	Violating a condition of a furlough.
309	Violating a condition of a community program.
310	Unexcused absence from work or any program assignment.
311	Failing to perform work as instructed by the supervisor.
312	Insolence towards a staff member.
313	Lying or providing a false statement to a staff member.
314	Counterfeiting, forging, or unauthorized reproduction of any document, article of identification, money, security, or official paper (may be categorized in terms of greater severity according to the nature of the item being reproduced, e.g., counterfeiting release papers to effect escape, Code 102).
315	Participating in an unauthorized meeting or gathering.
316	Being in an unauthorized area without staff authorization.
317	Failure to follow safety or sanitation regulations (including safety regulations, chemical instructions, tools, MSDS sheets, OSHA standards).
318	Using any equipment or machinery without staff authorization.
319	Using any equipment or machinery contrary to instructions or posted safety standards.
320	Failing to stand count.
321	Interfering with the taking of count.
324	Gambling.
325	Preparing or conducting a gambling pool.
326	Possession of gambling paraphernalia.
327	Unauthorized contacts with the public.

	Medium Level Offences (cont.)
328	Giving money or anything of value to, or accepting money or anything of value from, another inmate or any other person without staff authorization.
329	Destroying, altering, or damaging government property, or the property of another person, having a value of $100.00 or less.
330	Being unsanitary or untidy; failing to keep one's person or quarters in accordance with posted standards.
331	Possession, manufacture, introduction, or loss of a non-hazardous tool, equipment, supplies, or other non-hazardous contraband.
332	Smoking where prohibited.
333	Fraudulent or deceptive completion of a skills test (e.g., cheating on a GED, or other educational or vocational skills test).
334	Conducting a business; conducting or directing an investment transaction without staff authorization.
335	Communicating gang affiliation; participating in gang-related activities; possession of paraphernalia indicating gang affiliation.
336	Circulating a petition.
396	Use of the mail for abuses other than criminal activity which do not circumvent mail monitoring; or use of the mail to commit or further a Moderate category prohibited act.
397	Use of the telephone for abuses other than illegal activity which do not circumvent the ability of staff to monitor the frequency of telephone use, the content of the call, or the number called; or to commit or further a Moderate category prohibited act.
398	Interfering with a staff member in the performance of duties is most like another Moderate severity prohibited act. This charge is to be used only when another charge of Moderate severity is not accurate. The offending conduct must be charged as "most like" one of the listed Moderate severity prohibited acts.
399	Conduct which disrupts or interferes with the security or orderly running of the institution or the Bureau of Prisons most like another Moderate severity prohibited act. This charge is to be used only when another charge of Moderate severity is not accurate. The offending conduct must be charged as "most like" one of the listed Moderate severity prohibited acts.

	Low-Level Offenses
402	Malingering, feigning illness.
404	Using abusive or obscene language.
407	Conduct with a visitor in violation of Bureau regulations.
409	Unauthorized physical contact (e.g., kissing, embracing).
498	Interfering with a staff member in the performance of duties. This charge is to be used only when another charge of Low severity is not accurate. The offending conduct must be charged as "most like" one of the listed Low severity prohibited acts.
499	Conduct that disrupts or interferes with the security or orderly running of the institution or the Bureau of Prisons is most like another Low severity prohibited act. This charge is to be used only when another charge of Low severity is not accurate. The offending conduct must be charged as "most like" one of the listed Low severity prohibited acts.

APPENDIX 2B. SANCTIONS FOR SHOTS

	Sanctions for Maximum Level Offenses
1	Recommend parole date rescission or retardation.
2	Forfeit and/or withhold earned statutory good time or non-vested good conduct time (up to 100%) and/or terminate or disallow extra good time (an extra good time or good conduct time sanction may not be suspended).
3	Disallow ordinarily between 50% and 75% (27–41 days) of good conduct time credit available for a year (a good conduct time sanction may not be suspended).
4	Forfeit up to 41 days of earned First Step Act (FSA) Time Credits (see 28 CFR part 523, subpart E) for each prohibited act committed.
5	Disciplinary segregation (up to 12 months).
6	Make monetary restitution.
7	Monetary fine.
8	Loss of privileges (e.g., visiting, telephone, commissary, movies, recreation).
9	Change housing (quarters).
10	Remove from program and/or group activity.
11	Loss of job.
12	Impound inmate's personal property.
13	Confiscate contraband.
14	Restrict to quarters.
15	Extra duty.
	Sanctions for High-Level Offenses
1	Recommend parole date rescission or retardation.
2	Forfeit and/or withhold earned statutory good time or non-vested good conduct time up to 50% or up to 60 days, whichever is less, and/or terminate or disallow extra good time (an extra good time or good conduct time sanction may not be suspended).
3	Disallow ordinarily between 25% and 50% (14–27 days) of good conduct time credit available for a year (a good conduct time sanction may not be suspended).
4	Forfeit up to 27 days of earned FSA Time Credits for each prohibited act committed.
5	Disciplinary segregation (up to 6 months).
6	Make monetary restitution.
7	Monetary fine.
8	Loss of privileges (e.g., visiting, telephone, commissary, movies, recreation).
9	Change housing (quarters).

10	Remove from program and/or group activity.
11	Loss of job.
12	Impound inmate's personal property.
13	Confiscate contraband.
14	Restrict to quarters.
15	Extra duty.

Sanctions for Medium-Level Offenses	
1	Recommend parole date rescission or retardation.
2	Forfeit and/or withhold earned statutory good time or non-vested good conduct time up to 25% or up to 30 days, whichever is less, and/or terminate or disallow extra good time (an extra good time or good conduct time sanction may not be suspended).
3	Disallow ordinarily up to 25% (1–14 days) of good conduct time credit available for a year (a good conduct time sanction may not be suspended).
4	Forfeit up to 27 days of earned FSA Time Credits for each prohibited act committed.
5	Disciplinary segregation (up to 3 months).
6	Make monetary restitution.
7	Monetary fine.
8	Loss of privileges (e.g., visiting, telephone, commissary, movies, recreation).
9	Change housing (quarters).
10	Remove from program and/or group activity.
11	Loss of job.
12	Impound inmate's personal property.
13	Confiscate contraband.
14	Restrict to quarters.
15	Extra duty.

Sanctions for Low-Level Offenses	
1	Disallow ordinarily up to 12.5% (1–7 days) of good conduct time credit available for year (to be used only where inmate found to have committed a second violation of the same prohibited act within 6 months); Disallow ordinarily up to 25% (1–14 days) of good conduct time credit available for year (to be used only where inmate found to have committed a third violation of the same prohibited act within 6 months) (a good conduct time sanction may not be suspended).
2	Forfeit up to 7 days of earned FSA Time Credits (only where the inmate is found to have committed a second violation of the same prohibited act within 6 months; forfeit up to 14 days of FSA Time Credits (only where the inmate is found to have committed a third violation of the same prohibited act within 6 months).

3	Make monetary restitution.
4	Monetary fine.
5	Loss of privileges (e.g., visiting, telephone, commissary, movies, recreation).
6	Change housing (quarters).
7	Remove from program and/or group activity.
8	Loss of job.
9	Impound inmate's personal property.
10	Confiscate contraband.
11	Restrict to quarters.
12	Extra duty.

CHAPTER 3: THE US DEPARTMENT OF JUSTICE

Undesirable behavior is not criminal unless a society, through its legal system, deems it so. In some countries, drug 'crimes' do not exist because unwanted drug behavior has not been defined as criminal. Instead, behavioral and health professionals use *harm-reduction* strategies to mitigate unwanted behavior. Empirical studies by the *National Institutes of Health* (NIH) and others show that addiction is a health issue, not a criminal issue, and should be treated as such.

Introduction
According to the NIH, *harm reduction* techniques help people who use drugs avoid adverse effects, such as infection or overdose. In addition, *"many understand harm reduction as a way to meet people where they are with kindness and respect."*[19] Research shows that involuntary addiction treatment is not effective and can increase the risk of overdose.[20] Harm reduction is powerful because it allows people with substance use disorders to make their own decisions about their lives and health, which in turn increases rates of treatment success in long-term recovery. *"Harm reduction has nothing to do with condoning the behavior. It has to do with reducing the harm. And frankly, from my perspective, that's what public safety is...every person in this community who uses drugs...deserves respect and dignity. We want to make sure people stay alive. They can't recover if they are dead."*[21]

Harm Reduction International describes it as *"policies, programs, and practices that aim to minimize negative health, social, and legal impacts associated with drug use, policies, and laws."*[22] More simply, if a person

---

[19] National Institute on Drug Addiction (2021). What is Harm Reduction? *National Institutes of Health*, Dec. 1.
[20] Werb, D., Kamarulzaman, A., Mecham, M.C., Rafful, C., Fischer, B., Strathdee, S.A. & Wood, E. (2016). The Effectiveness of Compulsory Drug Treatment: A Systematic Review. *International Journal of Drug Policy*, 28, 1-9.
[21] FJP (2021). Drug-Induced Homicide Prosecutions. *Fair and Just Prosecution*. Quoted: Sarah George States Attorney, Chittenden County, Burlington, VT.
[22] *Harm Reduction International*. What is Harm Reduction? https://hri.global/what-is-harm-reduction/

with substance use disorder is not ready for treatment, their lack of readiness does not make them less deserving of health care and support.

The US employs methods that are the opposite of harm reduction strategies for those with substance use disorders. Drug use is a crime in the US; having drugs on your person or in your car or house is a crime. Those who associate with drug users are viewed with suspicion and are to be avoided. If an addict dies of an accidental overdose, someone must go to prison. The *Department of Justice* (DOJ), rather than the *US Department of Health and Human Services* (HHS), oversees all forms of drug use, possession, and distribution; the consequences are lengthy prison sentences. The DOJ has not embraced harm reduction strategies in any form. Many in the US feel that people with an addiction should suffer the consequences of their actions, even if that means death—this lack of empathy is a consequence of the criminalization of addiction and the resulting criminal addict.

> **There is no crueler tyranny than that which is perpetrated under the shield of the law and in the name of justice.**
> Charles-Louis de Secondat, Baron de la Brede et de Montesquieu (1748). *The Spirit of the Law.*

What if, for example, it was illegal for those with diabetes to eat sugar? Let's say it is not only unlawful but a *criminal* felony because eating sugar comes with known risks that can lead to accidents involving others. Then, those people with diabetes who give in to sugar cravings would become criminals, and society would soon come to believe they deserve punishment. Criminalizing and punishing sugar-eating diabetics will never solve the medical problem involving insulin imbalances. Diabetes cannot be punished into extinction, and neither can drug addiction because both are medical problems rather than criminal behavior. Punishing individuals for a medical condition is inhumane and ignorant. Additionally, 55% of those addicted to opioids started with prescriptions received from *medical* doctors. Once the medical condition of addiction is triggered, it assumes a life of its own that can only be described as insanity.[23]

The US began its *'war on drugs'* under President Nixon with the *Comprehensive Drug Abuse Prevention and Control Act of 1970* (21 USC §§801), usually referred to as the *Controlled Substances Act of 1970* (CSA). Later, under President Regan, the *Anti-Drug Abuse Act* (ADAA) *of 1986* was enacted to increase the penalties for violations of the CSA. The ADAA raised spending for drug enforcement by $1.7 billion and targeted traffickers by instituting mandatory minimum sentences for high-level drug crimes. The purpose of the ADAA was to completely eradicate international drug crops to stop the flow of illegal drugs into the US. To that end, Congress included the *Drug-Induced Homicide* (DIH) laws in the ADAA to prosecute and sentence drug traffickers to no less than 20 years in prison.

Throughout the 1980s and 1990s, prescriptions for opioids gradually increased until 1996, when Perdue Pharma introduced OxyContin to the market. It was not widely known at the time that physical dependency on opioids can occur in as few as 3-5 days.[24] Prescriptions surged, and the use of opioids to treat chronic pain became widespread and commonplace. Not surprisingly, lawsuits followed in the early 2000s as more people began to die from overdoses. Nearly all the early lawsuits were against Perdue Pharma, but later, others followed, e.g., CVS, Walgreens, and Walmart. Even with clear indications that many became dependent on opioids, legally, through prescriptions, the DOJ punishes them with the same severity as traffickers.

Today, the US continues its 50-plus-year obsession with punishment and revenge-seeking as the primary methods used to reduce overdose deaths, discourage opioid sales and use, and protect society.

---

[23] APA (2023). Opioid Use Disorder. *American Psychiatric Association.* https://www.psychiatry.org/patients-families/opioid-use-disorder#:~:text=Opioid%20Use%20Disorder%20Symptoms&text=Taking%20larger%20amounts%20or%20taking,or%20recovering%20from%20its%20effects.

[24] Hays, L.R. (2004). A Profile of OxyContin addiction. *Journal of Addictive Diseases,* 23(4), 1-9.

Department of Justice Structure

The DOJ was formed in 1789 to assist the president and cabinet in matters concerning the law.[25] The DOJ comprises more than 40 component organizations and employs more than 115,000 people. Headquartered at the Robert F. Kennedy Building in Washington, DC, the department maintains field offices in all 50 states, US territories, and more than 50 countries. **Figure 3.1** below shows most division offices and agencies housed under the DOJ. The divisions and offices shown to the left of the bracket are under the direction of the *Associate Attorney General* (AAG), who reports to the *Deputy Attorney General* (DAG). Note that the DOJ is part of the executive branch, not the judicial branch. The judicial branch comprises the *Supreme Court* and the *Federal Judicial Center*, which covers all federal courts.

The offices, divisions, or agencies listed to the right of the bracket report directly to the DAG, who reports to the *Attorney General* (AG). None of the offices, divisions, or agencies are ranked above the others; they all operate independently. The DAG oversees the units most involved with drug oversight, including Interpol, the *Federal Bureau of Investigations* (FBI), the *Drug Enforcement Agency* (DEA), the *Bureau of Prisons* (BOP), and the Marshal Service.

---

[25] Encyclopedia of American Politics (2024). *U.S. Department of Justice*.

Figure 3.1.   **DOJ Organizational Chart**

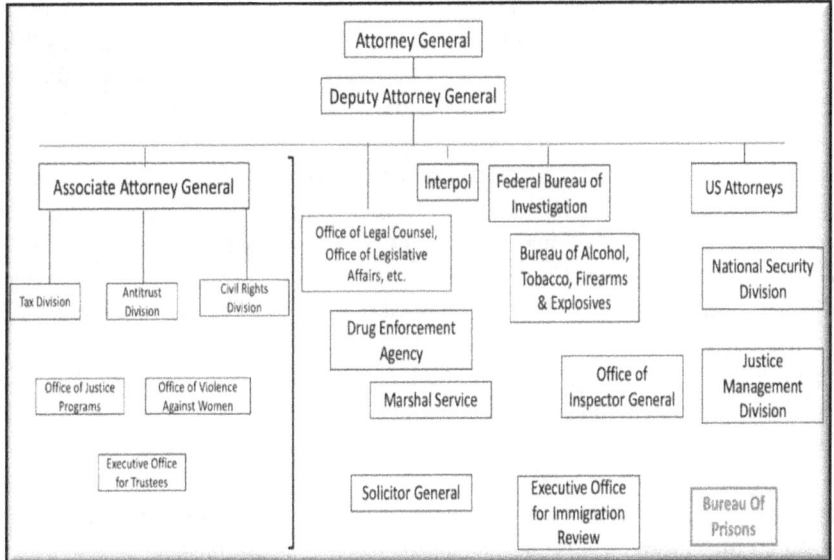

Sources of Fentanyl

Under the 1970 CSA, Congress gave the DEA the authority to regulate fentanyl, which had been used medically since 1959. Due to its potency, the *United Nations* (UN) placed fentanyl under international control in 1964 and has received reports of 153 fentanyl-related products, as well as thousands of other fentanyl analogs.[26]

In early 2019, the DEA identified China as the primary source of illicit fentanyl. Fentanyl is typically manufactured in China and imported directly to Mexico, where traffickers mix it with heroin before distribution to the United States. DEA spokesman Rusty Paine stated: *"China is by far the most significant manufacturer of illicit designer synthetic drugs. There is so much manufacturing of new drugs, [it's] amazing what is coming out of China. Hundreds of [versions], including synthetic fentanyl and fentanyl-based compounds."*[27] Louis Milione of the DEA's *Diversion*

---

[26] CRS (2024). China Primer: Illicit Fentanyl and China's Role. *Congressional Research Service*, Feb. 13. https://crsreports.congress.gov/product/pdf/IF/IF10890
[27] DEA (2020). Fentanyl Flow to the United States. *DEA Intelligence Report (Unclassified)*, January. https://www.dea.gov/sites/default/files/2020-

Control Center confirmed that *"China is the primary source of fentanyl."*[28] The DEA is also aware of illicit labs in Mexico producing fentanyl from precursor ingredients manufactured in China. Today, the DEA alleges that China-based chemical companies advertise and sell the chemicals needed to make fentanyl and ship those directly to the US and Mexico.[29]

Rumors suggest that fentanyl is being obtained from China to manufacture counterfeit opioid pills in the US, but the DEA has not found any evidence of operating labs. According to a DEA spokesperson, there is *"little evidence"* that fentanyl is added to heroin domestically.[30] Even if US dealers add fentanyl to heroin, it is likely to be done at the top of the distribution chain. Low-level sellers are typically unaware of the makeup of their product or its potency and have no reliable way to check. Yet, the law holds these people accountable and prosecutes them for murder if their supply results in an overdose death. Recent epidemiological research on the changing nature of the heroin market confirms that people at the bottom of the distribution chain are most often uninformed about the product and have no knowledge (until it is too late) that they are selling a product laced with fentanyl.[31]

In November 2023, President Biden met with China's Paramount leader, XI Jinping, to discuss renewing cooperation on drug control issues. Their agreement marked the first time in three years that the US and China had agreed to cooperate on drug control. It is too soon to observe the impact, if any.

While Mexico and China are the primary source countries for fentanyl and fentanyl-related products trafficked to the U.S., India is emerging as the

---

03/DEA_GOV_DIR-008-20%20Fentanyl%20Flow%20in%20the%20United%20States_0.pdf
[28] Benecchi, Liz (2021). Recidivism Imprisons American Progress. *Harvard Political Review*, August 8.
[29] CRS (2024). China Primer: Illicit Fentanyl and China's Role. *Congressional Research Service*, Feb. 13. https://crsreports.congress.gov/product/pdf/IF/IF10890
[30] DEA (2020). Fentanyl Flow to the United States. *DEA Intelligence Report (Unclassified)*, January. https://www.dea.gov/sites/default/files/2020-03/DEA_GOV_DIR-008-20%20Fentanyl%20Flow%20in%20the%20United%20States_0.pdf
[31] Compton, W.M., and Jones, C.M. (2019). Epidemiology of the U.S. Opioid Crisis: The importance of the vector. *Annals of the New York Academy of Science*, 1451(1), 130-143.

primary source of fentanyl powder and fentanyl precursor chemicals. By 2024, the number of countries involved in trafficking fentanyl had become more diverse, resulting in a more consistent global supply chain.[32]

The primary *use* country is the US, where more than 80% of the world's supply of opioids is consumed.[33]

Department of Justice Goals

Prosecutions for drug crimes and DIH cases have risen markedly since 2011 as prosecutors have increasingly focused on applying the harsh punishments meant for traffickers to friends, family, and co-addicts. The DOJ justifies harsh punishments as a successful tool in reducing opioid-related deaths, discouraging the sale and use of opioids, protecting the public, and penalizing offenders. Studies such as Carroll et al. (2021) and Peterson et al. (2019) found that now *most* prosecutions are being brought against individuals who are either low-level dealers or are friends, family, or co-users of the overdose decedent.[34] *"Often, these individuals are characterized in the media as profiteering "dealers" when, in reality, most people who use drugs also sell or deliver drugs to friends and relatives on occasion."*[35] Yet neither state nor federal laws distinguish between a person with an addiction, a user, and a dealer—the mischaracterization of a person with an addiction as a dealer results in many instances of the miscarriage of justice.

To summarize, the DOJ's stated goals of harsh punishment are to:
   1) *Reduce drug overdose deaths*,

---

[32] DEA (2020). Fentanyl Flow to the United States. *DEA Intelligence Report (Unclassified)*, January. https://www.dea.gov/sites/default/files/2020-03/DEA_GOV_DIR-008-20%20Fentanyl%20Flow%20in%20the%20United%20States_0.pdf

[33] Whitaker, Bill (2024). The Opioid Epidemic: Who is to Blame? *60 Minutes*, Sunday, June 23.

[34] i) Carroll, J. J., Ostrach, B., Wilson, L., Dunlap, J. L., Getty, R., & Bennett, J. (2021). Drug induced homicide laws may worsen Opioid related harms: An example from rural North Carolina. *International Journal of Drug Policy*, 97, 103406.

  ii) Peterson, M., Rich, J., Macmadu, A., Truong, A. Q., Green, T. C., Beletsky, L., ... & Brinkley-Rubinstein, L. (2019). "One guy goes to jail, two people are ready to take his spot": Perspectives on drug-induced homicide laws among incarcerated individuals. *International Journal of Drug Policy*, 70, 47-53.

[35] Beletsky, L. (2019). America's favorite antidote: drug-induced homicide in the age of the overdose crisis. *Utah Law Review*, 833.

2) ***Discourage the sale and use of opioids***,
3) ***Protect the public***, *and*
4) ***Punish offenders***.

Each is examined below to determine the DOJ's success or failure in achieving the four goals.

Goal 1: Reduce Drug Overdose Deaths

The *Centers for Disease Control and Prevention* (CDC) is unable to track overdose deaths in real-time, so its published data is at least one year old, obscuring what is currently happening on the ground. The CDC is still tallying the death toll from drug overdoses in 2022 and 2023. A CDC November 2023 report stated a new record of 109,000 overdose deaths for the 12 months covering April 2021 to April 2022, driven principally by fentanyl.[36] Two-thirds of the deaths were due to fentanyl overdoses. Without comprehensive real-time data, *"...we are driving blind,"* said John P. Walters, the drug czar during the Clinton and Bush administrations. *"This is like tracking the epidemic by visiting cemeteries. We're not measuring what's coming into the country in real-time. We're not measuring what's happening with the health consequences and where to put resources to buffer those health consequences. Our drug-control strategy is an embarrassment, and it doesn't begin to propose a way of reversing this problem."*[37]

Table 3. 1 illustrates the failure of existing policies to reduce overdose deaths by showing the number of overdose deaths in each decade beginning with the 1970s.

---

[36] Centers for Disease Control (2022). Drug Overdose Deaths in the U.S. Top 109,000 Annually. *National Center for Health Statistics*, Feb. 17.
[37] Walters, John P. (2003). White House, President George W. Bush, *Office of National Drug Control Policy*, Director John P. Walters.

Table 3.1.	Overdose Deaths		
A	B	C	D
Year	Overdose deaths	Year	Overdose deaths
1970	7,101	2000	17,415
1979	2,544	2009	37,004
% Change	-64%	% Change	112%
Total Deaths	61,446	Total Deaths	287,238
1980	2,492	2010	38,329
1989	5,035	2019	70,630
% Change	102%	% Change	84%
Total Deaths	35,760	Total Deaths	536,478
1990	4,506	2020	91,799
1999	16,849	2023*	112,000
% Change	274%	% Change	22%
Total Deaths	83,099	Total Deaths	310,789

*Complete count unavailable at this time
Source: CDC Mortality files 1970-2023

The 1970s began with the most significant number of overdose deaths (7,101) seen until 1993. The lax drug environment of the 1960s slowly started to wane in the 1970s. By the end of the decade, the annual number of overdose deaths had declined to 2,544, a 64% decline and the only decade of decrease in the sample period. Even so, a total of 61,446 people died during the 1970s due to drug overdoses. In response, Congress passed the CSA in 1970 and created the DEA on July 1, 1973. Two years later, Congress ratified the *Drug and Drug Abuse Act of 1972* and, in 1973, the *Misuse of Drugs Act*.

The results of the 1980s decade are less straightforward. From 1980 to 1989, there was an increase of 102% in overdose deaths. However, the total number of deaths (35,760) in the 1980s was 42% lower than in the previous decade. In 1984, the *Crime Control Act* targeted various aspects of criminal sanctions related to drug trafficking. Criminal asset forfeiture penalties were expanded and increased, and the law established a determinate sentencing system for drug offenses. Congress passed the ADAA in 1986, which initiated mandatory minimum sentences with *strict liability* clauses.[38] At that time, prosecutors were focused only on traffickers and major drug dealers as targets for these tough sanctions.

The public can observe the outcomes of the DOJ's efforts by reviewing the data from the decades that followed. The decade of the 1990s resulted in a total number of overdose deaths of 83,099, with an increase of 274% from 1990-1999. During the 1990s, OxyContin prescriptions were proliferating, and opioids were easy to obtain. Then, the number of fatalities began to skyrocket, and by the end of 2009, the total number of people lost to drug overdoses was 287,238. This large number shocked society at large and created an atmosphere of fear towards heroin and fentanyl. From 2000 to 2009, overdose deaths had increased another 112%, causing medical practitioners, lawmakers, and families to demand reform, but their goals were very different. The medical community wanted funding to research and treat people with drug addiction, lawmakers wanted harsher laws, and the families of the deceased wanted revenge. Prosecutors began going after low-level dealers, but nothing helped; the numbers kept climbing.

Between 2010 and 2019, the number of fatalities from drug overdoses almost doubled when compared to the previous decade, resulting in more than half a million people (536,478) dead. More people died in this one decade than in the last four combined. This frightening trend has continued in the first four years of the 2020 decade; 310,789 already passed due to drug overdoses. It will be 2029 before the public can observe another entire decade, but if this pace continues, the death toll will exceed 1 million. Overdose deaths are out of control, and the harsher punishments/revenge strategy has not made a dent in the rapid increase.

Due to the introduction of OxyContin in the early 1990s, by the end of the decade, lawsuits and criminal liability standards were being applied to large pharmaceutical companies, forcing them to pay attention to the damage caused by opioids. The American fentanyl crisis deepened during the coronavirus pandemic. From 2019 to 2022 alone, fatal overdoses surged by 55%, and an estimated 196 Americans were dying each day from the drug. A recent report from the *American Medical Association's Advocacy Resource Center* (2022) observed that "...[t]he crisis in opioid overdose deaths has reached epidemic proportions in the United

---

[38] Liability is strict when the crime does not require proof of fault for the offense or any relevant moral culpability.

States..."[39] Even casual observation of the overdose death rates makes it evident that the DOJ strategy, applied to drug users, has been a failure.[40]

Hudack (2021) bluntly summarizes the waste and loss:[41]

> *"The war on drugs, not the war in Afghanistan, is America's longest war. It has used trillions of American taxpayer dollars, militarized American law enforcement agencies (federal, state, and local), claimed an untold number of lives, railroaded people's futures (especially among Black, Latino, and Native populations), and concentrated the effort in the country's most diverse and poorest neighborhoods. The war on drugs has been a staggering policy failure, advancing few of the claims that presidents, members of Congress, law enforcement officials, and state and local leaders have sought to achieve. The illicit drug trade has thrived under prohibition and harsher punishments; adults of all ages and youth have access to illicit substances. Substance use disorders have thrived, and policymakers' efforts to protect public health were fully undermined by a policy that disproportionately focused, if unsuccessfully, on public safety. It is time for an American president to think seriously about broad-based policy change to disrupt the manner in which the United States deals with drugs."*

Of all the opioids available, the tragic truth is that fentanyl is the cheapest, most lethal drug ever to hit the US black market. Never has the US seen such a dramatic rise in drug overdose deaths or such desperate efforts to prosecute *anyone* standing nearby. Deaths involving synthetic opioids, including both fentanyl and illicit fentanyl analogs, represent at least 60% of all deaths from drug overdoses. Too often, in times of crisis, policies are

---

[39] *American Medical Association* (2022). Nation's Drug-Related Overdose and Death Epidemic Continues to Worsen, May 12.

[40] **i)** Wagner, P., & Rabuy, B. (2017). Following the money of mass incarceration. *Prison policy initiative, 25.*

ii) Lopez, German (2017). Mass incarceration doesn't do much to fight crime. But it costs an absurd $182 billion a year. A new report suggests mass incarceration costs even more than previously thought. *Vox*, Jan. 27.

[41] Hudak, John (2021). Biden should end America's longest war: The War on Drugs. *Brookings*, Friday, Sept. 24.

implemented to appease voters and families but ultimately do not solve the problem.

In 1971, when the US began its war on drugs, overdose deaths were 6,771; the CDC estimates the 2023 death toll will be 112,000.[42] It is no surprise that the public is alarmed by opioid abuse, but **Table 3.1** above leaves little doubt that the current approach has not reduced overdose fatalities.

"Every past drug epidemic has been about an increase in the number of users; this one is about a massive increase in death."[43]

Goal 2: Discourage Opioid Sale and Use

The second goal of the DOJ's use of harsh punishment is to send a message to drug sellers that the consequences will be harsh. The success or failure of discouraging opioid sales can be inferred by examining usage rates, rates of addiction, and drug arrests.

The federal government discourages opioid use by using CDC-published guidelines for prescribing opioids for chronic pain. In addition, the CDC publishes a considerable amount of educational materials on the topic of drug abuse. Further, while the federal government does not have a plan to address prescription abuse, states have implemented prescription drug laws and have monitored opioid abuse over the past 20 years. Neither the federal nor state governments offer any treatment programs for those with substance use disorder. If imprisoned, there may be opportunities to access evidence-based treatments, including *Medication-Assisted Treatment* (MAT). MAT is used in federal prisons, although admittance to the program can take years.[44] The federal government has also invested in the availability of lifesaving drugs such as naloxone.

> Scott was incarcerated for 4.5 years before he was admitted to the MAT program.

Even so, the primary tool used to discourage opioid sales and use is harsh punishment through extended sentences. The logic is that long sentences will dissuade users and sellers if they see others serving long sentences.

---

[42] Actual numbers will be available at the end of 2024.
[43] DeWeerdt, S. (2019). Tracing the US opioid crisis to its roots. *Nature*, *573*(7773), S10-S10.
[44] Scott was incarcerated for 4.5 years before he was admitted to the MAT program.

The fundamental problem with this logic is that it does not work and displays a complete lack of understanding of severe opioid addiction. Opioid addicts see their friends dying from fentanyl overdoses and still *knowingly* risk their death in a weird game of *Russian roulette* for a fentanyl high. Punishment cannot get any harsher than death, but even death does not stop the person with an addiction. *"We are the people who see our friends die and then seek out the strand of fentanyl that killed them, believing it must be really good* [strong] *stuff."*[45]

Drug offenses are regularly prosecuted in both state and federal courts; therefore, a potential offender has no means of knowing in which court system they would likely be charged, much less what punishment would be applied. More importantly, the reality of being arrested rarely penetrates the addict's mind; the primary focus of each day is the search for drugs. Therefore, using the threat of punishment as deterrence is pointless. People with addiction disorders are not 'criminals'; they are suffering from a profound psychological and mental disorder that contributes to their inability to understand society's threats.

To the extent that sentencing policies may deter some criminals, research shows that increases in the certainty or severity of punishment are much less likely to produce the same result in people with an addiction. One of the mental distortions suffered by those with a substance use disorder is the unshakable belief that nothing 'bad' will happen to them. Therefore, threats of more severe punishment do little, if anything, to deter addictive behavior. Since most offenders do not believe they will be apprehended, extending the length of the sentence is scarcely a deterrent. Mandatory minimum penalties are ineffective because they increase the severity of consequences without impacting behavior.[46]

According to the *Bureau of Justice Statistics National Survey on Drug Use & Health* (NSDH, 2000-2023), not only have overdose deaths increased dramatically, but so have rates of addiction. Unlike overdose deaths, comparisons of addiction rates to the 1970s, 1980s, or 1990s are not possible because the NSDH did not begin collecting such data until 2000. **Table 3.2** shows that in the first decade of the new century, 2000-2009,

---

[45] Gary Scott Hancock (2021).
[46] Congressional Research Service (2023).
https://crsreports.congress.gov/product/pdf/LSB/LSB10910. Feb 2.

rates of addiction rose by a population-adjusted 51%. This increase pales in comparison to the

Table 3.2.		Rates of Addiction		
Year	# of People Addicted	% Chg. in addiction	% Chg in Population	Population Adjusted Addiction
2000	14,000,000			
2009	21,800,000	56%	9%	51%
2010	22,600,000			
2019	57,200,000	153%	6%	144%
2020	59,300,000	16%	-	16%
2022	68,700,000		Total % Chg	= 391%
Source: *National Survey on Drug Use & Health (2000-2023)*				

2010-2019 decade, when addiction rates rose by an enormous 144%. Despite the increase in harsh punishments, rates of addiction have soared. In the first three years of the 2020-2029 decade, the number of people addicted increased by 16%. Overall, the data set demonstrates that addiction rates rose 391% from 2000 to 2022.

The *National Center for Drug Abuse Statistics* has only reported heroin usage as a separate category since 2011, so the data set does not include the first decade of this century. Over the period 2011 to 2022, heroin usage rates increased by 93.5%, as shown in **Table 3.3**. The four years in bold print show moderate decreases in heroin use, particularly over the 2017-2019 period. Most of the increase occurred in 2014 and during 2020-2022, when COVID-19 had much of the country locked down. Everything from visiting friends to going to work was stressful. Businesses sent employees home to work in isolated environments. Heroin use rose by 21.1% in 2020, another 21.8% in 2021 and 9.2% in 2022. It may be that the stress of the rapidly changing COVID-19 environment sent many people over the edge. Although users increased by 9.2% in 2022, the rate of increase slowed. More recent numbers have not yet been published, and 2022 has not yet been verified. More time must pass before researchers can accurately evaluate the impact of COVID-19 on heroin usage.

Table 3.3. Nationwide Annual Heroin Usage		
Year	Users	%Chg
2011	620,000	
2012	669,000	7.9%
2013	681,000	1.8%
2014	914,000	34.2%
2015	828,000	-9.4%
2016	948,000	14.5%
2017	886,000	-6.5%
2018	808,000	-8.8%
2019	745,000	-7.8%
2020	902,000	21.1%
2021	1,099,000	21.8%
2022	1,200,000	9.2%
	Total =	93.5%
Source: The National Center for Drug Abuse Statistics. https://drugabusestatistics.org/heroin-statistics/		

Heroin usage and rates of addiction have soared despite increases in DIH arrests and total drug arrests. **Table 3.4** presents the data for arrests and shows that from 2011 to 2021, DIH arrests increased by 183%, and total drug arrests increased by 139%. In 2020 and 2021, arrests for all crimes decreased dramatically due to COVID-19. Prisons even released inmates in response to the health crisis. Despite the COVID-19 pandemic, DIH arrests in 2020 grew by 45%, and total drug arrests rose by 24%. DIH arrests declined slightly in 2021, as did total drug arrests, but more data is needed to evaluate the trend post-COVID-19. Given the public's heightened fears surrounding fentanyl, it is not unreasonable to assume arrests will continue to rise.

Since 2018, both law enforcement and drug addiction treatment centers have noticed a new trend with illicit fentanyl; it has transitioned from a drug that people hoped to avoid to one that the most advanced opioid addicts actively seek.[47] Advanced heroin users must either buy larger quantities to satisfy their growing addiction or switch to a stronger, more potent drug, fentanyl. This shift from heroin to the more potent fentanyl

---

[47] Erika Edwards (2022). Once Feared, Illicit fentanyl is now a Drug of Choice for many Opioid Users. *NBC News*, Aug. 7.

underscores the problem of opioid tolerance. The *National Institute of Health* (NIH) publishes statistics on the use of a wide variety of drugs in this country, including heroin, but does not currently track fentanyl use. Even so, tolerance to opioids is built with repeated use; therefore, it is reasonable to assume that heroin survivors will eventually matriculate to fentanyl.

Table 3.4.		Drug Arrests		
Year	DIH Arrests	% Chg in DIH	Total Drug Arrests	# Chg in Total
2011	61,214		1,512,769	
2012	60,015	-2%	1,508,112	-0.31%
2013	86,307	44%	2,248,887	49%
2014	103,831	20%	2,582,341	15%
2015	121,486	17%	3,095,426	20%
2016	136,909	13%	3,441,956	11%
2017	142,342	4%	3,592,841	4%
2018	139,235	-2%	3,562,746	-1%
2019	127,623	-8%	3,049,743	-14%
2020	185,664	45%	3,793,911	24%
2021	173,410	-7%	3,614,537	-5%
%Chg	183%			139%
Media Cloud. https://tools.mediacloud.org/#/home. Accessed August 13, 2022				

To summarize, the data in this section demonstrates that the sale and use of opioids has increased. Despite increases in DIH and total drug arrests, rates of addiction and heroin usage have soared.

Goal 3: *Protect the Public*

While it is unclear whether the DOJ's objective has been to protect all of the public or only some groups, most Americans would assume that the DOJ aspires to protect all of society. However, much evidence suggests that those who have spent time in prison are no longer considered worthy of protection, rehabilitation, or social acceptance, and neither are their families. Protecting all of society would mean providing safety to all members at a *reasonable cost*. Congress created laws to protect society from unwanted behavior but failed to protect those with behavioral difficulties.

The direct cost to taxpayers of supporting just the federal BOP is $8.816 billion in 2024.[48] The US holds over 1.9 million people in 1,566 state prisons, 98 federal prisons, 3,116 local jails, 1,323 juvenile correctional facilities, 142 immigration detention facilities, and 80 Indian country jails, as well as in military prisons, civil commitment centers, state psychiatric hospitals, and prisons in the US territories — at a system-wide cost of at least $182 billion each year, a 4.2% increase over the previous year.[49] This figure addresses the cost of operating prisons, jails, parole boards, and probation agencies. This cost estimate ignores policing and court costs. The estimate also does not include the costs families pay to support incarcerated loved ones or the costs families have incurred for attorneys. The cost of imprisonment is only a fraction of the economic burden on society. In addition to the $182 billion spent annually on corrections in the US, 1.9 million imprisoned citizens are unable to work and pay taxes.

Additionally, *"[t]he toll that prisoners' families must pay remains an often-overlooked cost,"* according to Hedwig Lee, professor of sociology at Washington University in St. Louis, MO.[50] *"In many cases, a male partner or spouse is the one sent to prison, depriving their family of a major wage earner,"* says Lee. People of color are also five times more likely to be incarcerated than white people. What this means, Lee notes, is that a financial burden is placed on the entire family, often on families that can least afford it. Millions more have completed their sentences but live with a criminal record that limits their ability to gain employment, pay taxes, or find housing.

Communication, visits, commissary, and care packages can cost families up to $800 per month to support loved ones in prison.[51] Research indicates

---

[48] DOJ (2024). Federal Prison System FY 2024 Budget. *Department of Justice*, https://www.justice.gov/d9/2023-03/29-bop_bs_section_ii_chapter_omb_cleared_3.8.23_1045.pdf

[49] Sawyer, Wendy and Wagner, Peter (2024). Mass Incarceration: The Whole Pie 2024. *The Prison Policy Initiative*, March 14. https://www.prisonpolicy.org/reports/pie2024.html#:~:text=Together%2C%20these%20systems%20hold%20over,centers%2C%20state%20psychiatric%20hospitals%2C%20and

[50] Anderson, Francis (2020). The Hidden Costs of Incarceration. *Washington University*, St. Louis, July 9.

[51] The cost of travel varies widely with some loved ones living near the prison, while others must travel more than 1000 miles. The costs of flights, hotels, and eating out can add a significant amount to the total.

that some family members spend as much as 25% of their income paying for such items.[52] Each email and phone call to an incarcerated individual costs money. The total cost

> To visit Scott, our drive is 700 miles (round trip) with one night in a hotel, once a month. The cost per visit is approximately $300 which includes gas, food and lodging. Our typical monthly costs for commissary are $400, $10 on communication and $50 or more on books, magazines and other reading material.

depends on the frequency and length of the communications and whether the prison is state or federal. Some families must pay for airline tickets because the distance is too far to drive, and generally, at least one or two nights (depending on the structure of the visits) in a hotel is needed. Then there is the commissary, the part of every week (or two weeks) all inmates look forward to. The commissary holds various clothing items, shoes, household cleaners, soap, toothpaste, and other hygiene products. There is also a variety of snack foods available, and sometimes sodas. Prisons and jails have limits on the amount an inmate can spend at the commissary to avoid hoarding and selling inside the prison. A wealthy inmate, for example, could buy all the snacks in the commissary and then sell them to inmates at outrageous prices. Finally, some families send care packages so their loved ones can enjoy receiving something in the mail. Prisons and jails are very strict about packages entering the prison; the standards must be met, or the mailroom will reject the package.

Of course, many families cannot afford these expenditures, so they must restrict communication, go without visits, and deprive their loved ones of needed items from the commissary. Unfortunately, the time and money spent on travel do not guarantee being able to see a loved one—prisons close at the last minute for many reasons. COVID was the most common reason for being turned away during 2020-2021; since then, the most common cause is insufficient staffing.

> We see Scott, on average, 1 out of every 3 visitation attempts.

---

[52] Pettus-Davis, C., Brown, D., Veeh, C., & Renn, T. (2016). The economic burden of incarceration in the US. *Institute for Advancing Justice Research and Innovation. Washington University in St. Louis.*

Once family members realize the time and money spent to see their loved one has been wasted, the pain on their faces is heartbreaking to witness. It is no surprise that family members of prisoners are more likely to suffer from mental and physical health complications.[53] Women who have a spouse arrested are more likely to experience depression, have reduced life satisfaction, and have a higher risk of heart disease, for example. Children with an incarcerated parent are more likely to have depression, anxiety, or *Post Traumatic Stress Disorder* (PTSD) and to develop weight or heart problems later in life.[54]

The title of Lopez's 2017 article summarizes his findings on the societal benefits of harsh punishment: *"Mass incarceration doesn't do much to fight crime. But it costs an absurd $183 billion per year."*[55] Lopez's analysis evaluates the cost of imprisonment in jails, state prisons, and federal prisons and takes a broader view to include other actors in the criminal justice system. For example, he included the following costs: courts, parole, probation agencies, prosecutors, and indigent defense services. Also included are health care costs for prisoners, policing for criminal law, construction of criminal justice facilities, food for inmates, and costs to families. The only item not considered is the tax revenue forgone on income lost due to imprisonment.

According to the CDC's *Surgeon General's Report*, 61.2 million people (or 22% of people ages 12 and older) in the US have some sort of drug or alcohol abuse problem. It is likely that everyone in this country knows someone or is related to someone who has a substance abuse disorder. Yet only 10% of those with a drug or alcohol abuse problem seek treatment due to the social stigma and legal consequences surrounding addiction and

---

[53] van de Weijer, S. G., Besemer, K. L., & Dennison, S. M. (2021). Family member incarceration and physical health problems: A longitudinal study among Australian households. *SSM-Population Health, 14*, 100810.

[54] Wildeman, C., Goldman, A. W., & Lee, H. (2019). Health consequences of family member incarceration for adults in the household. *Public Health Reports, 134*(1_suppl), 15S-21S.

[55] Lopez, German (2017). Mass incarceration doesn't do much to fight crime. But it costs an absurd $182 billion a year. A new report suggests mass incarceration costs even more than previously thought. *Vox*, Jan. 27.

substance abuse.[56] These social and legal consequences stem from the early 1970s when the war on drugs criminalized drug use. Addicts were no longer people who needed help; they were criminals. Given the consequences of being labeled a criminal, few want to risk seeking assistance.

Peterson (2019) says, *"The rationale of seeking to protect people is often given to justify harsh sentences for fentanyl distribution, yet there is no research or data set that supports this justification."*[57] Yet addiction is widespread, with no respect for income level, education level, or anything else. It cuts across all societal and cultural boundaries and cannot be isolated or hidden as a minor problem. The *National Survey on Drug Use and Health* differs from the *US Surgeon General's Report*, saying that of those who need treatment for substance use disorders, only 6.5% receive treatment in a medical facility.[58] Both reports agree that the main reason for the large gap between the number of people with addiction and those seeking treatment is that people with addiction and those who care for them fear the social or legal consequences if they seek treatment. The reports highlight another problem with treating addiction as a criminal matter rather than a health issue: those who need help are too afraid and ashamed to come forward, compounding the cycle of drug abuse and addiction.

Similarly, critical tools like naloxone and syringe services are often restricted or underfunded at the community level, limiting access for people who are at high risk of overdose. Naloxone is a lifesaving injection for those who overdose on opioids; it reverses the effects of the drug. Syringe services provide clean needles to those who inject drugs to prevent the spread of disease. There is no national estimate of the lives saved by naloxone, but several news reports suggest the number is substantial. For

---

[56] Surgeon General (2016). Facing Addiction in America: The Surgeon General's Report on Alcohol, Drugs, and Health Full Report. *US Department of Health and Human Services.* https://pubmed.ncbi.nlm.nih.gov/28252892/

[57] Peterson, M., Rich, J., Macmadu, A., Truong, A. Q., Green, T. C., Beletsky, L., ... & Brinkley-Rubinstein, L. (2019). "One guy goes to jail, two people are ready to take his spot": Perspectives on drug-induced homicide laws among incarcerated individuals. *International Journal of Drug Policy, 70,* 47-53.

[58] *National Survey on Drug Use and Health* (2000-2020). Substance Abuse and Mental Health Services Administration. https://www.samhsa.gov/data/data-we-collect/nsduh-national-survey-drug-use-and-health

example, the *Tennessee Department of Mental Health & Substance Abuse Services* reported that from October 2017 through March 2023, more than 450,000 units of naloxone were distributed, and at least 60,000 lives were saved due to naloxone. The number of lives saved is likely much higher since the department suspects underreporting due to stigma and fear.[59] In 2014, before naloxone was widely distributed, managers at 136 organizations that work with people who have a substance abuse disorder completed a survey on the naloxone distributed. From 1996 through June 2014, surveyed organizations provided naloxone kits to 152,283 laypersons and received reports of 26,463 overdose reversals.[60]

Some states have legal barriers that *restrict* access to naloxone, and in states where barriers do not exist, naloxone does not always reach those at the highest risk of an overdose. President Biden's *National Drug Control Strategy* advocates harm reduction strategies to meet people where they are and engage them in care and services.[61] It also calls for actions that will expand access to evidence-based treatments that have been shown to reduce overdose risk and mortality.

On November 1, 2023, the *US Sentencing Commission* (USSC) moved forward with multiple amendments to the *First Step Act* (FSA), reducing sentences for non-violent drug offenders.[62] President Trump signed the FSA into law on December 21, 2018; it was a welcomed reform. Unfortunately, it does not apply to DIH convictions because they are considered violent offenses.

Prosecutors say society needs more prisons built, longer sentences imposed, and more drug users incarcerated. Economists ask, at what price?

Even after the COVID-19 thinning of prison populations, the US still maintains the highest incarceration rates in the world. Before the deaths

---

[59] *Tennessee Department of Mental Health & Substance Abuse Services* (2014). Regional Overdose Prevention Specialists.
[60] CDC (2015). Opioid Overdose Prevention Programs Providing Naloxone to Laypersons-US 2014. *Morbidity and Mortality Weekly*, June 19.
[61] *The White House Fact Sheet* (2022). White House National Drug Control Strategy that Outlines Comprehensive Path Forward to Address Addiction and the Overdose Epidemic, April 22.
[62] USSC (2023). Amendments to Sentencing Guidelines. *United States Sentencing Commission*, April 23.

caused by COVID-19, the US represented 5% of the global population, with 25% of its prisoners. After 1,134,660 deaths and the release of thousands of prisoners, the US now represents 4.25% of the world population with 20% of its prisoners. The strategy of rehabilitation through long-term imprisonment is a lazy, intentionally ignorant approach that has been proven, year after year, to produce the opposite of the desired results.

Protecting all of society means providing safety to all members *at a reasonable* cost. Society has not been protected from the ravages of illegal drugs flowing into the US, yet the price is astronomical.

Goal #4: Punish the Offender
"We have known for decades that addiction is a medical condition, a treatable brain disorder, not a character flaw or a form of social deviance. Yet, despite the overwhelming evidence supporting that position, drug addiction continues to be criminalized. The US must take a public health approach to drug addiction now, in the interest of both population well-being and health equity."[63] The use of harsh sentences is covered throughout this book; this section focuses on the question: *does harsh punishment deter offenders from re-offending?*

The *Crime Museum* puts it like this: *"The basic idea of rehabilitation through imprisonment is that a person who has been incarcerated will never want to be sent back to prison after they have been set free."*[64] *Unfortunately, research has consistently shown that time spent in prison does not successfully rehabilitate most inmates, and the majority of criminals return to a life of crime almost immediately."*[65] In fact, according to the *American Psychological Association* (APA), prisons in the US deliberately turned away from rehabilitation in the mid-1970s as the country adopted a *"tough on crime"* approach that focused on punishment.

---

[63] Volkow, N. D. (2021). Addiction should be treated, not penalized. *Neuropsychopharmacology, 46*(12), 2048-2050.
[64] Crime Museum (2022). Rehabilitative Effects of Imprisonment. *The Crime Museum.* https://www.crimemuseum.org/crime-library/famous-prisons-incarceration/rehabilitative-effects-of-imprisonment/
[65] Crime Museum (2022). Rehabilitative Effects of Imprisonment. *The Crime Museum.* https://www.crimemuseum.org/crime-library/famous-prisons-incarceration/rehabilitative-effects-of-imprisonment/

"The approach has created explosive growth in the prison population," the APA explains, *"while having at most a modest effect on crime rates."*[66]

After the passage of the 1970 CSA, Congress abandoned rehabilitation practices in the penal system. In 1989, the Supreme Court upheld federal sentencing guidelines that removed rehabilitation from serious consideration when sentencing offenders.[67] Defendants were sentenced strictly for the crime, with no recognition given to factors such as amenability to treatment, personal history, efforts to rehabilitate oneself, or alternatives to prison.

Socially, people with an addiction are viewed as the lowest rung of society, 'gutter people' who get what they deserve. People with an addiction are widely considered to have no willpower. Nevertheless, Snoek, Levy, and Kennett (2016) argue that willpower is much less critical to explaining recovery than the prevailing views suggest.[68] When society believes that the real issue is willpower, it is not surprising that so many blame the addict for their lawless failings rather than recognize a medical problem. This perspective causes many to see harsh drug laws as an essential tool for controlling the overdose crisis and to see harsh sentences as justified punishment for the addict's depraved behavior.

The academic and scientific communities have not accepted this justification because the data does not support the conclusion that harsh drug laws effectively protect public welfare. Despite the growing record of failure, the justice system appears to be unquestioningly devoted to a failed strategy of punishment and retribution, ignoring significant evidence that it has caused the situation to worsen.

The US not only has the highest incarceration rates in the world but also the highest *recidivism* rates. *Recidivism* is the relapse of criminal or drug behavior that results in the re-arrest, reconviction, and re-imprisonment of

---

[66] Benson, Etienne (2003). Rehabilitate or Punish? Psychologists are not only providing treatment to prisoners; they're also contributing to debate over the nature of prison itself. *American Psychological Association*, July/August, Vol. 34, No. 7, page 46.
[67] Mistretta v. United States, 488 U.S. 361 (1989).
[68] Snoek, A., Levy, N., & Kennett, J. (2016). Strong-willed but not successful: The importance of strategies in recovery from addiction. *Addictive Behaviors Reports, 4*, 102-107.

an individual. On average, when the US BOP releases 5 prisoners, 4 of them will eventually return to prison. However, in Norway, only 1 in 5 will return to prison.[69] America's recidivism crisis is far more alarming than any other country studied. The high US recidivism rate demonstrates that US prisons are as ineffective as they are inefficient, a sobering reality that calls for a reimagined criminal justice system. The best approach to preparing those addicted to drugs for reintegration into society is to shift the goal from punishment to medical treatment and rehabilitation. By turning the goal of drug incarceration towards rehabilitation, recidivism rates can be lowered by investing in mental health care, devising personalized education plans, and creating a work pipeline.[70]

Perhaps the most reliable tool to judge the success of harsh punishment versus a medical approach to drug addiction is to compare the recidivism rates of various countries. **Table 3.5** shows the 2023 recidivism rates in selected countries. Apart from Russia and the US, the countries listed use a harm-reduction approach to drug addiction.

Table 3.5. Recidivism Rates	
Country	Recidivism Rate
Norway	20%
UK	24%
Denmark	27%
Sweden	30%
Finland	31%
France	31%
Germany	40%
Japan	49%
Russia	60%
USA	78%
Source: National Library of Medicine, National Center for Biotechnical Information, 2023.	

Norway has the lowest recidivism rate in the world, followed closely by the UK and Denmark. The Nordic countries, along with much of Western

---

[69] DOJ (2022). A. Second Chance: The Impact of Unsuccessful Reentry and the Need for Reintegration Resources in Communities. *Department of Justice*, April, Vol. 15, No. 4.
[70] Benecchi, L. (2021). Recidivism imprisons American progress. *Harvard Political Review*, 8.

Europe, now use harm-reduction techniques to address drug problems. Those countries have much lower recidivism rates than countries such as Russia or the US, where the punishment/revenge approach is used to curtail drug crimes. The US has the highest recidivism rate in the world, indicating a complete failure of the criminal justice system to function as intended. Cycling the same people into and out of prison is an active, daily demonstration of the failure of the current approach to curbing undesirable drug behavior.

To further examine the success or failure of imprisonment to modify behavior, a review of the states with the highest and lowest incarceration rates is noteworthy but not scientific. According to the *World Population Review-2023*, the ten states with the highest incarceration rates are Alaska, Mississippi, Louisiana, Arkansas, Oklahoma, Alabama, Delaware, Arizona, Idaho, and Texas.[71] **Table 3.6** lists the states in decreasing order of incarceration rates in column A, with Alaska having the highest per capita prison population and Massachusetts having the lowest. Column B shows the crime rate rank, indicating, for example, that Alaska has the eleventh highest crime rate in the US, and Massachusetts has one of the lowest crime rates in the country, ranked at 49th.

Seven of the ten states with the highest prison populations also have the highest crime rates, ranking in the top *twenty*. More strikingly, seven of the ten states with the lowest prison populations have crime rates in the lowest *ten* ranking states. The numbers do not indicate causality; they are offered as an interesting observation.

The historical information provided in this section provides evidence that the US criminal justice system has completely failed to manage drug use and addiction outcomes. In other words, taxpayers do not receive the level of protection for which they have paid.

---

[71] https://worldpopulationreview.com

State	Prison Population-Ranked	Crime Rate-Ranked
A	B	C
10 Highest Prison Population States		
Alaska	1	11
Mississippi	2	23
Louisiana	3	2
Arkansas	4	5
Oklahoma	5	6
Alabama	6	18
Delaware	7	26
Arizona	8	14
Idaho	9	47
Texas	10	15
10 Lowest Prison Population States		
Connecticut	41	21
Rhode Island	42	44
Vermont	43	45
Utah	45	12
New York	46	41
New Hampshire	47	50
Minnesota	48	22
New Jersey	49	46
Maine	50	48
Massachusetts	51	49

Table 3.6. Comparison of Crime and Prison

*The District of Columbia was included as a separate state.

To summarize, harsh punishments have produced increased drug overdose deaths, increased drug sales, increased drug addiction, increased recidivism, and imposed unreasonable societal costs. Of the four DOJ-stated goals, they have succeeded at only one: punishing and repunishing the same offenders. Until the US realizes it is dealing with a medical issue, not a criminal issue, the problems related to overdose deaths, addiction, recidivism, and high costs will not be resolved.

Legal Points at Issue

Before 2008, law enforcement considered death by drug overdose as accidental or as *'death by misadventure'* – widely considered to be unintentional, involving no violation of law or criminal negligence. When death was ruled *by misadventure*, it meant the deceased had voluntarily engaged in a risky activity, resulting in death. There was no crime involved in the death. But things have changed radically since that time. Now, an overdose death means someone is going to prison, likely for a minimum of 20 years.

The primary legal points are corollaries to the DIH laws contained in the ADAA of 1986. The corollaries to the overdose laws are:

i) The *felony murder doctrine* of *strict liability* and
ii) Mandatory minimums.

The DIH charge establishes that a *homicide* occurred rather than an accident *by misadventure*, which then triggers the *felony murder doctrine* (FMD). Invoking the FMD triggers the judiciary's application of *strict liability*. Congress sets mandatory minimum sentences rather than the judiciary.

The Felony Murder Doctrine

The FMD is a principle that allows a defendant to be charged with first-degree murder for a death that occurs during a felony, even if the defendant is not the killer. Most drug crimes and many weapons crimes are subject to the FMD. The FMD is an exception to the standard rules of homicide. Typically, a defendant can be convicted of murder only if a prosecutor shows that the defendant acted with the intent to kill or with reckless indifference to human life. However, under the FMD, a defendant can be convicted of murder even in the absence of intent or reckless disregard.

In general, proof of the underlying offense and the cause of death will be sufficient to obtain a conviction under this approach.[72] The waiving of the responsibility requirement, regardless of a person's intent or mental state, means that the defendant's motive, or *mens rea*, is not considered,

---

[72] Neil, Mark. Prosecuting Drug Overdose Cases: A Paradigm Shift. *National Association of Attorneys General.* https://www.naag.org/attorney-general-journal/prosecuting-drug-overdose-cases-a-paradigm-shift/

effectively denying the defendant the due process *guaranteed* by the US Constitution.[73]

Because the crime of DIH is considered felony murder, *strict liability* applies. Liability is strict when the crime does not require proof of fault for the offense or any relevant moral culpability.[74] When death by misadventure is converted into first-degree murder with no evidence needed, the punishment rendered will likely be disproportionate to the crime for which the offender is responsible. It does not matter whether the accused or an accomplice caused the death. Nor does it matter whether the death occurred accidentally or without negligence. Most scholars oppose the concept of strict liability for reasons commonly pertaining to the unfairness of a defendant being held liable for something unrelated to the defendant's intentions (or lack thereof). Even so, US courts and legislatures support strict criminal liability because they feel it prevents further deaths. Imposing liability on persons who intended no harm puts them in the same legal category as those who acted deliberately to hurt someone. The *Proportionality Doctrine* in the Eighth Amendment to the US Constitution prohibits punishment that is disproportionate to the crime.[75] Logically, this should prohibit a 20-year sentence for a death by misadventure.

After a deep dive into the development of strict liability offenses, such as DIH laws, Phillips (2020) found that knowledge of the accused's criminal intent is an indispensable part of due process protections provided in homicide law. *"Ignoring the accused's mens rea is troubling because, according to criminal law principles, 'intent to harm' is required to impose culpability. DIH laws are strict liability offenses, requiring no intent toward the resulting death. This research asserts that criminal intent is an indispensable due process protection in homicide law. Further, DIH laws, though not facially unconstitutional, are functionally anti-constitutional and inconsistent with the spirit of due process."*[76]

---

[73] Mens Rea is Latin for *'guilty mind.'* Mens rea, intent and motive have the same meaning here.
[74] Duff, R. A. (2005). Strict liability, legal presumptions, and the presumption of innocence. *Appraising strict liability*, *125*, 125.
[75] The *Proportionality Doctrine* states that the punishment should be proportional to the crime committed.
[76] Phillips, K. S. (2020). From overdose to crime scene: The incompatibility of drug-induced homicide statutes with due process. *Duke Law Journal*, *70*, 659.

In 2021, the Washington State Supreme Court, in *State v. Blake*,[77] considered the constitutionality of the strict liability standard imposed by the state's drug possession statute.[78] The court ruled that it violates due process because the statute, which has substantial penalties for *"innocent, passive conduct,"* exceeds the legislature's police power. The state supreme court ruled on February 25, 2021, that the state's strict liability law is unconstitutional because it does not require proof that a defendant knew they possessed a controlled substance.[79]

The legal questions around DIH laws, as they relate to the FMD, have been explored elsewhere by legal historians, epistemologists, and criminal law theorists. The resulting consensus is nearly unanimous regarding felony murder and other provisions that are corollaries to DIH laws: they are flawed laws and have created harmful criminal justice policies.[80,81] Even so, DIH laws are rapidly expanding beyond the federal government to the states. In the 2023 legislative session alone, 46 states introduced hundreds of fentanyl crime bills, according to the *National Conference on State Legislatures*.[82] Virginia lawmakers codified fentanyl as "*a weapon of terrorism."* An Iowa law makes the sale or manufacture of less than five grams of fentanyl, roughly the weight of five paper clips, punishable by up to 10 years in prison. Arkansas and Texas recently joined some 30 states, including Pennsylvania, Colorado, and Wyoming, that have DIH statutes, allowing murder prosecutions even of people who share drugs socially that contain lethal fentanyl doses.[83] Other states bring charges of first-degree murder, second-degree murder, or manslaughter in DIH cases.

---

[77] State v. Blake, 481 P.3d 521 (Wash. 2021)
[78] Washington Rev. Code § 69.50.4013 (2015).
[79] Weiss, Debra C. (2021). Cataclysmic decision striking down strict liability drug law puts past convictions at risk in this state. *American Bar Association Journal*, March 15. https://www.abajournal.com/news/article/cataclysmic-decision-striking-down-strict-liability-drug-law-puts-past-convictions-at-risk-in-this-state
[80] Coyne, C. J., & Hall, A. R. (2017). Four decades and counting: The continued failure of the war on drugs. *Cato Institute Policy Analysis*, (811).
[81] Lamb, H. R., & Weinberger, L. E. (1998). Persons with severe mental illness in jails and prisons: A review. *Psychiatric services*, 49(4), 483-492.
[82] NCSL Legislative Summit, Indy (2023). https://www.ncsl.org/events/ncsl-legislative-summit-2023
[83] Hoffman, Jan (2023). Harsh New Fentanyl Laws Ignites Debate Over How to Combat Overdose Crisis. *The New York Times*, June 1.

The surge in the utilization of harsh punishments is particularly alarming because it produces the opposite results as desired and is at direct odds with the findings of academic research, health sciences reports, and successful recovery programs. Rather than helping, the rash of state legislation has the potential to compound the problems of increasing overdose deaths, rates of addiction, and costs to society.

According to *Fair & Just Prosecution*, in response to the opioid crisis gripping our country, *"...numerous states have been pursuing charges against drug dealers in situations where someone has overdosed on the drugs they received. Not only are prosecutors looking to press drug charges against these dealers, but surprisingly to most people, these prosecutors are looking to hold them responsible for murder. Whether by advancing new state legislation or reviving existing state statutes, prosecutors in at least twelve states are pursuing these charges, as is the federal government under the Controlled Substances Act."*[84] Rather than offering any sort of deterrence effects, these homicide statutes are inappropriately holding drug addicts and users strictly liable for homicides due to the lack of a mens rea requirement in the law.[85,86,87] The number of overdose deaths is increasing, and the statutes are not working as intended. Instead, they are needlessly punitive and succeed only in ruining additional lives. Despite adverse outcomes, current judicial conduct suggests that punishment for the sake of punishment is the path chosen by the DOJ.

Mandatory Minimums
The 1909 federal criminal code revision eliminated most mandatory minimums enacted during the 1800s to usher in a period of discretionary

---

[84] FJP (2022). Drug Induced Homicide Prosecutions. *Fair & Just Prosecutions.* https://fairandjustprosecution.org/wp-content/uploads/2022/07/FJP-Drug-Induced-Homicide-Brief.pdf

[85] FJP (2022). Drug Induced Homicide Prosecutions. *Fair & Just Prosecutions.* https://fairandjustprosecution.org/wp-content/uploads/2022/07/FJP-Drug-Induced-Homicide-Brief.pdf

[86] NACDL (2019). Advocacy Calls on Drug Induced Homicide Laws. *National Association of Criminal Defense Lawyers*, Oct 19.

[87] DPA Report (2017). An Overdose Death is Not Murder: Why Overdose Laws are Counterproductive and Inhumane. *The Drug Policy alliance.* https://drugpolicy.org/wp-content/uploads/2023/05/Overdose_Death_Is_Not_Murder_Report.pdf

judgment.[88] Rather than have mandatory minimums, the consensus at the time was to allow judges the discretion to rule based on the individual information available for each case. By the mid-twentieth century, a well-respected commentator observed that *"[t]he individualization of penal dispositions, principally through the institutions of the indeterminate sentence, probation, and parole, is a development whose value few would contest."*[89]

However, within a few decades, attitudes shifted again, driven by concerns that broad discretion for judges had led to unjustifiable sentences, some too lenient, others too severe.[90] State legislative bodies moved to curtail discretionary sentencing by implementing the 1984 sentencing reform measure, which abolished indeterminate sentencing at the federal level and created a determinate sentencing structure through the federal sentencing guidelines. Two years later, the *Anti-Drug Abuse Act* of 1986 was passed and established higher mandatory minimums than the 1984 act because federal legislators felt the penalties were not severe enough. By 1994, all 50 states had enacted at least one mandatory sentencing law.[91]

A mandatory minimum sentence, created by Congress or a state legislature, sets the shortest prison time a court must impose on a convicted defendant, no matter the offense or the offender's unique circumstances. Typically, mandatory minimums apply to gun and drug crimes and are based only on the possession or presence of a gun or the type and weight of the drug involved.

The issue of mandatory minimums has been researched extensively over the past three decades and deserves more attention. To that end, Chapter 6 is devoted entirely to motive and mandatory minimum sentences.

---

[88] Doyle, Charles (2013). Federal Mandatory Minimum Sentencing Statutes. *Congressional Research Service*, Sept. 9.
[89] Kadish, S. H. (1962). Legal norm and discretion in the police and sentencing processes. *Harvard Law Review*, 904-931.
[90] Brown, G. M. (1988). Do Judicial Scarlet Letters Violate the Cruel and Unusual Punishments Clause of the Eight Amendment. *Hastings Const. LQ, 16,* 115.
[91] Parent, Dale, Dunworth, Terrence, McDonald, Douglas and Rhodes, William (19970. Mandatory Sentencing. The Office of Justice Programs, *U.S. Department of Justice,* Jan.

Retribution vs Restorative Justice

Retribution is the oldest justification for punishment, and the concept is central to the philosophy offered by Hegel.[92] The fact that the individual has committed a wrongful act justifies punishment that should be *proportional to the wrong committed.*

Historically, there are two schools of thought on retribution and punishment. The *Old Testament* school of thought follows the instructions in Exodus 21:23, to *"give life for life, eye for eye, tooth for tooth, hand for hand, foot for foot, to punish an offender.*[93] But more than 3,400 years later, Martin Luther King Jr. responded, *"The old law of 'an eye for an eye' leaves everybody blind. It destroys communities and makes humanity impossible. It creates bitterness in the survivors and brutality in the destroyers..."*[94,95]

For centuries, psychologists have been exploring the "mental machinery" behind punishment and revenge. Behavioral scientists have observed that revenge increases hostility instead of quenching it, so harming an offender is not enough to satisfy a person's vengeful spirit. They have also found that revenge often creates a cycle of retaliation instead of delivering justice because one person's moral compass rarely aligns with another's. The upshot of these insights is a better sense of why the pursuit of revenge has persisted through the ages despite the adverse outcomes.[96] *"People who are more vengeful tend to be those who are motivated by power, authority, and the desire for status."* price (2009) says, *"They don't want to lose face."*[97]

---

[92] Dydk, S.W. (1898). Hegel's conception of crime and punishment. *The Philosophical Review,* 7(1), 62-71.
[93] *New American Standard Bible* (2022). Exodus 21:23-25.
[94] King, Coretta Scott (2021). *The Words of Martin Luther King, Jr.* William Marrow Paperbacks, Oct. 19, pp 1-128.
[95] The date of Exodus was 1446 BC according to *Bible.org.* https://bible.org/article/introduction-book-exodus. There is much disagreement on the exact date.
[96] Jaffee, Eric (2011). The Complicated Psychology of Revenge. *Psychological Science,* Oct. 4.
[97] Price, M. (2009). Revenge and the people who seek it. *American Psychological Association,* June, *40*(6), 43-45.

Restorative justice seeks to restore human relations rather than tear them apart and is often defended with references to *New Testament* values like reconciliation, forgiveness, and mercy. Advocates of the retribution approach to addiction ridicule the values of restorative justice, indicating a lack of understanding of the process.[98] Marshall (2020) expanded and deepened previous work on the dichotomy of the *Old* and *New Testament* views of justice by arguing that "*...justice is satisfied, not by retributive punishment but by repentance, restoration, and renewal.*"[99]

A restorative justice system first determines the harmful impact of a crime on both the victim and perpetrator. Once the harm is established, the possibility of repairing the damage is assessed to provide the perpetrator with avenues for accountability. Restorative systems are designed to transform individuals—victims and offenders—and pinpoint the root causes of the crime, including social systems and structural issues. Once identified, these systemic problems can be faced, addressed, and potentially overcome to foster fair systems and healthier, safer communities.[100]

The foundational principles underlying restorative justice include:

1. Relationships
At the core of every restorative justice process is a damaged relationship. The person who caused harm has negatively impacted another person's life and community. Leading fulfilling lives and creating desirable communities becomes more challenging without solid relationships. The complex relationship that exists between the perpetrator and the victim requires time and a therapeutic approach to unravel. Once the person who caused harm accepts accountability for their actions and begins to make amends, the relationship can begin the healing process.

---

[98] Rosenblum, A., Marsch, L. A., Joseph, H., & Portenoy, R. K. (2008). Opioids and the treatment of chronic pain: controversies, current status, and future directions. *Experimental and clinical psychopharmacology*, 16(5), 405.
[99] Marshall, C. D. (2020). Restorative justice. *Religion matters: The contemporary relevance of religion*, 101-117.
[100] Three Core Elements of Restorative Justice. *Restorative Justice.org*. https://restorativejustice.org/what-is-restorative-justice/three-core-elements-of-restorative-justice/

2. Respect

Respect is vital to relationships and essential to the restorative justice process. Respect keeps the process safe. All involved parties are trusted to respect themselves and others at all process stages. Deep listening skills are employed, assumptions are set aside, and concentration is focused on listening to the speaker. Understanding the perspective of the parties involved forms the foundation for respect. It is unnecessary to agree with each party's perspective, but it is essential to understand.

3. Responsibility

For restorative justice to be effective, each participant must recognize and accept responsibility for the damage inflicted. Everyone is asked to be honest with themselves and to search deeply to discover how they participated in the situation. Even if the damage was unintentional, the person who caused harm must take responsibility for their actions. Ultimately, taking responsibility must be a personal choice and cannot be imposed on someone.

4. Repair

After respect and responsibility are established, the next step toward healing is the repair process. The offender is expected to repair the damage fully when possible. Not all damage can be restored; an overdose death cannot be 'repaired' because a loved one is gone forever, leaving an enormous hole in the family. In these cases, the victim's family is taught to resist thoughts of revenge, punishment, and blame to move forward with a better understanding of the consequences of addiction. The offender can regain their self-respect and respect for others through working to repair the damage.

5. Reintegration

The community allows the offender to accept responsibility and begin reintegration to complete the process. Reintegration encourages collaboration between the community and the offender rather than turning toward coercion and isolation. This process recognizes the assets the offender brings to the table and what they have learned. By accepting responsibility and agreeing to repair the damage, the offender creates a space to rebuild trust and to be reintegrated into the community.

The disparity between the punishment-revenge approach and the restorative-justice approach to addiction could not be more striking. Narrowing this chasm is necessary for criminal justice reform but is far from the most challenging. The most difficult aspect of reform is changing society's views of people who are suffering from addiction. The US has spent 50-plus years convincing society that drug users are criminals rather than those needing intensive medical and mental health attention.

Every dollar spent on arresting, prosecuting, and imprisoning persons with an addiction is a dollar that is not spent on interventions that are proven to decrease overdose deaths. Harm reduction programs and treatments, particularly the treatment of opioid use disorder with medications, have been proven to save lives.[101] If society is ever going to end this overdose crisis, it will be by using harm reduction strategies and effective treatment for people with an addiction.

Recommendations

The US should move to decriminalize drugs and institute restorative justice practices to help all parties heal from the trauma involved. The data is clear; the drug problem in the US has become worse over the past 50 years despite spending trillions of taxpayer dollars. Newer, more dangerous drugs have infiltrated the black-market supply, more people are using, more are becoming addicted, and many more are dying. The current situation is one of untold anguish and despair for all parties involved. The loved ones of those who die bear the enormous burden of an irreplaceable loss. The families and communities of those who are incarcerated are also destroyed by the challenge of having a loved one who is alive but is

---

[101] i) Irvine, M. A., Oller, D., Boggis, J., Bishop, B., Coombs, D., Wheeler, E., ... & Green, T. C. (2022). Estimating naloxone need in the USA across fentanyl, heroin, and prescription opioid epidemics: a modelling study. *The Lancet Public Health, 7*(3), e210-e218.

ii) Santo, T., Clark, B., Hickman, M., Grebely, J., Campbell, G., Sordo, L., ... & Degenhardt, L. (2021). Association of opioid agonist treatment with all-cause mortality and specific causes of death among people with opioid dependence: a systematic review and meta-analysis. *JAMA psychiatry, 78*(9), 979-993.

iii) Linas, B. P., Savinkina, A., Madushani, R. W. M. A., Wang, J., Yazdi, G. E., Chatterjee, A., ... & Barocas, J. A. (2021). Projected estimates of opioid mortality after community-level interventions. *JAMA Network Open, 4*(2), e2037259-e2037259.

effectively dead to the world. Revenge may provide temporary relief, but it leaves the family empty, bitter, and alone. Too often, the so-called 'dealer' turns out to be another addict lost in their disease, and the system happily destroys their lives and families, as well. It is time for a fresh approach, focusing on wellness and seeking to make each party whole. The families of DIH victims cannot replace their loved ones, but they can learn to understand and accept the consequences of addiction to a deadly drug without the need to blame themselves, their loved ones, or a third party. Both victims and offenders can begin healing when they take responsibility for their actions.

The criminalization approach to curbing unwanted drug behavior has fueled the most tragic overdose crisis this country has ever seen; it is killing and incarcerating loved ones by the thousands. It has been a complete and total failure by every measure. Drug decriminalization means that people would no longer be stigmatized, arrested, or incarcerated for personal drug use. Instead, the savings from reduced enforcement could be reinvested into addiction services and social support. The services and support include voluntary treatment, housing, employment, harm reduction, recovery centers, and peer support groups.

A Word from Scott

As with most people, I grew up believing that American justice meant you are innocent until proven guilty, you have the right to due process, the right to an attorney, etc. As I grew older, I never interacted with any state or federal justice system, so I had no reason to believe otherwise. It wasn't until the DEA arrested me in 2019 for a drug-induced overdose death that I had firsthand experience with either state or federal judicial systems. In my case, I was never assumed innocent; my guilt was established upon arrest, and no further investigation was ever done. No one tells you that all attorneys lose their cases against federal prosecutors. If you find an attorney who has won a federal criminal case, hire them immediately because the defense winning is an almost impossible task. Defense attorneys go into federal court KNOWING they will lose before the negotiations or trial begins. Their goal is to go through the motions of pretending to be an attorney while knowing it is a lost cause. I used to be pissed off at my worthless defense attorney until I realized that all defense attorneys lose to federal prosecutors. It doesn't change that I had a lousy

attorney, but it would not have mattered. All the cards are in the prosecutor's hands; they can do whatever they want.
Unless you have been charged, processed, and sentenced to federal prison, it is impossible to thoroughly understand the level of corruption, inconsistencies, and the prosecutor's power. My advice: If you ever are accused of a federal drug crime, you ARE going to prison. Don't waste any money on a defense attorney; just take the one assigned by the court.

Summary

This chapter identified and discussed the four goals of the *Department of Justice* regarding harsh punishment for drug violations. The first goal of the DOJ is to reduce drug overdose deaths. The data showed that overdose deaths have rapidly multiplied over the past 50 years. Researchers and health organizations now characterize the current period as an *'overdose death crisis.'*

The second stated goal of the DOJ is to discourage opioid sales and use. The data presented shows addiction rates and heroin usage rates have increased dramatically this century despite an increase in drug arrests.
The third goal of the DOJ is to protect society. The US spends $182 billion per year for prisoners in exchange for a 78% recidivism rate. Society has paid enormous sums of money to incarcerate and punish drug addicts, and in return, the US has the worst recidivism rate in the world. The DOJ has successfully implemented excessively harsh punishments, but they have backfired, leaving society with nothing in return for the costs born.

The fourth and final stated goal of the DOJ is punishment. The evidence overwhelmingly shows that harsher punishments have not rehabilitated offenders. The US has the highest recidivism rates in the world, indicating the most dysfunctional system known. Using the FMD, applying strict liability and mandatory minimums raises constitutional issues regarding how the justice system treats the defendant.

Research demonstrates that addiction is a *health* issue, not a *criminal* one, and should be treated as such. Additionally, harsh punishments have failed to accomplish *ANY* of the DOJ's stated goals.

The Criminalization of Addiction

This chapter recommends that the US adopt a harm-reduction approach to drug crimes and abandon the failed punishment/revenge approach to treating a medical condition.

APPENDIX 3. OVERDOSE DEATHS IN EACH YEAR

Yr	O.D.s 000	Pop. 000	Yr	ODs 000	Pop. 000	Yr	Ods 000	Pop. 000
1970	7.1	203,458	1990	4.5	248,922	2010	38	308,745
1971	6.8	206,783	1991	5.2	253,088	2011	41.3	311,592
1972	6.6	206,783	1992	6	256,606	2012	41.5	313,914
1973	6.4	211,362	1993	7.4	260,024	2013	44	316,128
1974	6.5	213,437	1994	7.8	263,241	2014	47	318,857
1975	7.2	215,457	1995	8	266,386	2015	52	321,418
1976	6.8	217,615	1996	8.4	269,540	2016	63.6	323,127
1977	6.1	219,808	1997	9.1	272,776	2017	70.2	325,719
1978	5.5	222,102	1998	9.8	276,033	2018	67.4	327,167
1979	2.5	224,635	1999	16.9	279,040	2019	70.6	328,239
Total	61.5	2141440	Total	83.1	2645656	Total	535.6	3194906
% Chg	-64%	-58%	% Chg	274%	245%	% Chg	84%	80%
1980	2.5	226,624	2000	17.4	281,421	2020	91.8	329,484
1981	2.7	229,487	2001	19.4	284,968	2021	107	331,900
1982	2.9	231,701	2002	23.5	287,625	2022	109*	333,271
1983	2.9	233,781	2003	25.8	290,107	2023	112	335,821
1984	3.3	235,922	2004	27.4	292,805	2024		
1985	3.6	238,005	2005	29.8	295,516	2025		
1986	4.2	240,190	2006	34.4	298,380	2026		
1987	3.9	242,395	2007	36	301,231	2027		
1988	4.9	244,652	2008	36.5	304,094	2028		
1989	5	247,002	2009	37	306,771	2029		
Total	35.8	2,369,759	Total	287	2,942,918	Total	311	1,330,476
% Chg	102%	94%	% Chg	112%	103%	% Chg	22%	22%

Source: CDC Mortality files 1970-2020

*Complete count currently unavailable

CHAPTER 4: OPIOID ADDICTS *CAN'T* BE DEALERS... *even if they want to*

This chapter discusses the medical condition of opioid addiction and its impact on the brain's normal functioning. The demands of a drug dealer are reviewed through the eyes of three dealers who wrote anonymously on *Quora*. The medical condition is then reviewed, considering the demands of being a drug dealer to determine the addict's ability to perform the tasks.

Introduction

The primary criterion that distinguishes a charge of *Drug-Induced Homicide* from other, more minor, drug charges is the accused *must be a drug dealer*. It is the *dealer* component of the charge that results in such a lengthy mandatory minimum sentence of 20 years in federal prison. It is also the *dealer* segment of the charge that makes it impossible for advanced opioid addicts to be guilty under DIH laws. It is helpful to begin with a working definition of a *drug dealer*. Entering 'drug dealer' into a search engine produces these top two definitions:

1. An individual or group who sells or supplies controlled drugs/substances of any type or quantity. The label can be used for small-time dealers who sell small amounts to offset the costs of their drug use, as well as highly organized groups that operate like an organized crime business.

2. A person who sells illegal drugs.

Neither definition is constructive when trying to understand the business model for drug dealers. For example, in stock trading, dealers are called *specialists* who own an inventory of specific stocks and use stockbrokers to sell to the public for a percentage commission. A stockbroker transacts with the public and does not own an inventory of stocks. Instead, the broker brings the buyer and seller together for a mutually agreeable trade. Similarly, the automobile industry involves car dealers and car sellers. The automobile dealership owns the inventory of cars, and the salespeople sell the car for a percentage commission but never own the vehicle.

In the context of illegal drugs, the word 'dealer' applies to ALL levels of the hierarchy displayed in **Figure 4.1.**, because, at each level, all individual players must buy and *own* their inventory of drugs. *Traffickers* illegally bring drugs into the US and sell them to high-level dealers inside the country. With opioid distribution, traffickers are the ones most likely to cut heroin with fentanyl to increase profit margins. The fact that the heroin has been cut is not information relayed to the high-level dealer who is now selling heroin laced with fentanyl. Should the high-level dealer cut the heroin again, the results could be deadly.

The drug dealer hierarchy in **Figure 4.1** shows the *Drug Kingpin's* crown at the top of the pyramid. [102] There is one Kingpin for *each* distribution channel, resulting in multiple drug lords. Just below the Kingpin are the traffickers in a relatively narrow box, indicating that there are very few traffickers relative to the other categories of dealers. Traffickers deliver illegal heroin to high-level dealers in the US, shown as a larger, wider box, indicating a significant number of high-level dealers relative to traffickers.[103] The high-level dealers then sell the drugs to a much larger group of medium-level dealers. Medium-level dealers may control a state's or city's drug market, while high-level dealers may control a region. Low-level dealers are the largest and most diverse dealer group at the bottom of the pyramid. Low-level dealers include city dealers, neighborhood dealers, and block dealers.

Addicts selling to other addicts are not a part of the drug dealer hierarchy because they enter the market as *buyers* and only sell from their personal stash if absolutely necessary. They do not move the product through the sales distribution channel.

---

[102] *Kingpin* and *Drug Lord* are used interchangeably
[103] There are also low-level traffickers inside the U.S. who move drugs from one part of the country to another.

Figure 4.1 **Drug Dealer Hierarchy**

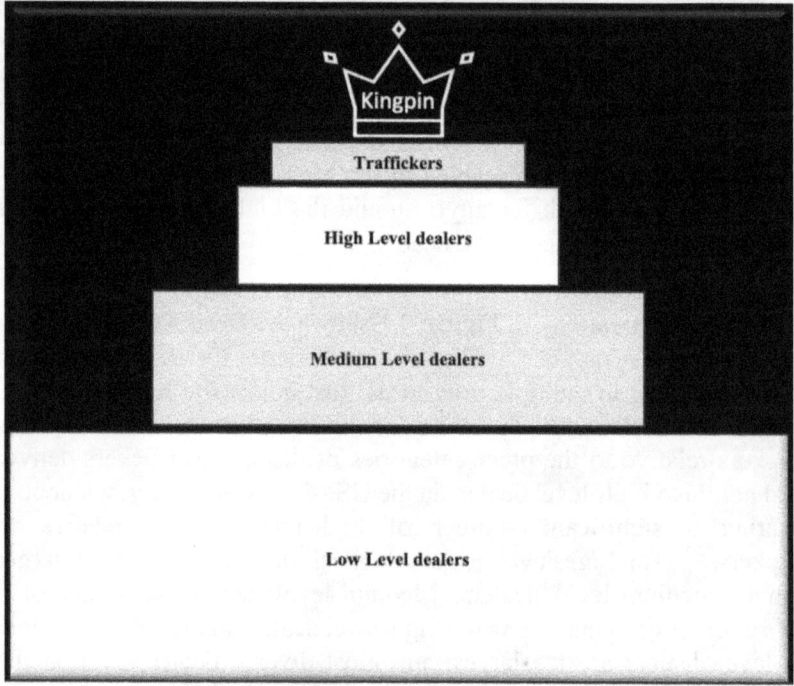

After an exhaustive DOJ and USSC literature search, no definitions were found for the various dealer levels in use. However, an examination of *US Code 21 § 802* reveals the following definitions:

1. *Traffickers* who import illegal drugs into the country, and
2. *Dealers* who sell (or give) drugs to someone else, whether for profit or not. Under *US Code 21* definitions, there is no distinction between a drug Kingpin and a person with an addiction who shares drugs with friends.

Fentanyl is approximately 10% of the cost of heroin on the 'street,' as shown in **Table 4.1**.[104] Since fentanyl is roughly 50 times stronger than heroin, an equivalent dose would be 1/500 of the wholesale price of heroin. Most US dealers do not realize their heroin has been cut with fentanyl, so it is no surprise that most users are also unaware. The law does not distinguish between traffickers, such as the infamous Oscar Noe Medina Gonzalez[105], head of the Medina cartel, and people like Scott, who share drugs with fellow addicts.

This chapter focuses on matters that prevent advanced opioid addicts from performing as dealers.

Table 4.1	Price of Heroin vs. Fentanyl	
Weight	Heroin	Fentanyl
0.1 g	$5-$20	$0.50-$2
1 g	$60-$200	$6-$20
1 oz	$1,000-$1,500	$100-$150
Source: *Zinnia Health*, 2023		

Advanced Opioid Addiction

Due to its potency, a tiny amount of fentanyl can be deadly. Just two milligrams can cause an overdose death. It is not only potent but highly addictive. A person can become addicted to fentanyl with the first dose. It cannot be smelled or tasted, making it nearly impossible to tell if other drugs have been laced with it unless special fentanyl test strips are used.[106] Fentanyl enters the brain more rapidly than other opioids because of its ability to quickly pass the blood-brain barrier, which is why fentanyl has been used for immediate pain relief in emergency medicine since the 1950s. Hospitals administer fentanyl as an anesthetic drug during surgeries.

---

[104] Hill, Rebecca (2023). How Much Does Heroin Cost? (The Street Prices). *Zinnia Health*, Sept. 14.
[105] For more information on Oscar Gonzalez go to https://www.dea.gov/fugitives.
[106] Cultivating Health (2023). Fentanyl Facts, Overdose Signs to Look for, and how you can Help Save a Life. *University of California Davis Health*, Jan. 11.

Receiving fentanyl in a medical setting does not change its highly addictive properties. Nearly all opioids are *highly* addictive, in large part because they activate powerful reward centers in the brain. Opioids trigger the release of potent endorphins, creating intense feelings of ultimate peace, bliss, and well-being.[107] As the opioid effect begins to fade, the user begins to crave that peaceful feeling once again, which leads to repeated use of the drug. The repeated use of opioids leads to addiction, both physical and psychological.

Drug addiction is a *"chronic, relapsing disorder characterized by compulsive drug seeking and drug using, despite adverse consequences."*[108]

Since 2013, fentanyl has been manufactured in underground laboratories in China to be mixed into the illicit drug supply via Mexico and into North America.[109] In some regions, such as the East Coast, fentanyl has been blended into the underground heroin supply for so long that it has replaced heroin altogether.[110] Over the past several years, fentanyl has emerged in the drug markets west of the Mississippi River.[111] A growing number of people are accidentally consuming fentanyl in the form of counterfeit prescription opioid pills. In the best-case scenario, these people are unknowingly developing tolerance to fentanyl. In the worst case, death occurs due to overdose.

---

[107] Cultivating Health (2023). Fentanyl Facts, Overdose Signs to Look for, and how you can Help Save a Life. *University of California Davis Health*, Jan. 11.

[108] NIDA. 2020, July 13. Drug Misuse and Addiction. *National Institute of Drug Abuse*, Retrieved from https://nida.nih.gov/publications/drugs-brains-behavior-science-addiction/drug-misuse-addiction on 2023, July 18.

[109] Ciccarone, Daniel (2017). Fentanyl in the US Heroin Supply: A Rapidly Changing Risk Environment. *International Journal of Drug Policy*, July. https://doi.org/10.1016/j.drugpo.2017.06.010.

[110] Kilmer, Beau, Bryce Pardo, Toyya A. Pujol, and Jonathan P. Caulkins. 2022. Rapid Changes in Illegally Manufactured Fentanyl Products and Prices in the United States. *Addiction*, 1–5. https://doi.org/10.1111/add.15942.

[111] Health Alert Network (2020). Increase in Fatal Drug Overdoses Across the United States Driven by Synthetic Opioids Before and During the COVID-19 Pandemic. *Health Alert Network*, December 17, 2020. https://emergency.cdc.gov/han/2020/han00438.asp?ACSTrackingID=USCDC_511-DM44961&ACSTrackingLabel=HAN%20438%20-%20General%20Public&deliveryName=USCDC_511-DM44961.

As tolerance emerges, the same dose of opioids stops triggering the same intense flood of good feelings. Now, the user must take more of the drug to achieve the old "high"—except the original high is never again achievable.[112] Unfortunately, the compulsive search for the high persists as deterioration destroys the part of the brain needed to stop the cycle of abuse. The addiction has now taken over the addict's entire life. Addicts frequently combine their opioids with other substances, such as alcohol or methamphetamines, which magnifies the effect of each, increasing the risk of overdose.

For the brain, the difference between "everyday rewards" and "drug rewards" can be described as the difference between someone *"whispering into your ear and someone shouting into a microphone."*[113] Just like turning down the volume on a radio that is too loud, the brain adjusts to the overwhelming surges in dopamine (and other neurotransmitters) from opioids by producing less dopamine or by reducing the number of receptors that can receive signals. As a result, dopamine's impact on the brain's reward circuit becomes abnormally low, reducing the user's ability to experience pleasure.[114] This is why addicts eventually feel flat, lifeless, depressed, and unable to enjoy things that were previously pleasurable. Now, the drugs must be taken just to bring the dopamine levels back to normal, making the problem worse; tolerance creates a vicious cycle.[115]

Health experts know that the mechanisms involved in the development of tolerance can eventually lead to profound changes in neurons and brain circuits, potentially severely compromising the brain's long-term health.[116] In addition to impairing cognitive function, long-term drug abuse can trigger adaptations in habit or unconscious memory systems. Conditioning

---

[112] Cultivating Health (2023). Fentanyl Facts, Overdose Signs to Look for, and how you can Help Save a Life. *UC Davis Health*, Jan. 11.
[113] National Institute on Drug Abuse. (2007). Drugs, brains, and behavior: The science of addiction. *National Institute on Drug Abuse, National Institutes of Health, US Department of Health, and Human Services.*
[114] Volkow, N. D. (2010). Drugs, brains, and behavior: The science of addiction. *Safespace,*, 255-169. https://safespace.org/drugs-brains-and-behavior-the-science-of-addiction/
[115] Ghoshal, Malini (Nov 21, 2019). Understanding Drug Tolerance. *HealthLine*. https://www.healthline.com/health/drug-tolerance
[116] National Institute on Drug Abuse. (2007). Drugs, brains, and behavior: The science of addiction. *National Institute on Drug Abuse, National Institutes of Health, US Department of Health, and Human Services.*

is one example of this type of learning when cues in a daily routine or environment become associated with the drug experience; this can trigger uncontrollable cravings whenever the person is exposed to these cues, even if the drug itself is not available. This learned response is exceptionally durable and can affect a former drug user even after many years of abstinence. Drug addiction erodes self-control and the ability to make sound decisions while producing intense impulses to take drugs.[117]

Opioid use, even short-term use, can lead to addiction and, too often, to overdose. Anyone who takes opioids risks developing an addiction. There is no way to predict who is susceptible to opioid abuse, but personal history and the amount of time invested in drug use play a role. Legal or illegal, stolen or shared, opioids are responsible for most overdose deaths in the US today.[118] Substance use disorder is a progressive disease; no one begins opioid use with heroin or fentanyl. A person may start with alcohol, recreational drugs, or, most commonly, a prescription for painkillers. Substance abuse can happen to anyone regardless of age, sex, race, income, or level of education. Anyone can be prescribed opioids, anyone can become addicted, and anyone can overdose.

Given the prevalence of opioid use, it is helpful to be aware of both the physical and behavioral signs of abuse.

Physical Signs
Heavy opioid use is characterized by the user feeling tired much of the time, causing them to sleep off and on throughout the day. The user's physical appearance deteriorates, as they are too tired to shower or bathe and too exhausted to care if they brush their teeth or hair. If they ever cared about their appearance, they no longer do. When high, the pupils of the eyes are usually small, and the user will have a decreased respiratory rate. In addition, most users will experience substantial weight loss, although in some cases, weight gain occurs.

---

[117] National Institutes of Health (2015). Biology of Addiction: Drugs and Alcohol Can Hijack Your Brain. *NIH News in Health*, Oct. https://newsinhealth.nih.gov/2015/10/biology-addiction.
[118] *Mayo Clinic*. How Opioid Addiction Occurs. https://www.mayoclinic.org/diseases-conditions/prescription-drug-abuse/in-depth/how-opioid-addiction-occurs/art-20360372

> Scott was one of those who lost *a lot* of weight. Towards the end of his years of liberty, he looked like a skeleton, and I knew he was close to death. Being arrested temporarily saved his life...now he must figure out how to save himself in a system that exacerbates his addition.

Other physical signs of addiction include intense flu-like symptoms such as nausea, vomiting, sweating, shaky hands, feet, or head.[119] Opioid addicts who have graduated to injecting heroin or fentanyl will wear long sleeves and pants year-round to hide the needle marks on their arms and legs.

Behavioral Signs
In addition to the changes in the physical appearance of the person with an addiction, there are behavioral changes as well. Signs that indicate the person with an addiction has progressed to injecting heroin or fentanyl include missing (or burnt) spoons, shoelaces, belts, or syringes. Additionally, opioid addicts exhibit a changed attitude combined with a different personality. They cease to take responsibility for paying their bills, medical appointments, eating, showering, or any other activity that does not involve the pursuit of drugs. They blame others for their shortcomings, as well as for their drug addiction. It is their boss's fault they were fired; it is their spouse's fault they missed appointments; it is their parent's fault they are on drugs, and on and on and on. Nothing is *ever their* fault.

It is unusual to see advanced opioid addicts who are happy and joyful. They are more often bitter, angry people who cannot accept responsibility for their lives. Opioid addicts tend to avoid old friends and family unless they need money. Old friends are less important than the new, "sketchy" friends—unless the old friends are also users. The point is addicts surround themselves with other addicts and avoid everyone else. Hobbies or sports that used to be important are no longer of interest. Interests move away from active engagements toward passive activities such as video games and watching television.

---

[119] New York State. Opioids: Recognizing the Signs. *Department of Health.* https://www.health.ny.gov/community/opioid_epidemic/signs.htm

Those who have an opioid use disorder often forget to take prescribed medication and could have additional behavioral issues related to those missed doses. Criminal behavior may begin when the addict runs out of money. Often, stealing from family occurs first because it feels safe from criminal prosecution. They will steal money, as well as any prescriptions valued in the black market, that are then sold for cash to buy their drug of choice.

> In my son's case, he became very isolated and secretive. He had lived in our basement while going through college, but in his last year at home, he did something very strange. He moved his bed from the large appealing finished side of the basement to the small, dark, cluttered, unfinished side of the basement! Confined, secretive spaces seemed to be where he was most comfortable. Other behavioral changes I noticed in Scott included mood swings, irritability, nervousness, and difficulty concentrating on any conversation. Often, in the middle of a discussion, he would start talking about a completely unrelated topic. It seemed he had not heard one word of the discourse; he probably had not. As time passed and money became increasingly difficult to obtain, Scott began to steal from local stores—and me.

Consequences of Opioid Addiction

Natural Consequences

There are harsh natural consequences for opioid users that serve as punishment for their behavior. Researchers have found that opioids seize and destroy crucial brain regions that are meant to help humans survive.[120] Repeated use of opioids can damage the essential decision-making center in the prefrontal cortex area, the region needed to recognize the harms of using addictive substances.[121] How ironic that the brain region required to save the addict is the first one destroyed by opioid use.

---

[120] i) Verdejo-García, A., Bechara, A., Recknor, E. C., & Perez-Garcia, M. (2006). Executive dysfunction in substance dependent individuals during drug use and abstinence: an examination of the behavioral, cognitive, and emotional correlates of addiction. *Journal of the International Neuropsychological Society, 12*(3), 405-415.

ii) Naqvi, N. H., & Bechara, A. (2010). The insula and drug addiction: an interoceptive view of pleasure, urges, and decision-making. *Brain Structure and Function, 214*(5-6), 435-450.

iii) Crews, F. T., & Boettiger, C. A. (2009). Impulsivity, frontal lobes, and risk for addiction. *Pharmacology Biochemistry and Behavior, 93*(3), 237-247.

[121] National Institutes of Health (2020). White Matter of the Brain. *National Library of Medicine: MedlinePlus*, Sep. 16.

Those who continue to abuse opioids can expect the following:[122]

- → The onset of mental illness(es). Chronic drug abuse may occur as the result of a mental illness, and or a mental illness(es) can be created by drug abuse.
- → Suicidal thoughts and behaviors
- → Job loss
- → Academic failure
- → Deterioration of white and grey matter in the brain
- → Axoxia - an oxygen deficiency in the body's tissues. The nerve cells in the brain are extremely sensitive to lack of oxygen because of their high energy demand. Anoxia damages cells throughout the brain and may result in a coma.
- → Physical impairments to vision, bowel function, taste, and smell.
- → Legal problems
- → Toxic relationships
- → Reduced sexual pleasure
- → Financial difficulties
- → Death

The *American Psychiatric Association* (APA) identifies the following nine mental disorders severely impacted by chronic drug abuse.[123]

Schizophrenia is a serious mental disorder that causes people to interpret reality abnormally. Schizophrenia may result in some combination of hallucinations, delusions, and extremely disordered thinking and behavior that impairs daily functioning and can be disabling. People with schizophrenia require lifelong treatment. Adding opioids to schizophrenia is particularly harmful because opioids compound the severity of delusions and disordered thinking. It is akin to schizophrenia on steroids.

Bipolar disorder (formerly known as *manic depression*) is a *neurodevelopmental* condition that causes unusual shifts in a person's mood, energy, activity levels, and concentration. These shifts can make it

---

[122] *North Tampa Behavioral Health.*
https://www.northtampabehavioralhealth.com/addiction/fentanyl/effects-symptoms-signs/
[123] Definitions of all disorders are from the *National Library of Medicine.*
https://www.ncbi.nlm.nih.gov/books/NBK541052/

challenging to complete daily tasks. Opioids magnify mood swings to an extreme level.

Attention deficit hyperactivity disorder (ADHD) is a condition that is commonly diagnosed in childhood but often lasts into adulthood. Adults and children with ADHD may have trouble paying attention and controlling impulsive behaviors (such as acting without thinking), or they may be *overly* active. Since opioids cause users to be unable to control impulsive behavior or focus on the topic at hand, it is not surprising that opioids compound the symptoms of ADHD. Using opioids before the brain is fully developed arrests the growth of the brain, leaving the addict mentally *stuck* in adolescence.

Generalized anxiety disorder is a mental condition characterized by excessive or unrealistic anxiety about two or more aspects of life (work, social relationships, financial matters, etc.), accompanied by symptoms such as increased muscle tension, impaired concentration, and insomnia. Combining this disorder with opioid use heightens unrealistic anxieties and can lead to delusions.

Obsessive-compulsive disorder (OCD) is a condition that causes people to have recurring, unwanted thoughts, ideas, or sensations. For example, someone may believe that deadly germs exist everywhere and may repetitively wash their hands throughout the day. To get rid of the thoughts (e.g., germs everywhere), they feel compelled to do something repetitively (e.g., cleaning). The repetitive behaviors, however, change with opioid use. Whereas the addict may have compulsively washed his hands, he may now not care about that but has become obsessive about how his drugs are stored, hidden, or cleaned. Family and friends may not observe some new obsessions, as they are often performed secretly. Some families have been fooled into thinking that the OCD is improving because the old compulsions have been dropped, and the new ones are not visible.

Post-traumatic stress disorder (PTSD) is a mental health condition that is triggered by a terrifying event. This could be witnessing an event, such as the murder of a friend, or it could be experiencing terror oneself. Symptoms may include flashbacks, nightmares, and severe anxiety, as well as uncontrollable thoughts about the event. Opioids alone will not cause PTSD, but they amplify the symptoms.

Panic disorder is a condition that causes sudden episodes of intense fear that trigger severe physical reactions when there is no real danger or apparent cause. When a panic attack occurs, it feels like having a heart attack, losing control, or dying. Opioid abuse can compound feelings of danger and lead to rash actions in response to the sense of panic.

Antisocial personality disorder (ASPD) is a mental health condition causing a person to engage in manipulating, exploiting, or violating the rights of others. People with ASPD are often witty, charming, friendly, and good at insincere flattery. People with ASPD frequently tell friends or acquaintances, *"I love you!"* or *"You're the best friend I've ever had."* The primary goal is to manipulate other's emotions. Those with ASPD do not believe the law applies to them, so they frequently ignore it, disregarding their safety and that of others. When opioids are added to the mix, the ASPD person is treacherous; be prepared to go to prison if an ASPD person is part of your safe group.

Major depressive disorder is a condition that is diagnosed when an individual persistently exhibits a depressed mood, decreased interest in pleasurable activities, feelings of guilt or worthlessness, lack of energy, poor concentration, appetite changes, psychomotor retardation or agitation, sleep disturbances, or suicidal thoughts. Many of the symptoms of major depressive disorder are also symptoms of opioid abuse. Opioid abuse compounds this disorder, making it largely unmanageable and deadly due to high suicide rates.

Substance abuse affects more than one in four adults living with serious mental health problems. Substance abuse and mental health problems occur together frequently because certain substances *cause* addicts to experience mental illness. In addition, some mental illnesses *cause* people to become susceptible to excessive self-medication. Untangling the mystery of the causal relationship between drug abuse and mental illness is especially difficult because causality can flow in either direction. Mental health disorders and substance abuse share many similar underlying causes and behavioral traits.

Withdrawal Symptoms

There are severe consequences for using opioids, but for those already addicted, there are much *more dire* consequences for *NOT* using. People addicted to fentanyl who suddenly stop using will have debilitating physical, mental, and emotional withdrawal symptoms. Some of the symptoms can begin as early as a few hours after the drug was last taken and can last for weeks or months. Many advanced opioid addicts never recover and must remain on supervised medication for the rest of their lives.[124] Withdrawal symptoms include:

- → Severe muscle cramping
- → Bone pain
- → Dehydration
- → Inability to sleep
- → Inability to control bowels
- → Vomiting
- → Cold flashes with goosebumps
- → Uncontrollable leg movements
- → Overwhelming fear and anxiety
- → Hot flashes and profuse sweating
- → Headaches
- → Severe cravings for the drug
- → Death.[125]

Scott describes one of his withdrawal experiences when he could not obtain the fentanyl he needed:

"It had been 8 hours since my last use, and a feeling of dread began to overtake me. I needed another hit right now! I called my primary drug dealer and couldn't get an answer, so I moved through my phonebook, searching for other sources of fentanyl. I called 3 or 4 different dealers no answer. I knew what was coming; I was already getting the shakes and panicking. I was consumed by only one thought: where can I get some fentanyl? I began to sweat profusely and didn't feel like moving or doing anything. I gave up on the dealers, started calling other users, and finally found a friend who would sell to me, but there was a huge catch: I had to

---

[124] Medications such as suboxone, methadone or others.
[125] Darke, Shane, Larney, Sarah and Farrell, Michael (2016). Yes, People Can Die from Opiate Withdrawal. *Addiction*, 11 Aug.

come to his house to get the drugs. By now, the shaking was brutal, and I felt like I couldn't breathe. How would I get on the bus to my friend's house? My muscles were starting to cramp, and diarrhea made it difficult to even think about being in public. I was starting to get confused and could not figure out how to make this work. The only thing real to me at that moment was pain until it seemed like someone was there trying to tell me something, but I couldn't see their face or hear their words. I thought for sure I was going to die, and I was glad.

Then I felt the stick of a needle, and bliss overcame me. The pain disappeared, my body stopped shaking, and I was at peace."

Sharing drugs is how users help other users.

Medical Evidence

This section explores why advanced opioid addicts cannot be good students, workers, planners, organizers, or, more relevantly, drug dealers. To understand the absurdity of characterizing an addict as a dealer, one must understand the impact of advanced opioid addiction on the brain. The *National Institute of Health* defines drug addiction as "*a chronic, relapsing disorder characterized by*

> 1. *compulsive drug seeking,*
> 2. *continued use of the drug despite harmful consequences and*
> 3. *long-lasting changes in the brain.*"[126]

Impact on Brain

Many different parts of the human brain serve various essential functions. Each brain region has unique responsibilities that support cognitive and emotional processes. Addiction is considered both a complex brain disorder and a mental illness. It is widely accepted that addiction is the most severe form of full-spectrum substance-use disorder and is a medical illness caused by repeated use of a substance. *"A common misperception is that addiction is a choice or a moral problem, and all you have to do is stop. But nothing could be further from the truth,"* according to Dr. Koob,

---

[126] National Institutes of Health (2015). Biology of Addiction: Drugs and Alcohol Can Hijack Your Brain. *NIH News in Health*, Oct. https://newsinhealth.nih.gov/2015/10/biology-addiction.

director of the *National Institute of Alcohol Abuse and Drug Addiction*. "The brain actually changes with addiction, and it takes a good deal of work to get it back to its normal state. The more drugs or alcohol you've taken, the more disruptive it is to the brain."

Opioid-dependent individuals have significantly less gray matter in several regions of the brain that play a crucial role in *cognitive* and *affective processing*. *Affective processes* include all feelings and responses related to one's behavior, knowledge, and beliefs. Affect can alter both perceptions of situations and the outcomes of cognitive effort; affect can fuel, block, or terminate cognition.[127] All human actions and decisions occur in an emotional context, and therefore, cognitive functions are colored by one's emotional state.

There are seven areas of *cognitive* functioning: learning, thinking, reasoning, remembering, problem-solving, decision-making, and attention. **Figure 4.2** provides a picture of the brain with the location of the cerebrum, the cerebellum, the frontal lobe, and the insular system. The *cerebrum* and the *cerebellum* regions of the brain control cognition.

The *cerebrum* includes the *insular system* and the most significant part of the brain, the *frontal lobe*, also known as the *prefrontal cortex*. Continued use of opioids damages the essential decision-making center in the prefrontal cortex of the brain, a small area of the frontal lobe. This region of the brain is needed to recognize the harms of using addictive substances.[128] According to the *National Institute of Drug Abuse*, heroin, morphine, and fentanyl work by binding to the body's opioid receptors, found in areas of the brain that control pain and emotions.[129] The hijacking of pain and emotions starts the *chain of addiction*, with drug seeking and drug using taking over an addict's life. Increased opioid tolerance acts as a depressant, slowing the body's natural systems (e.g., respiratory

---

[127] Schnall, S., W. Affective Processes. *International Encyclopedia of Education*, 3rd ed. ISPN: 9780128156148
978-0-12-815614-8, pp. 449-455.
[128] National Institutes of Health (2020). White Matter of the Brain. *National Library of Medicine: MedlinePlus*, Sep. 16.
[129] National Institute on Drug Abuse (2021). Fentanyl Drug Facts, June 1. https://www.drugabuse.gov/publications/drugfacts/fentanyl.

and cardiac). This disruption can then lead to severe consequences such as stroke, heart failure, or death.

The *cerebellum* is a small part of the brain located at the bottom near the back of the head (see **Figure 4.2**). Research provides evidence that opioid dependence results in the breakdown of the *cerebellum* region of the brain.[130] Scientists have found that damage to the cerebellum makes it harder for a person to learn new words or skills, whereas damage to the frontal lobe retards learning, speech, reasoning, emotions, interpreting, touch, and vision.

The *insular system* of the cerebrum is responsible for sensory processing, decision-making, self-awareness, nervous system functions, emotions, motor control, and conscious desires. Damage to all these functions occurs with opioid abuse, resulting in both cognitive and decision-making impairments.[131] The cerebrum controls all higher-level functions, so damage can also interfere with other areas, such as depth perception and the ability to estimate the passage of time (*dyschronometria*).

The result for opioid addicts is a progressive inability to function as an average human being. Addicts cannot remember, so they cannot learn; they cannot reason their way to stopping the use of deadly drugs, so they cannot save their own lives. They cannot string together two sentences that make sense, so they cannot communicate; their emotional state is adolescent, so they cannot relate to the adult world. The advanced addict's damage is so complete that it is evident to everyone, confirmed by the addict's slurred words, unsteady gate, and inability to make eye contact.

---

[130] Scott C. Wollman, Omar M. Alhassoon, Matthew G. Hall, Mark J. Stern, Eric J. Connors, Christine L. Kimmel, Kenneth E. Allen, Rick A. Stephan & Joaquim Radua (2017). Gray matter abnormalities in opioid-dependent patients: A neuroimaging meta-analysis. *The American Journal of Drug and Alcohol Abuse*, 43:5, 505-517, DOI: 10.1080/00952990.2016.1245312.
[131] Desmond, JE, Gabrieli JD, Glover GH (1998). Dissociation of frontal and cerebellar activity in a Cognitive task: evidence for a distinction between selection and search. *NeuroImage*, 7 (4), 368–376.

Figure 4.2.   **Structure of the Brain**

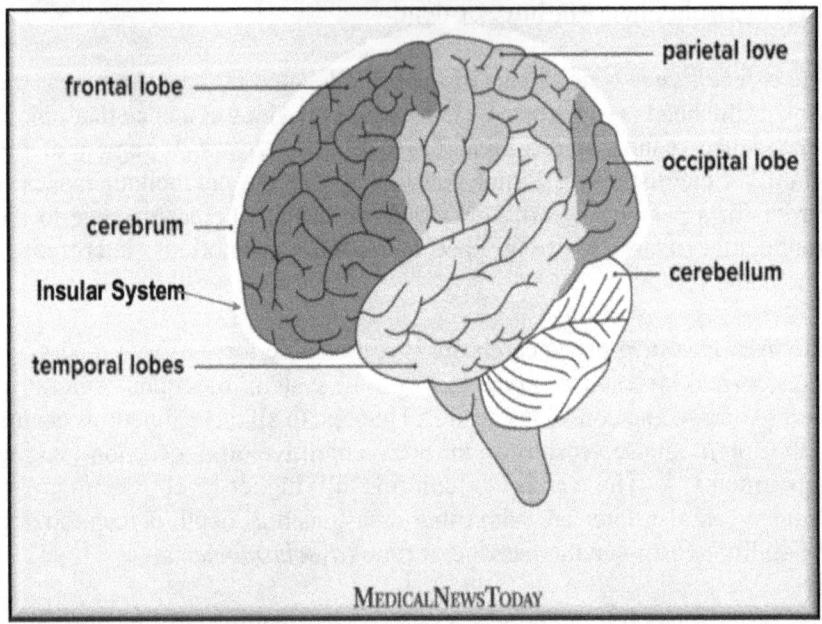

Shi et al. (2020) studied heroin-addicted men and demonstrated they have significantly less gray matter volume than non-addicted men. The loss of grey matter is mainly in the prefrontal cortex, a circuit in the brain's central nervous system called the *mesolimbic dopaminergic* region. The loss of this grey matter inhibits the addict's ability to control automatic urges by pausing and thinking before reacting. The study provides evidence that advanced opioid addiction is associated with the deterioration of the ability to control one's behavior, visual deterioration, and decreased touch perception.[132]

Not only is grey matter damaged by opioid use, but medical researchers have found that it also deteriorates the *white matter* in the brain. White matter comprises about *half* the brain and manages the learning and

---

[132] Shi H, Liang Z, Chen J, Li W, Zhu J, Li Y, Ye J, Zhang J, Xue J, Liu W, Wang F, Wang W, Li Q, He X. (2020). Gray matter alteration in heroin-dependent men: An atlas-based magnetic resonance imaging study. *Psychiatry Res Neuroimaging*, Oct 30, 304:111150. doi: 10.1016/j.pscychresns.2020.111150. Epub 2020 Jul 22. PMID: 32717665; PMCID: PMC8170872.

standard functioning areas by providing the connective tissues throughout the brain. It then coordinates communication between different regions of the brain.[133] When white matter deteriorates, as it does with opioid addicts, the result is a short-circuiting of:

1. problem-solving abilities,
2. learning capacity and
3. the ability to remember.[134]

Neuroscientists have only recently begun to understand the importance of white brain matter in thinking, learning, talking, and even walking. In a normal brain, white matter provides the essential connectivity needed to unite different regions into networks that perform various mental functions. When this connectivity is disrupted by disease or damage, the result is often an extraordinary disturbance of normal cognitive functioning. The scope and variety of syndromes that result from the destruction of white matter suggest that white matter is pivotal to all realms of human behavior, a contribution that scientists are just beginning to grasp.[135]

White matter is a vast, intertwining system of neural connections that joins all four brain lobes with the emotion center into a complex brain map, just being discovered by neuroscientists.[136] This suggests that no brain region acts in isolation. The brain's frontal lobe has the highest level of white matter because it has the highest degree of connectivity of any brain lobe. Clinical studies have shown that the maturation of white matter, particularly in the frontal lobe, strongly correlates with personality maturation, including factors such as motivation, demeanor,

---

[133] Wells, Diana (2018). White Matter Disease. *Healthline,* September 29, 2018. Medically reviewed by Seunggu Han, M.D.

[134] **i)** National Library of Medicine (2020). Opioid addiction. *National Institute of Health,* Jul 10. https://medlineplus.gov/genetics/condition/opioid-addiction/

   ii) National Institutes of Health (2015). Biology of Addiction: Drugs and Alcohol Can Hijack Your Brain. *NIH News in Health,* Oct. https://newsinhealth.nih.gov/2015/10/biology-addiction.

[135] Brain Facts. *Society for Neuroscience.* https://www.brainfacts.org/the-brain-facts-book?gad=1&gclid=Cj0KCQjw_O2lBhCFARIsAB0E8B9jUh9KmfyU7JCSF0w_o8uDP5KvE2CYRLBunOW2SfhjNyBcflo5Kx8aAvfDEALw_wcB

[136] The four brain lobes are: Frontal, Temporal, Parietal, and Occipital.

and executive function. The frontal lobe and personality maturation processes are not usually fully developed until 25 or 26 years of age.[137]

The most common effect of drugs on white brain matter is *white matter disease*, which causes white matter in brain tissue to deteriorate. White matter disease is characterized by deep lesions in the brain's white matter due to restricted blood flow.[138, 139] Schmidt showed that people with substance abuse disorders have *less* frontal lobe white matter, suggesting some of it had died.[140] When the white matter begins to die, communication between nerve cells becomes nonexistent, preventing the individual from functioning. Any disruption in cell communication directly affects things like emotions, thoughts, learning, speech, memory, and overall behavior.[141] *"Opioid drugs cause profound and long-lasting changes in the functioning of the brain that can persist long after opiate use has stopped."*[142]

To summarize, advanced opioid addicts incur significant damage to both the grey and white matter of the brain. This section has detailed the numerous consequences of opioid abuse on the brain, including the deterioration of the addict's capacity to plan, meet goals, display self-control, and remember events, dates, or context. A person with an addiction experiences difficulties with thinking and a reduced ability to reason due to cognitive decline. In addition to having impaired learning and problem-solving skills, the addict has impaired depth perception, vision, and walking abilities. Emotionally, the addict lacks maturity and experiences an increase in both impulsive and compulsive behaviors.

---

[137] Herlinger K., Lingford-Hughes A. (2021). Addressing unmet needs in opiate dependence: supporting detoxification and advances in relapse prevention. *BJ Psych Advances*, 1–11.

[138] World Health Organisation (2019). International Classification of Diseases, 11th Revision. Available at: https://icd.who.int/en

[139] Bora E., Yucel M., Fornito A., Pantelis C., Harrison B. J., Cocchi L., et al. (2012). White matter microstructure in opiate addiction. *Addict Biology*, 17, 141–148.

[140] Schmidt A., Vogel M., Baumgartner S., Wiesbeck G. A., Lang U., Borgwardt S., et al (2020). Brain volume changes after long-term injectable opioid treatment: a longitudinal voxel-based morphometry study. *Addict Biology*, **26**: e12970.

[141] (https://www.banyantreatmentcenter.com/2021/02/04/how-drug-abuse-affects-white-matter-in-the-brain-pompano/)

[142] Wollman S. C., Alhassoon O. M., Stern M. J., Hall M. G., Rompogren J., Kimmel C. L., et al. (2015). White matter abnormalities in long-term heroin users: a preliminary neuroimaging meta-analysis. *American Journal of Drug & Alcohol Abuse*, 41, 133–138.

Impact on Body

Beyond the impact of advanced opioids on the brain is the effect of the drug on the addict's body. Long-term users (2 months or longer) of fentanyl expose themselves to an array of physical problems. For example, a person who smokes fentanyl sets themselves up for severe long-term lung damage and respiratory problems.[143] Additionally, smoking fentanyl makes it almost impossible to control the dose, which increases the chances of a fatal overdose. If a person were to contract a serious disease like COVID-19 and then smoke fentanyl, it could easily cause immediate death.

Those who inject heroin or fentanyl are at risk of contracting diseases like HIV or hepatitis C. With continued injections, the addict will experience collapsed blood vessels, making it difficult to find a vein to inject. A permanently collapsed vein will never recover and cannot be repaired.[144]

> The last time Scott injected fentanyl was in February 2019, yet his veins are still problematic to locate even after more than 5 years of no needle use.

Frequently, addicts suffer from malnutrition and a lack of personal hygiene, making it much more challenging to fight viruses. Opioids can trigger a histamine release, causing intense itching as well as more serious consequences, such as a significant decrease in systemic vascular resistance and blood pressure. Fentanyl can cause modest changes in heart rate and blood pressure. However, mixing fentanyl with depressants, like benzodiazepines, can lead to significant cardiovascular changes, including decreased cardiac output and stroke, as well as dramatic decreases in blood pressure. More simply put, the combination can kill.

Organ damage is likely to occur in opioid addicts due to the dehydration, hypotension, and urine retention that occurs with heavy use. Chronic kidney disease is the most common problem for those who inject *due to*

---

[143] Delphi Behavioral Health Group. What Are the Short-Term and Long-Term Effects of Fentanyl Use? *DBHG* https://delphihealthgroup.com/opioids/fentanyl/short-long-effects/
[144] Pietrangelo, Ann (2019). What Can Cause a Blown Vein and How to Treat it. *Healthline*, Nov. 1.

skin popping, resulting in amyloidosis.[145] *Amyloidosis* is caused by an abnormal protein produced in the bone marrow that can be deposited in any organ. There is no cure for amyloidosis, and it can lead to life-threatening organ failure.

The body is not made to sustain massive quantities of daily opioids. When people with an addiction continue to use, it is no surprise that there are substantial health consequences. The behavioral changes incurred by addicts can also lead to more bodily injury, e.g., car accidents, falling, tripping, walking in front of moving traffic, etc. It is rare to see old heroin or fentanyl addicts; they do not live that long.

Relapse

Relapse occurs when a person **returns to drug use after a period of abstinence**. Opiates have the highest relapse rates of any drug, with one study reporting a 91% rate.[146] The study also found that at least 59% of those who had an opiate relapse would do so within the first week of sobriety, and 80% would relapse within a month after discharge from a detox program.

Studies show that using only abstinence to stop taking opioids is very likely to result in relapse, raising the risk of a fatal overdose.[147] Overdose

---

[145] Mallappallil, Mary, Sabu, Jacob, Friedman, Eli A., and Salifu, Moro (2017). What Do We Know about Opioids and the Kidney? *International Journal of Molecular Science,* Jan, 18(1): 223.

[146] Smyth, B. P., Barry, J., Keenan, E. & Ducray, K. (2010). Lapse and relapse following inpatient treatment of opiate dependence. *Irish Medical Journal. 103(6), 176–179.*

[147] i) Substance Abuse Center for Behavioral Health Statistics and Quality (2021). Results from the 2020 *National Survey on Drug Use and Health*: Detailed Tables. SAMHSA, October 25.

ii) Wheeler E, Jones TS, Gilbert MK, Davidson PJ (2015). Centers for Disease Control and Prevention (CDC). Opioid Overdose Prevention Programs Providing Naloxone to Laypersons - United States, 2014. *Morbidity & Mortality Weekly Report,* 64(23):631-635.

iii) Mattick RP, Breen C, Kimber J, Davoli M (2009). Methadone maintenance therapy versus no opioid replacement therapy for opioid dependence. *Cochrane Database System Review*, (3):CD002309. doi:10.1002/14651858.CD002209.pub2.

iv) Mattick RP, Breen C, Kimber J, Davoli M. (2014). Buprenorphine maintenance versus placebo or methadone maintenance for opioid dependence. *Cochrane Database System Re*view, (2):CD002207. doi:10.1002/14651858.CD002207.pub4.

v) The American Society of Addiction Medicine (2017). *Advancing Access to Addiction Medications.*

risk increases each time an addict quits using opioids for a while because tolerance is lowered. A lower tolerance level means a higher risk of overdose, particularly if the same quantity of drugs is taken as before the abstinence period. Even after one year or more of abstaining from opioids, many people relapse because of the depression, anxiety, and other negative emotions that accompany withdrawal. Suppressing these negative emotional states dramatically increases the addict's chance of staying clean. [148] Medications such as suboxone and methadone are used to suppress these negative emotional states, as well as the physical craving for opioids, without producing the same euphoria.

A *National Institute of Drug Abuse* (NIDA) study was designed to determine if six monthly injections of extended-release naltrexone (similar to suboxone) could blunt relapse rates in opioid-addicted men who were recently released from prison, on probation or parole, or with other criminal justice involvement.[149] Injections were administered at five locations in four major U.S. cities: two in New York and one each in Baltimore, Providence, and Philadelphia. The treatment group consisted of 153 participants who were given monthly injections of extended-release naltrexone, while 155 in the control group did not receive the drug or a placebo.[150] Both groups received motivational counseling and referrals to community treatment.

After six monthly injections, 64% of participants in the control group relapsed, while only 43% relapsed in the treatment group. In addition, members of the treatment group who did relapse used significantly less heroin and other opioids than those in the control group. Importantly,

---

vi) Centers for Disease Control and Prevention (2021). Prescription Opioids Overview. *CDC*. https://www.cdc.gov/drugoverdose/data/prescribing/overview.html. Published March 17.

[148] Vierkant, Valerie (2023). Researchers Identify Breakthrough In Understanding Fentanyl Abuse. *Texas A&M Today*, Feb 20.

[149] NYU Langone Health (2016). Opioid Relapse Rates Fall with Long-Term Use of Medication for Adults Involved in the Criminal Justice System. *News Hub*, March 30. https://nyulangone.org/news/opioid-relapse-rates-fall-long-term-use-medication-adults-involved-criminal-justice-system.

[150] Naltrexone is one of the main ingredients in suboxone, an intramuscular extended-release medication approved by the *Food and Drug Administration* to treat both opioid use disorder and alcohol use disorder.

across the six-month study period, there were no overdoses in the treatment group, compared with five in the control group.

Drug therapy is one of the most promising areas for solving the opioid death crisis.

The U.S. BOP portrays itself to the public as having numerous programs for inmates who are addicted to drugs. These programs do not exist in the way they are advertised to the public. For example, it took Scott four years of begging to get into the *Medically Assisted Treatment* (MAT) program. The MAT program consists of two things:

> **a)** a once-a-month trip to the nurse for an injection of suboxone and
> **b)** a once-a-week, 15-minute meeting with a mental health professional.

The absence of group support for those addicted and incarcerated in prison makes recovery from drug abuse almost impossible. The first self-help group allowed in federal prisons was AA in 1942, but over the years, as security concerns increased, self-help groups were phased out of federal and state prisons. Today, approved self-help groups can visit prison camps but are not allowed in any of the other security levels. Even so, local jails and detention centers have been exceptionally accommodating to self-help group visits on a regular basis.

A Drug Dealer's Life

Dealing drugs is not as simple as the sharing transactions between two people addicted to the same drug, and it is not for the lazy or faint of heart. The price of getting caught is extremely high and even higher for crossing a competitor or supplier. There is no room for doubt, indecision, or laziness. One careless move and Pablo Escobar's empire was gone. A successful drug dealer knows the product inside and out but does not use the drug themselves.

The *Cardinal Rule* of being a successful drug dealer is *"... **don't get high on your own supply**."*

As with other successful businesses, drug dealers need buyers and must create a need the consumer does not realize they have. Dealers frequently do this by allowing new people to sample the product for free. Dealers selling highly addictive drugs figure they will have a customer for life after the first dose. The business requires long hours, and the dealer must be there when the client calls. It is not good business to let customers go into withdrawal, especially since attempting to conduct a business transaction with someone in withdrawal is impossible. A person with an addiction trying to run such a business is already doomed for failure. The market is not expanded when people with an addiction only deal with other addicts. Compliance with the *Cardinal Rule* is utterly unrealistic for those with opioid use disorder.

In the drug business, it is vital to constantly improve processes, increase efficiencies, and update security measures. There are basic security measures, such as randomizing meeting places and creating unpredictable time patterns. Then, the dealer must undertake additional measures to secure the product and the location.

Next, the successful dealer must consider the competition and the territory to dominate. The territory can be one or more blocks, the entire city, or the state. A defined territory is critical; the dealer must prepare to fight to drive out the competition. The dealer must choose employees (other lower-level dealers) and *customers* more wisely than a legal business. The employees must be people who can be trusted with the knowledge of an illegally run enterprise. The dealer also needs to evaluate a potential employee's ability to operate under stress, capacity to create new contacts, and drug habits. It is a known rule never to hire someone who has an addiction or who will use the product. This rule is equivalent to legitimate businesses not wanting to hire employees who are known thieves.

Customers also know the dealer is running an illegal operation, and it is generally true that 10% of the clients will cause 90% of the problems. Dealers must learn to distinguish between 'good' clients and 'bad' clients to minimize losses and negative interactions. A drug dealer cannot turn to the law to resolve disputes for obvious reasons; resolving conflicts can be deadly. Finally, a successful dealer will form strategic alliances with other businesses and partners to build a referral base. In the drug business, the ultimate alliance is called a *cartel*.

From the above descriptions, a useful definition for a drug dealer is a businessperson who owns an inventory of drugs for sale and operates to maximize their wealth.

Having drawn parallels between a legally successful business and a successful drug dealer, the site *Quora* was searched to learn of any drug dealer experiences. There were a few posts, and, not surprisingly, all were under the name *"Anonymous."* Below are three different drug dealer experiences that demonstrate the skills needed to operate.

Anonymous Drug Dealer #1

"Selling drugs is exhilarating at first, but soon, the burden of being a 24-hour on-demand courier drags you into hell.

My background: I was a cocaine dealer for 6 years. My clients varied from grams to ounces, but most of my weight moved about an ounce at a time to 7 guys who stomped it and flipped it in grams and 8 balls.
I'm a businessman at heart, and during college, my roommate did a lot of coke. I mean he'd call in an 8 ball for him and his friends on a Friday afternoon, one late night, and one in the dawn hours of Saturday morning, and then he'd turn around and do it again on Saturday. I had dealt weed and smoked my fair share in high school, but cocaine was new to me. His dealer was a decent enough guy after he'd met me about 30 times, and one day, while I was walking into the apartment as he was leaving from one of his 6 trips for the weekend, I joked, "I should just buy a couple ounces and save you the trips." Half an hour later, I had an ounce of coke fronted to me for 48 hours; he must've really hated the revolving door he had at our place.

I made exactly zero dollars on that first ounce; he fronted it to me at exactly what he would have charged my roommate. The next weekend, we worked out a better deal; I took all the cash out of my bank account, bought another ounce of coke, and stood to make a quick 20% profit on it off my one built-in client. By 10 pm Friday, the original ounce was gone; having an ounce in the house was a great reason to have a party in my roommate's eyes. I bought my second ounce that night, and by the time classes started on Monday morning, that too was gone.

What started as a way to make a quick buck off my roommate's habit and his dealer's laziness quickly snowballed into supplying coke for five, ten, and then twenty people. Soon I was buying a couple of ounces a couple of times a week, sometimes up to an eighth of a kilo, usually on finals week. I was pushing the limits of what my dealer was willing to sell, and he wasn't eager to jump higher up the distribution chain or introduce me to his dealer; it took returning to my hometown over break and talking to friends to find a lead on someone who could get me more weight.

Meeting my new supplier was harrowing; I only knew one coke dealer, so I had no frame of reference on how he'd act or how I should act. Was he going to have a guy hold a gun to my head and grill me about whether I was a cop or not? Rip my shirt open and check me for a wire? Nothing of the sort happened. We didn't even talk about drugs the first time I met him at the bar he managed. By the second time he was willing to meet me, I assume he'd already had me checked out because talk immediately went to business: 4 ounces a week, 4 grand. The businessman in me couldn't agree fast enough: A 30% profit margin before I even cut it.

I profited just over $100,000 in my first full year of dealing. At 19, that's like making a quadrillion dollars a year. Things grew steadily, and soon I was getting called every 20 minutes to "come hang out," meaning "bring some coke, I'm going to try to get some for free, and then maybe I'll buy some." I don't mean 20 minutes for 8 hours a day; it was becoming a 24-hour job. Getting woken up at 3:30 am with the coy "Hey dude, wanna come chill?" got old. Quick. The money was great, but it was the most inconvenient job in the world; tired of doing all the on-call leg work, I decided it was time to get some employees.

Finding people to work for me was easy. Most were already my clients. Slowly, over the course of the next two years, I transferred almost all my business to them, roughly doubling my volume, halving my profits, but drastically reducing my exposure to something bad happening.

I never caught any heat in my time as a dealer. There were no raids, busts, or arrests, and only one close call when I went through a light as it turned red after dropping off the last of what I had on me. One of my guys did get busted and spent several years in jail because of it, but he was honorable enough to keep my name out of it. How lucky I was did not escape me; it wouldn't have taken much for me to get locked away for a long time.

In the end, having a child was what pushed me towards leaving the business. The transition from illicit work to legitimate work was rough, to say the very least. My first "real" career job at 22 paid just $12 an hour, $100 a day- I had made that before most people even woke up while selling drugs. I've never returned to the level of financial success I had while dealing. Every once in a while, when the stack of bills piles up high, I can't help but consider returning to it until I see my kids, and I think about the possibility of never being able to hug them again or watching them grow old through a pane of glass."

Anonymous Drug Dealer #2

"It's fucking stressful, and it's not what you think it is or how it is. I'm telling you from my perspective as a person who used to sell drugs for 20 years, which is a long time, an almost unheard-of stretch or career if you want to call it that. I've only had one legal job in my life for just under a year in 1999. I owned a clothing store for two years, 10 years ago. If I weren't doing what I was doing now, which I'll get into at the end, I would have zero experience in the world of employment, no college education and I got my GED from correspondence courses.

That would leave anybody with very few options to move forward in life and continue living a lifestyle remotely close to when I was hustling. The only jobs you can get hired for are warehouse and general labor work. Breaking your back for forty hours a week for a paycheck that you can make in a day becomes very unfulfilling and will quickly make anyone fall right back into their old ways. For people who have never experienced a day in my shoes or who think the life is completely different than what it's really like:

It's nothing but headaches, stress, and problems, and whoever thinks that it's easy money is wrong. You must be smart, always on your toes, watching your back, and available. Nobody will call you or turn to you if you're never around or inconsistent. Your phone is ringing all day, you're in your car all day, there were days when I was literally in my car for 19 hours, and the moment you sit down to just relax or eat, you're right back on the road.

On top of all that, you'll take losses; losses are inevitable-- sometimes you'll be in the hole, and you've lost more than what you put in. It's like gambling you can make a shit ton of money just as fast as you can lose it. There will be people who owe you money that you have to chase and harass because you owe money for whatever it is you're selling, so now, you're getting pressured to cover the balance because you want to be in good standing with your people.

You must always be aware of things happening around you, such as snitches or people who want to rob you because you're doing good. You start having trust issues with people over money, and even if you work within a team, some people's envy will get the best of them when they are a part of your team. It's so hard to leave the life, especially if it's the only life you know as a means of income. I used to think that I would never do anything else other than what I was doing until I had my son. The last time my freedom was on the line, I had to seriously think about the risks and rewards involved, what direction my life had gone, and which direction I needed to go in. The amount of time that I was fighting for people in the life isn't all that bad, which was 7–9 years, and if you're doing what I did at some point, you're going to deal with the law. The only reason why I changed was it's a good possibility that if I were to be locked up, say for even 7 years, there's a possibility of something happening to one of my parents while locked up. I don't think I would be able to deal with myself if I wasn't there prior to anything happening or when it occurs, and it's not something I want to think about.

Also, I can't let my son go through the trauma of my absence; I have a unique bond with him. I just realized how much it affects my own family and how much they will have to suffer for my choices and selfishness. Without letting this drag on, I'll tell you what it's like in a nutshell. It's fun, exciting, gives you financial freedom, and you get respect, girls, but it's also a headache, stressful as shit; you'll lose sleep, friends, money, and your freedom. It's not what you think it is, and there's no such thing as a happy old drug dealer. It's a tradeoff; you can make a lot of money, but your quality of life will take a hit, and you will suffer. I can't imagine what it's like to be at the top level, be 60 years old, do multimillion-dollar deals, and not be stressed. Because when you have $100k worth of drugs in a bag in your trunk, even after the deal is done, there's a period when you still have that adrenaline pumping in you.

It's just fucked, but to be honest, if I had nothing to lose or to worry about, like my family, I wouldn't have stopped. I'm only on here because I was on house arrest recently. If I hadn't been on house arrest, I would never have had the time to talk about all the shit I do on here. I'm telling you that once you're involved in the life like I was, it becomes almost impossible to get out, and it takes life changing events to make you get out."

Anonymous Drug Dealer #3

I sold heroin, crack cocaine, and oxycodone from the age of 16 up until I went to prison at age 28. It's far more complex than running a Fortune 500 corporation, because the risks and locate real estate (open areas to sell your product). Evaluating potential employees isn't as simple as running an online background check; you must reach out to other dealers to find out their reputation and, most importantly, whether they have been to prison. If they have been to prison, that's a plus. Once you've been inside, you're never afraid of a bust because you know what to expect. Worse comes to worse, and they are loyal enough to shed blood for you in a turf war. People who don't pay are maimed or killed; at least, that's the way it is in Baltimore, and we don't mess around; we use enforcers.

I was a heroin dealer before this fentanyl epidemic came about. We cut 10 grams of raw heroin with 5 grams of morphine and 8.5 grams of Quinine Benita. Quinine must sit out for two days and be exposed to oxygen to neutralize the molecular structure so that it won't overpower the opiate rush. When injected, it adds warmth and euphoria but won't disturb the high. When fentanyl started hitting the streets in 2010, I had been eating it for years, so I was already familiar with the product.

I was great at measuring fentanyl HCL powder so no one would overdose and die from my dope--then we all would be in Leavenworth looking stupid. I did precisely 2 grams of Carfentanil to 10 grams of Mannitol; then I would test 0.001g on myself to see if it was the right potency and add or subtract more Mannitol as necessary. I made nearly $2500 nightly...and that's just the smack business. When I added cocaine to my inventory, I would get 1/2 ounce for $500. Then my girl cooked it; she was a pro at cooking. We made close to $3,000 on each $500 investment.

The Criminalization of Addiction

The Oxycodone business was smooth as a newborn infant's ass. My mother was on pain management and got 120 30mg Oxys per month, each selling for $40 or $4,800 per prescription; I used this money to start my heroin and cocaine business.

That's the smooth parts of the game now; let's get to the problems. One employee started smoking crack heavy, I mean HEAVY; he ended up never getting paid because he was working just for the crack. He smoked everything I gave him to sell, which was 100 vials to each hitter. One day, he ran off with a pack of hitters; this is where your enforcer comes in. I paid $500 to have him beaten and brought back to me weeping and saying that 'crack got him bad he wants to go to rehab, can I please help him get treatment.' I did help him, but that showed weakness in front of my crew, a huge problem. I corrected it by going to one of my crew's stores and shooting three dudes who had moved in without my permission. I didn't shoot to kill; I just showed them I would use a pistol if necessary and don't fuck with me or my money.

Then, after all that bullshit, there are the plain-clothes cops, we call them knockers. We hire lookouts to get the makeup of the cars and who's in it; if it's two stocky white dudes in a Crown Victoria with crew cuts, then they are waiting for us to make a transaction.

The money coming in is great, but you also have high expenses. You must put aside about $20,000-$50,000 in bail money for your crew and keep a lawyer handy with monthly payments of about $2,500. Then, no matter what the charge, he's already detained. Maximum security measures must be taken since prison is the alternative. High-technology security systems for the property (depending on size) are vital and run in the $100,000 range. Then there are the paid human lookouts, burner phones, and a hundred other things I can't think of right now. Then, some crew went to prison, and I sent them money for commissary and gave their girlfriends heroin and suboxone to smuggle to them on visiting day.

Holding all of this up is so fucking stressful I swear I had grey hair in my beard by age 23, lol. But I loved those guys, and they loved me. After all that, it was a fucking probation violation that sent me to prison. I was sentenced to 8yrs, 8 months, and 14 days, but I only served 3 miserable years before being released.

So that's it, my inside story of drug dealing.

None of the necessary skills described for being a successful *low-level* drug dealer are manageable by advanced opioid addicts. Drug dealers operate their businesses in a highly charged, illegal environment that requires extreme caution at all levels of operations. The descriptions offered above indicate drug dealers need to take the initiative to develop a steady supply line for drugs and undergo delicate negotiations with dangerous people. Drug dealers must also hire employees and collect funds from sketchy people while avoiding the attention of neighbors and the police. It is a very time-consuming career path with no vacations or weekends off. A dependable car is necessary for a dealer who must be available 24/7 and know how to solve distribution and delivery issues. In addition, dealers need to know how to manage a high stress level and be aware of things happening around them.

> Scott did not own, or have access to, a car during the period he was supposedly a dealer.

The opioid addict does not have *any* of the skills required to be a drug dealer. The cognitive, physical, and emotional deterioration of an advanced opioid addict prohibits the possibility of being able to function as a dealer—or anything else. Recall opioid addicts are unable to perform even the necessary daily activities to care for themselves (e.g., taking a shower, paying a bill, or cooking a meal), are unable to remember simple engagements, are unable to plan or organize, and are cognitively confused. They mostly sleep. Labeling addicts as 'dealers' is a clear mischaracterization of the reality in which they exist. Misleading labels are dangerous as they often provoke unfounded and unfair judgments about the addict, who may have wished at some point that he was a dealer but is simply not capable of managing an inventory of drugs.

Opioid addicts, often finding themselves unemployed after being fired from multiple jobs, fantasize about easy money: money for drugs. Being a dealer sounds easy enough to addicts, and they believe (incorrectly) it does not require sobriety, so it appears to be a good fit with the fantasy of easy money. Scott described his experience:

> "A few years back, I thought dealing drugs was the answer to my money problems. I thought it would provide steady access to drugs, and I could make some money at the same time. It did not work out that way, though. Instead, I ended up owing the dealer $330, money I did not have. I had used the drugs to pay back some of my friends and used the remainder for myself. Some rough-looking guys showed up at my house with a gun and told me to figure out how to get the money NOW or else.
> So, no, dealing didn't work out for me, but I continued to share with friends. I've never met a heroin or fentanyl addict who doesn't share drugs with friends; it's in their best interests to do so. In the eyes of the law, I guess all opioid addicts are dealers, and that includes all the deceased ones as well."

The first challenge for the addict is grappling with distributing a drug that the addict is desperate to consume. Too often, the addict uses the drugs to either get high or pay other addicts for past drug sharing, or more likely, both. With the drugs for distribution depleted, a cash problem arises for the addict, who now finds himself in debt to his dealer with no way to repay the total amount. Unfortunately for the person with an addiction, many drug dealers do not even want to have them as customers. Addicts frequently become the victims of their dealers. According to Jacques, Allen, and Wright (2014), *"...we find that dealers typically "rip-off" people who are addicted to drugs because they are unlikely to realize what has happened, and most are unwilling to retaliate or complain."*[151] Real dealers perceive addicts as needy and not worth the trouble they cause. No one wants to be around addicts, including dealers. They are trying to run a business, not a daycare facility.

On one hand, mental health professionals describe addiction as a complex brain disorder and a cognitive illness. On the other hand, prosecutors take bows for locking addicts in prison for decades. This large discrepancy in perspectives makes it nearly impossible to have a sound policy regarding the treatment of addicts. The DOJ focuses on punishment and revenge, while mental health professionals focus on rehabilitation. Prosecutors depriving the mentally ill of their liberty for 20 years or longer violates the Eighth Amendment, which prohibits the government from imposing

---

[151] Jacques, S., Allen, A., Wright, R. (2014). Drug dealers' rational choices on which customers to rip-off. *International Journal of Drug Policy, 25*(2), 251-256.

a penalty that is either barbaric or too severe for the crime committed. If the crime committed was drug sharing among addicts, one addict dying does not make the survivor a killer.

The research findings detailed in this chapter indicate that it is *physically* and *mentally* impossible for an advanced opioid addict to be a dealer in any meaningful sense of the label. The demands of being a dealer, as outlined by three anonymous drug dealers, are far beyond the ability of fentanyl addicts.

Recommendations

The profound ignorance of the legal community regarding advanced opioid addiction must be directly addressed. Educating Congress and the legal community about the limitations of those addicted to opioids is critical to avoiding the prosecution of those who cannot perform the accused tasks.

An educated Congress would be the first step towards decriminalizing drugs. Decriminalizing drugs does not imply there should be no consequences; there should be. When a crime is committed involving a person with an addiction, the case should be sent to a *Drug Court*. The consequences of the addict's crime should sentence them to confinement in a federal or state rehabilitation facility that follows the restorative justice practices described at the end of Chapter 3. Perhaps these actions could be the beginning of a change in societal attitudes toward those who are physically and psychologically addicted to drugs.

It is the *dealer* component of the DIH charge that results in such a lengthy mandatory minimum sentence of 20 years in federal prison, and it is also the reason advanced addicts cannot be guilty of the crime. When people are being incarcerated for a crime they are incapable of committing, it is time to start educating our legislators.

A Word from Scott
This addict cannot be a dealer because...

My main problem when I attempted to sell drugs was not being able to move my product fast enough. It needed to be lightning fast because otherwise, I would be sitting there with a bunch of the drugs I'm addicted to. *While sitting there, I would start getting dope sick, so what do you do? You fold and do the drugs to mitigate the sickness. Then I had a new problem because I had fewer drugs to sell, and I started feeling like maybe I should not sell all the drugs because I would need them when I got dope sick again.*

Inevitably, I didn't have the money to pay the dealer when promised. You can't NOT pay your drug dealer; that's not an option unless you want to get robbed or shot or both. It does not take long for your 'career' as a dealer to end if you have no money to pay for the product. People who were okay with fronting you the product won't do that anymore because getting payment from you was such a big hassle. This put me right back where I started, searching for drugs to keep from getting sick. The way the drug market works, it removes addicts quickly.

If you have an addiction, don't bother with trying to deal in the drug you are addicted to, it won't work. Save yourself the time, money, and danger of trying.

Summary

This chapter explored the reasons why advanced opioid addicts cannot be competent dealers. Since 2013, fentanyl has been made in underground laboratories and has been mixed into the illicit drug supply. Growing numbers of people are unintentionally consuming fentanyl in the form of counterfeit prescription opioids. In the best-case scenario, these people are unknowingly developing tolerance to fentanyl. In the worst case, death occurs due to overdose or body malfunction.

Advanced opioid addicts already live in a world of harsh natural consequences; there are even more severe consequences for *NOT* using. People addicted to fentanyl who stop using will have severe physical, mental, and emotional withdrawal symptoms that persist for years. The medical evidence shows that advanced opioid addicts incur significant damage to both the grey and white matter of the brain. The brain is essential to normal human functioning, and people with an addiction do not have access to a normal brain. This chapter discussed the numerous consequences of opioid brain damage, including the deterioration of the addict's capacity to plan, meet goals, display self-control, and remember events, dates, or context. The addict experiences difficulties with thinking and a reduced ability to reason due to cognitive decline. In addition to having impaired learning and problem-solving skills, the addict has impaired depth perception, vision, and walking abilities. Emotionally, the addict lacks maturity and experiences an increase in both impulsive and compulsive behaviors.

Other medical evidence shows that organ damage is likely to occur in opioid addicts due to the dehydration, hypotension, and urine retention that comes with heavy use. Chronic kidney disease is the most common problem for those who inject due to skin popping. The skin popping is due to amyloidosis, a disease that causes an unwelcome protein to accumulate in organs, affecting the heart, kidneys, nervous system, digestive tract, liver, and spleen.

Psychologists have noted that opioid addicts not only show physical changes but also display a changed attitude combined with a different personality. Addicts cease to take responsibility for their bills, medical appointments, and any other activities that do not involve the pursuit of drugs. They blame others for their shortcomings, as well as their drug addiction. It is their boss's fault that they were fired, their spouse's fault they missed an appointment, their parent's fault they are on drugs, and on and on and on. Nothing is *ever their* fault.

Dealing drugs is not as simple as the sharing transactions between two people addicted to the same drug. The skills required to be a drug dealer include but are not limited to planning, thinking, driving, conversing coherently as well as organizing deliveries, weighing drugs, always being available, etc. Addicts do not possess the abilities needed to be dealers of any consequence; at most, they buy and sell small quantities of drugs with like-minded addicts. The stories from two anonymous drug dealers revealed a fast-paced life full of time demands and security measures. Good judgment is required to select good buyers and those who can work for the business. Advanced opioid addicts do not have good judgment, cannot remember simple assignments, and become unable to care for themselves, much less customers.

The misguided targeting of addicts arises because the US legal system ignores that it is physically and psychologically impossible for an advanced opioid addict to be a drug dealer of any consequence. Perhaps the most obvious reason a person with a fentanyl disorder cannot be a fentanyl dealer is the Cardinal Rule: *"... don't get high on your own supply."* A person with an addiction attempting to run a demanding drug business is doomed for failure; that would be like putting the fox in charge of the hen house.

CHAPTER 5: CULPABILITY MATTERS

Introduction
Prior to 2008, overdose deaths were widely viewed by the legal community as accidental deaths, with no one legally liable. Although there have been no changes in the law, societal attitudes changed after the release of newer, more deadly drugs, resulting in frightening rates of overdose deaths. The legal community attempted to allay the public's fears by arresting and prosecuting more people. By 2011, arresting and convicting an overdose victim's friends and family under DIH laws was the norm. The views of the legal community had shifted, in the blink of an eye, from accidental death to strict liability homicide. The deceased was no longer an addict who died by their own hand but a victim of the person who provided the drugs.

Both views are extreme and fail to capture the nature of the culpability of the deceased and the responsibility of the surviving addict. Overdose deaths are accidental. The surviving addict is responsible for providing the illegal drug to the deceased. The deceased is responsible for buying the drug and determining the amount and method of ingestion. Neither person enters the transaction expecting death to be the outcome, but both know it is possible.

Self-Harm vs. Suicide
Self-harm includes any actions that an individual undertakes that create intentional, unnecessary damage to their body, e.g., cutting, burning, asphyxiation, poisoning, drug addiction, etc., and are not covered by another psychological condition. Drug addiction is a particularly complicated area of self-harming behaviors. There are two basic types of self-destructive behavior: suicide and non-suicidal self-injury (NSSI).[152] Halicka & Kienia (2018) say that NSSI has always been present in societies and is believed to afflict approximately 10% of nearly every society around the globe equally. Despite the enormous scale of the phenomenon, research into the details of NSSI behaviors is limited.

---

[152] Halicka, J., & Kiejna, A. (2018). Non-suicidal self-injury (NSSI) and suicidal: Criteria differentiation. *Advanced Clinical Experimental Medicine, 27*(2), 257-261.

The taking of one's life, whether intentionally or through self-harming actions, is a tragedy. O'Carroll (2022) argues that, as a society, we are not equally compassionate about every death because it matters *how* one dies, either by accident or suicide, drugs or no drugs. He argues that a hierarchy of empathy determines the level of care given to those who die as a result of their actions.[153] Those who clearly and purposefully take their life receive the most social sympathy, while those who die recklessly by drug overdose garner the least. As a group, people who die from NSSIs generate the least social sympathy since their actions are intentional, and the risks are known in advance.

Gratz (2003) defines NSSI as the intentional self-induced harming of one's body, resulting in tissue damage to relieve extreme depression, stress, or negative thinking.[154] This definition could also apply to many suicides, except death occurs rather than merely tissue damage. It is not easy to distinguish between a death by suicide and a death by an NSSI overdose because the difference depends on the intent of the deceased. Additionally, the emotional states of a suicidal person and an NSSI individual are quite similar; both suffer from deep depression and anxiety.

O'Carroll (2022) argues that the issue of intent is paramount to philosophers, ethicists, families, and lawyers. The motive of the deceased determines their moral or legal culpability. O'Carroll says that if they committed the act accidentally, then they are *'innocent.'* However, if they committed the act intentionally, they are *'guilty.'* If they acted recklessly and knew that their actions could result in the undesired outcome but still acted, irrespective of the risk, they are usually *'guilty of a lesser crime.'*

This last category, *'guilty of a lesser crime,'* applies to most deceased overdose victims. From the Middle Ages until the late 19th century, suicide was viewed, through the lens of religion, as a sin of such magnitude that often the deceased was denied a burial on church grounds.[155] Consequently, it was essential to decide whether a person had committed

---

[153] O'Carroll, A. (2022). The suicide hierarchy. *British Journal of General Practice*, 72(723), 490-491.
[154] Gratz, K. L. (2003). Risk factors for and functions of deliberate self-harm: An empirical and conceptual review. *Clinical Psychology: Science and Practice*, *10*(2), 192.
[155] O'Carroll A. (2022). The suicide hierarchy. *The British Journal of General Practice*, 72(723), 490–491. https://doi.org/10.3399/bjgp22X720857

intentional suicide, given the implications for the destination of their corpse and celestial soul. Today, it is still important from a legal perspective to decide whether someone acted intentionally--for example, in the case of life insurance. During the late 19th century, the emphasis shifted from morality to a "psychosocial" understanding of suicide, but intent was still a core requirement.[156]

Moller, Tait & Byrne (2013) say that people become involved with self-harming behaviors, such as attempted hanging, impulsive self-poisoning [drug abuse], and cutting because they are experiencing intolerable internal tension.[157] Risk factors include socioeconomic disadvantage and psychiatric illness—particularly depression, substance abuse, and anxiety disorders. The risk of repeated self-harm and eventual suicide is very high. More than 50% of people treated at a hospital after a self-harming episode will commit suicide within approximately nine years. Psychiatric illness, lethal methods, and excessive secrecy are all indicators of a high suicide risk.

Today, attitudes towards suicide have evolved and are more nuanced; the act is no longer simply illegal or immoral. It is a tragedy of unquantifiable proportions, which leaves a devastated family and a hole in the community. The knowledge that the person was highly depressed does not provide any relief. Likewise, the loss of someone who died recklessly because of a drug overdose is equally tragic but leaves a much broader path of wreckage behind because, for every overdose death, someone must now go to prison. The imprisonment involves another person, family, and community whose lives have been forever shattered.

NSSI is expressed in various forms, from relatively mild, such as scratching, plucking hair, picking scabs, and nail-biting, to relatively severe forms, such as cutting, burning, or even beating oneself.[158]

---

[156] Jones, Robert A. (1986). *Emile Durkheim: An Introduction to Four Major Works.* Beverly Hills, CA: Sage Publications, Inc., 82-114.
[157] Moller, C. I., Tait, R. J., & Byrne, D. G. (2013). Deliberate self-harm, substance use, and negative affect in nonclinical samples: a systematic review. *Substance Abuse, 34*(2), 188-207.
[158] de Oliveira Teixeira, S. M., Souza, L. E. C., & Viana, L. M. M. (2018). Suicide as a public health issue. *Revista Brasileira em Promocao da Saude, 31*(3).

According to Shneidman (2001), suicide involves not so much the desire to kill the body but the wish to end consciousness.[159] The same could be said about those who die from drug overdoses; they wish to lose consciousness, not their life. Some reports characterize aggressive acts against one's own body, such as fentanyl abuse, as indicative of especially severe psychopathological problems.[160]

For drug-use behavior to be classified as an NSSI, the following must hold:

1) The drug is self-administered while knowing physical harm is possible, but without suicidal intent, on five or more days in the past year. The drug is taken to alleviate at least one of the following:
   a. To relieve negative thoughts or feelings.
   b. To resolve interpersonal problems, or
   c. To cause temporary positive feelings or emotions.

2) The drug behavior is associated with at least one of the following:
   a. Negative thoughts, feelings, or interpersonal problems immediately before taking the drug.
   b. Preoccupation with the drug.
   c. Frequent urges to take drugs.

3) The drug behavior is not socially sanctioned.

4) The drug behavior causes significant clinical distress or impairment.

5) The drug behavior does not occur exclusively in the context of another disorder and cannot be accounted for by another mental or medical disorder.

While philosophers, church authorities, scholars, and families are interested in knowing the deceased's intent, the *Department of Justice* is

---

[159] Shneidman, E. S. (2001). Comprehending suicide. *Landmarks in 20th-century Suicidology*.
[160] O'Carroll, Austin (2022). The Suicide Hierarchy. *British Journal of General Practice*, 72 (723); 490-491.

not. In the eyes of the DOJ, the deceased is an innocent victim, regardless of their intent, and someone must pay for the "murder."

US vs. Hancock

Scott stated, *"...the request by my girlfriend to 'take care' of TG was wearing thin. It was always an urgent request, so it was a hassle to find someone with fentanyl quickly. I never once reached out to TG; she always contacted me. At first, it wasn't too bad, but later, as her addiction grew, she needed more. I tried to do that for a while, but it was so annoying that I had reached the point of needing to talk to TG about finding herself a drug dealer rather than relying on friendship. I felt bad about rejecting her, so I kept putting off the conversation. Now I wish I hadn't."*

Scott's case provides an appropriate example of the culpability issue—recall from the background of the *US vs. Hancock* case and the actions taken.

1. TG initiated the interaction with Scott by first *texting* him to ask him to get five pills (*beans*) of fentanyl.

2. Then TG *drove* 25 miles to Scott's house,

3. TG *paid* $20 cash for the drugs and then *drove* 25 miles back to her aunt's house.

4. TG was alone when she chose to inhale (*snort*) the fentanyl despite having been told by Scott that it was strong.

5. TG chose to snort *two* pills instead of one or none, resulting in her overdose death.

6. The autopsy revealed that TG had multiple other drugs in her system that interact negatively with fentanyl, something Scott had no way of knowing, but TG did.[161]

---

[161] Fentanyl Interactions, *Drugs.com*. https://www.drugs.com/drug interactions/fentanyl.html.

7. The prosecutor's *discovery* materials indicated TG had no life-saving drugs (e.g., naloxone) available to counteract the overdose, even though this practice is now common among opioid addicts.[162] In this one respect, opioid users are more fortunate than other drug users because there is an opioid antidote that prevents an overdose death.

TG's activities make it evident that she was actively involved in seeking fentanyl. Despite TG's multiple confinements in rehabilitation centers for opioid abuse, neither she nor her family had any naloxone available.

All people with an addiction are victims of their drug use, and when addicted to a drug as lethal as fentanyl, that often means death will soon follow. Scott was close to death himself when the DEA arrested him. Despite several emergency room visits to see Scott when he had overdosed, being angry with his dealer(s) never came to mind. If Scott did not obtain drugs from one dealer or friend, he would have found another who would supply him. It was impossible for a dealer to 'push' drugs on Scott because he was constantly *seeking* them.

According to Scott, heroin and fentanyl addicts understand their activities are both illegal and potentially fatal. Even the threat of death is not enough to overpower their opioid addiction. Scott's actions did not trigger TG's drug-seeking behavior. Instead, it was the progression of her advanced opioid addiction that caused TG to contact a fellow addict for drugs. When asked about other addicts' knowledge of the high likelihood of death, Scott said:

"Well, everyone knows fentanyl can kill you, but once you start using it and get addicted to it, you notice you haven't died after using it multiple times, and it's done nothing but make you feel good, so you try to just use it as carefully as you can by going off how much you used last time and how it made you feel last time. The thing is, you are going to use either way, <u>no matter what,</u> because the withdrawal is horrific and is every dope fiend's worst fear-- there is absolutely nothing worse. Addicts spend 100% of their time trying to secure enough drugs to not go through withdrawal.

---

[162] Freeman, P. R., Hankosky, E. R., Lofwall, M. R., Talbert, J. C. (2018). The changing landscape of naloxone availability in the United States, 2011–2017. *Drug and Alcohol Dependence, 191,* 361-364.

Naturally, you'd rather get high than go through withdrawals, so no matter what, you are going to use it, even though you know it may kill you. It's like after you get addicted to it, you deny that it can kill you. As for me, I had overdosed on it a bunch of times and ended up in the hospital and never died, so I am like, well, it hasn't killed me, and if it does, who cares? My life is already fucked up–I spend all my time chasing the dragon to avoid the pain of withdrawal. What's one more life, even if it's mine?"

It is rare in DIH cases for autopsies to show the presence of only one drug; typically, there is a mix of prescription and non-prescription drugs in the bloodstream.[163] The drug mixtures can make it extremely difficult for a toxicologist to obtain clean results as to which drug, or drug mix, was the actual cause of death.[164] Fentanyl is known to interact negatively with at least 551 different drugs, 246 of which cause interactions categorized as major, 302 as moderate, and only three as minor.[165] Common medications for such things as depression, ventricular arrhythmias, antihistamines, muscle relaxants, hypertension, and edema have been shown to negatively interact with fentanyl, either increasing its potency or exacerbating its symptoms. Legal drugs such as alcohol and cannabis also contribute to the toxicity of fentanyl, making it impossible for the surviving addict to have gauged, in advance, the toxicity and tolerance levels of the deceased.[166]

One person cannot gauge the dangers of sharing drugs with another person without knowledge of what has already been ingested. Each person alone knows their tolerance level and the other drugs already in their system. The federal justice system deals with this dilemma using the *'but for'*

---

[163] National Institutes of Health (2015). Biology of Addiction: Drugs and Alcohol Can Hijack Your Brain. *NIH News in Health*, Oct. https://newsinhealth.nih.gov/2015/10/biology-addiction.

[164] Davis, Gregory G. (2013). National Association of Medical Examiners Position Paper: Recommendation for the Investigation, Diagnosis and Certification of Deaths Related to Opioid Drugs. *National Association of Medical Examiners*. https://name.memberclicks.net/assets/docs/a8f3230e-d063-4681-8678-e3d15ce9effb.pdf

[165] Fentanyl Interactions (2022). *Drugs.com*. https://www.drugs.com/drug-interactions/fentanyl.html.

[166] Cannabis is legal in 36 states of the 14 remaining states 3 have decriminalized marijuana for first offense. Of the remaining 11 states, Georgia, Texas, and Wisconsin have decriminalized marijuana only in certain cities and counties. Iowa allows some medical cannabis, but the rules are unclear. Kentucky-misdemeanor for 8oz or less. Of the remaining 6 states, Kansas, South Carolina, and Wyoming classify marijuana as a misdemeanor with no mention of the amount or weight.

standard created in the *US vs. Burrage* (2014) case. The Burrage standard was applied in Scott's case as follows: *"...but for the presence of fentanyl, the deceased would still be alive."*

Addiction recovery groups, books, and organizations are clear and consistent on how to allocate responsibility for people with substance use disorders. The process would start, for example, with Scott taking responsibility for his actions but NOT for the actions of TG. The group, *Alanon*, is designed to help people learn to avoid taking responsibility for others' actions; it is unhealthy behavior. Scott was responsible for the action of providing five beans of fentanyl to TG but was not responsible for the eight actions taken by TG. After TG secured the drugs, she had many choices available; she could have decided to discard the drugs, sell the drugs, give the drugs to a parent or trusted sponsor, snort one pill instead of two, or take the pills by mouth as a lower risk option. She did none of those things.

TG was not seeking fentanyl because of a weakness in her character; instead, like Scott, she was the victim of a progressive disease triggered by opioids. She and her family paid the ultimate price for her choices. Socially, many believe that those with a substance use disorder deserve to be punished for that reason alone, except when an addict dies from an overdose. Then, the judicial apparatus recasts the deceased addict as a blameless victim having no culpability in their death. In contrast, the surviving addict is demonized, shamed, and imprisoned for a minimum of 20 years. Harshly punishing people with an addiction fails to acknowledge that all people with a substance use disorder are victims of their drug use.

In the case of *US vs. Hancock*, there was no evidence suggesting that Scott prompted any communication with TG to exchange fentanyl. TG was 20-25 miles away from Scott when she consumed the fentanyl, so he could not have influenced her choice of snorting as the delivery method or her decision to administer two pills instead of one or none. Scott said, *"Five years later, I still hold much resentment and anger towards TG for not listening to me when I told her this fentanyl was stronger than usual. Ignoring me cost her life, but it cost mine, too. How do you get over that while you're sitting in prison? I know I eventually need to accept the outcome to find peace, but I'm not there yet."*

No legal consideration is given to the driving force in the transaction, namely the deceased or the motive of the surviving addict. One of many reasons the judicial system is failing to reduce opioid deaths is its targeting of the wrong offenders.

Overdose Death is Not Murder

According to the Department of Justice, there are three types of murder: first-degree murder, second-degree murder, and manslaughter. First-degree murder requires advanced planning and malicious intent, e.g., plotting to murder your spouse for the insurance payout. Second-degree murder is a killing that occurs during the commission of a felony; it requires malicious intent but not premeditation, e.g., killing someone while robbing a bank. For these two types of murder, the *mens rea* of the defendant is the intent to kill, intent to inflict serious bodily harm, or acting with reckless disregard for human life. First-degree murder charges will likely result in life in prison or the death penalty, while second-degree murder is punishable by not less than ten years in prison to life. The term of imprisonment is influenced most heavily by the defendant's motive.

Some deaths result during the 'heat of passion,' defending oneself from an attack, or the result of an accident and are categorized as manslaughter. There are two types of manslaughter charges: voluntary and involuntary. Voluntary manslaughter means a death that occurs during the heat of passion or while defending oneself. It requires an intentional act or one that is likely to cause death or great bodily harm. Involuntary manslaughter, in contrast, means a death was unintentional and the result of recklessness or criminal negligence, such as driving under the influence of alcohol. At the federal level, voluntary is punishable by imprisonment for not more than ten years or a fine under Title 18, or both, and involuntary manslaughter is punishable by imprisonment of not more than six years or a fine or both.[167]

The crucial distinctions made between first and second-degree murder and voluntary versus involuntary manslaughter are based on the defendant's *mens rea*. Motive is the most important factor considered in murder-related trials. Hessick (2006) puts it this way, *"Motive plays an important*

---

[167] United States Department of Justice Archives. https://www.justice.gov/archives/jm/criminal-resource-manual-1537-manslaughter-defined

role in criminal law. It is necessary to prove liability, a key component of several defenses. It has been a traditional consideration at sentencing. Motive's role in criminal punishment has grown through the adoption of hate crime sentencing enhancements and the rise of substantive sentencing law. Motive has an important role in punishment theory, as it reinforces the centrality of shared moral judgments, which are indispensable to any criminal law system. Yet despite motive's increasing importance in criminal law, its treatment is inconsistent and incomplete." [168]

Despite the critical importance of motive in determining a reasonable punishment, it is legally sidelined in DIH cases by using the 1986 strict liability standard applied to drug overdose cases. Given the mental, physical, and emotional condition of opioid addicts, they are unable to reason through the consequences of their actions, much less predict the actions of another addict.

Levels of Culpability

Below are four stories that illustrate different aspects of culpability. Notice the difference between the first three stories and the last story of a dealer who showed depraved indifference to human life. The stories highlight the importance of considering the defendant's motive and the victims' culpability in drug cases.

1. <u>**A Father's Story**</u>: *"It was almost dawn. My phone was ringing over and over, but it was the loud banging at the door that woke me up. It was my mother. She had come to tell me that my 19-year-old daughter was dead from a drug overdose. It was hard to process those words in that moment. My initial despair and grief shifted to rage. I wanted the person who gave my daughter the drugs to pay. It didn't matter if it was her boyfriend or friends—I wanted to hurt and punish that person."*

   "I had these feelings despite knowing that the person who gave my daughter the heroin, which was likely contaminated with fentanyl, was not responsible for my daughter's death. What is responsible for the hundreds of thousands of deaths from drug overdose is a

---

[168] Hessick, C. B. (2006). Motive's role in criminal punishment. *Southern California Law Review*, *80*-89.

broken drug policy, a system that prioritizes punishment over treatment, and a culture of prohibition that leads to drug use while alone and in shame. As a person who uses drugs, I know that no one person is to blame but myself."[169]

2. **A Story of Reconciliation**: *"My daughter, Elisif Janis Bruun, at age 24, died of a drug overdose on February 11, 2014, while attending Cooper Riis, a healing community in North Carolina. She obtained the drugs by contacting Sean Harrington, a friend living in a cardboard box under a freeway overpass in Philadelphia. She convinced him to mail her heroin upon her sending him a money order. Sean, an addict, not knowing Elisif was "in rehab," did as he was asked. Elisif, who had been at Cooper Riis for three months and seemed to be thriving, had earned the privileges of independence, so it was not difficult for the greeting card containing heroin to get through to her. She received the drugs, took them, and died."*

"The police authorities in North Carolina easily built a case tracing the distribution of the lethal dose of drugs to Sean Harrington: there were text messages, the money order record, and the greeting card itself. Per North Carolina law (and through persistent efforts of the District Attorney's prosecutorial offices), Sean was arrested, charged with second-degree murder, and extradited to Polk County, North Carolina, to face charges with a maximum penalty of 52 years in prison. After spending nearly two years in jail awaiting trial, Sean was released. The prosecutors elected not to proceed with charges because they did "not have the cooperation of the victim's family." We – my wife and two daughters and I – are the "victim's family," and we certainly did not cooperate with the prosecution. Instead, we established a relationship with Sean and his family, and, as expected, found we had much more in common with them – their suffering, their compassion – than with the District Attorney in Polk County."

"I fundamentally believe homicide charges around drug distribution misplaces blame: the disease is the culprit in almost all cases, not the provider. Sean, and so many like him, are often victims themselves,

---

[169] Vincent, Louise (2019). Reframing the Blame for the War on Drugs. *Open Society Foundations*, May 10. https://www.opensocietyfoundations.org/voices/reframing-blame-war-drugs

not perpetrators. The Sean's of the world need — and benefit from — treatment, not shame and blame. Yes, everyone needs to be held accountable for their actions, even with addiction at play. Still, the action Sean ought to have been held accountable for (and arguably was, with nearly two years in jail) was illegal distribution through the mail and certainly not murder. Sean has so much to offer as a citizen, not despite what he has been through, but because of what he has been through."

"Elisif died of her disease. Blaming is a toxic slippery slope that sets one on a misguided path without peace. As a slippery slope, why stop the blame at Sean? Why not blame the healing community Elisif was in for not effectively screening mail? Why not blame their psychiatrist for not embracing medication-assisted recovery (no Suboxone prescriptions for Elisif)? Why not blame me for knowing Elisif had phone numbers in her phone and trusting (despite her illness) that she was safe from using those numbers in the recovery program she herself sought? I blame none, for all did what we judged best before a dastardly illness. Judgment, our judgment — all of ours — is flawed, but not legally so, just humanly so. We do our best. The disease kills."

"We want to throw blame around, and there is ostensibly plenty to go around – and it's so easy to blame a young man suffering from addiction and living in a cardboard box under a freeway who, in his illness, thought he was helping a fellow hurting soul. We want to blame people because the disease is so ugly, and we are so powerless. We don't want to look at that because there's so little we can do about it, but we can punish a person. So, we do. That's called scapegoating. It's misguided and does not one iota set the world aright: it compounds pain and limits the opportunity to offer healing to so many. Sean is empowered to offer healing through sharing his story (I have seen that already), and he wants to be a force for good. He deserves that opportunity. We deserve the opportunity to have him in our midst."
"Locking him up would deprive us. It would deprive me of a beautiful kind of redemption: Sean as a force for good... Sean just having the opportunity to have a life... that's a redemption in the face of something no degree of punishment can ever return: my daughter."

"My daughter, who would have been the very first to lay culpability at her own illness-driven behavior, had more sense about what's real than the prosecutors in that regard. Elisif was ill, and so was Sean. They both deserve(d) life. Neither deserves(d) blame. Sean, in the meantime, rather than seeing his own life destroyed by a lifetime of incarceration, has demonstrated through his own behaviors the value of a compassionate approach to those in his circumstances. In my activism since Elisif's death, I have engaged in an effort to use arts programming and public engagement to challenge the stigma associated with mental illness and substance use, making the world a more healing place."

"In early 2017, I had the opportunity to hold an event where Sean spoke, offering his own story as a testimony of another way (besides punitive and scapegoating incarceration). Here is what Sean said about his learning of our family's attitude as he concluded his remarks that evening to an audience of more than 100 people:"

Sean: *"When I learned of Peter and his family's stance, I couldn't believe it. I thought this man had to hate me and rightfully should hate me because that was easier for me to understand. Yet he didn't because he knew that I held no malice towards his daughter; he understood intimately the way addiction ruins the lives of the sick and suffering. His compassion has made it possible for me to have a future, and I am eternally grateful for that. As a result of these events, I'm able to be coming up on three years off drugs, and that is something I never imagined being able to say. I owe that to Peter, Elisif, and the rest of their family because they were responsible for giving me a second chance when I was at a point in life where I didn't think I deserved one. Yet, this has helped to give me a purpose. I hope that the experiences that have affected me, my family, Elisif, Peter, and the Bruun family can be used to help prevent more families from enduring the pain and hardship that we have endured. I hope that Elisif's story and my story can be carried to those people who are still sick and suffering and be used as a source of strength, hope, and experience so that those people can one day find a way out of addiction. I feel like that is the best way to help keep Elisif's memory alive. Thank you for giving me this chance."*

"And lest one question the value beyond the private exchange between my family and the Harrington's, a typical response from a member of the audience is evidenced in an email I received from someone who had been a friend of Elisif's, who was in attendance that evening and who works at a treatment center in Baltimore, who wrote of the event that it "will stick with me forever. The enormity of your forgiveness and the transcendent love were tangible and profound. It was a gift to everyone present."

"Nobody would have been happier at this outcome than Elisif, and none of it possible if Sean were in prison."[170]

3. **A Typical Story**: *"Peter Kucinski and Amy were sweethearts in high school and now had a beautiful child. She and Peter struggled with substance abuse and used heroin regularly. Amy began using heroin after developing an addiction to prescription painkillers following a back injury. Peter used heroin for years before Amy's injury and helped her transition to heroin once she began experiencing symptoms of withdrawal between prescription refills."*

"Amy and Peter alternated driving into the city to buy drugs, and on the day of Peter's death, Amy caught a ride with a friend who purchased the heroin and drove her home. On the way home, Amy snorted a ten-dollar bag of heroin and then gave Peter his own ten-dollar bag. Peter snorted the bag of heroin in the bathroom of their home and then went to sleep. Amy and a friend later noticed that Peter was no longer breathing. They called 911, and paramedics rushed Peter to the hospital, where he died shortly after that. Two months later, the State of Illinois charged Amy with a DIH, and a judge set her bail at one million dollars. Later, Amy was convicted and sent to prison for 20 years."[171]

4. **Depraved Indifference to Life**. *"According to evidence presented at his trial, thirty-two-year-old Aaron Broussard ordered one hundred*

---

[170] An Overdose Death is Not Murder: Why Drug Induced Homicide Laws are Counterproductive & Inhumane. *The Drug Policy Alliance*. Nov 2017 booklet copyright owned by DPA. https://drugpolicy.org/sites

[171] Beavers, A. (2023). Drug-Induced Homicide: A Comprehensive Statutory Proposal. *Northeastern University Law Review Online*.

grams of 4-FA, an analog drug resembling that of amphetamine and MDMA, from his suppliers in China. Broussard's suppliers shipped him one hundred grams of ninety- nine percent <u>pure fentanyl</u>. For one month, Broussard sent packages containing fentanyl to over twelve customers throughout the US who ordered and expected to receive a controlled substance analog like Adderall."

"Broussard claimed that he did not know he was distributing fentanyl, but at trial, the prosecution noted that he continued to sell the drugs after learning some people had become seriously ill and nearly died. In fact, Broussard contacted his suppliers in China to request a discount on his next drug delivery because of this issue. Moreover, a similar mix-up occurred in August 2015, after which Broussard was "repeatedly told to test his drugs," though he never did. Eleven people died because of ingesting the fentanyl Broussard sold to them as an Adderall analog. A federal jury consequently convicted Broussard on seventeen counts, including distribution of fentanyl resulting in death." [172]

The story of the father who lost his daughter shows the various emotions involved when grappling with a child's culpability in their death. The second story about Elisif shows the results that can occur with a restorative justice process. It is a beautiful story of people's lives destroyed and remade due to Elisif's family. Note that the story holds all parties accountable for their part, but not for others, in the most loving way possible.

The third story is typical of many stories about victims of the DIH laws. Both Peter and Amy were adults who chose to use heroin and participated equally. This story is typical because it involves two people with an addiction; one dies of an overdose, and the other goes to prison. This sad story is repeated thousands of times every year as more people are charged with DIH crimes. The one case worthy of legal attention is Broussard's. He displayed apathy towards human life by ignoring all the warning signs and failing to take corrective action. Cases like Broussard's are used to represent one of the rationales behind DIH laws. The problem is that not

---

[172] Murray, Emily (2022). Federal Jury Convicts Minnesota Man for Distributing Fentanyl that Caused 11 Overdose Deaths. *The Drug Enforcement Agency*, April 1.

all overdose deaths involve depraved indifference to human life, as the other cases show.

Recommendations

When the culpability of the deceased is evaluated, it becomes clear that the survivor cannot be 100% responsible for the overdose death. When a person with opioid addiction has advanced to seeking heroin or fentanyl, they are beyond the point where they can take *'no'* for an answer. Instead, the person with an addiction will keep desperately searching until the drug is found. Those seeking such potent opioids treat the pursuit as a life-or-death matter. In overdose cases, the responsibility for taking the drug lies 100% with the deceased unless there is evidence of forced participation.

Rather than ignoring the issue of culpability completely or pretending the deceased addict was an innocent bystander, the DOJ needs to address the issue of culpability in overdose death cases directly. Additionally, the DOJ should restore the constitutional protections of due process in DIH cases. Restoring constitutional rights would remove strict liability and reestablish motive as a critical determinant in the punishment.

A Word from Scott

According to the US federal system, drug dealers or providers are strictly liable for the deceased's death when it involves a drug overdose. Strict liability means the death is 100% the responsibility of the person who gave or sold drugs to TG. The federal government essentially eliminates TG's responsibility for her actions to obtain and use fentanyl. The government's stance on overdose deaths is illogical and unreasonable. I was responsible for living a life that rotated around fentanyl and all that implies. I lost multiple jobs, never had any money, had no car, and only had a roof over my head because my mom and Paul paid for it. I wanted to be a dealer, but I couldn't cut it—I took all the drugs for myself. I led a life that made it feel like a favor to give someone fentanyl, and for that, I am responsible. I am not responsible for being a dealer, and I am not the reason TG died of an overdose. Fentanyl addicts will do anything *to obtain the drug, NO MATTER WHAT, so I know TG would have found another way; she had no choice.*

I was a junky addicted to the same drug TG was looking for, and I 100% never intended any harm to come to her. Unfortunately, most decisions made that day were entirely beyond my control. I believe overdose deaths are tragic accidents that are not the fault of anyone. The urge to use is a physical and mental craving that grabs your soul ... and then sucks it out.

Summary

In the US, an accident of any kind is not legally considered as a first- or second-degree murder...unless it involves a drug overdose. The taking of one's life, whether intentionally by suicide or by accident through one's self-harming actions, is a tragedy of epic proportions for the families and friends of the deceased. It is equally tragic for the family who loses a loved one to prison for 20+ years. There is no closure for the family who loses a loved one to prison; they are forever suspended in time, being forced to watch their child being tortured, half alive and half dead. My son's death would have been much easier to deal with than the long-term anguish of his incarceration.

It is not easy to distinguish between a death by suicide and death by an NSSI overdose because it all depends on the intent of the deceased. Additionally, the symptoms of a suicidal person are much the same as those of an NSSI individual, making it difficult for loved ones to distinguish between the two. Both suffer from deep depression and anxiety, and all too often, the result is death.

It is human nature to want to lash out and blame someone, *anyone,* when the death of a loved one occurs—especially the death of a child. Everyone wants to believe that their child or loved one was a drug fatality because of the actions of a drug provider, not because of *their own needs and actions*. Federal prosecutors too often concur with the family of the deceased by casting the departed as an innocent victim. In contrast, the surviving addict is cast as a murderous dealer. Nothing could be farther from the truth—on both counts. The deceased was not an innocent bystander who was physically forced to seek out and consume drugs, and the surviving addict was not a murderer. Federal and State laws have so far failed to address the issue of participation in one's overdose death, and prosecutors bow to the wishes of the deceased's family. Justice in a grieving family's hands is often expressed as mindless revenge based on little knowledge. Revenge and blaming are toxic to mental health.

CHAPTER 6: MOTIVE & MANDATORY MINIMUM SENTENCES

This chapter delves into the research findings on the impacts of disregarding motive and imposing mandatory minimum sentences in DIH cases.

Introduction

Congress designed *Drug-induced Homicide* laws to punish drug traffickers and high-level drug dealers. Still, as previously discussed, DIH laws are used just as often against non-dealers in response to the opioid death crisis. There are tens of thousands of people sitting in prisons, in the throes of painful withdrawals, mourning the loss of their loved ones or friends, plus dealing with the loss of their own lives because of society's misdirected anger and revenge. In a national survey, Stanforth, Kostiuk, and Garriott (2016) found more than 40% of those who reported having sold drugs also said they have a substance use disorder.[173] Four years later, the *Health in Justice Action Lab* (2020) at *Northeastern University* analyzed DIH news stories and found that 50% of people who were charged under drug-induced homicide laws were friends, partners, or family members who also had addiction issues.[174] Crowley (2017) found that 50% of all overdose death convictions involved co-addicts; he attributes this to the expansion of the belief that severe punishment will reduce the problem.[175]

DIH laws are among the most devastating and misguided tools used in the war on drugs because the laws remove constitutionally guaranteed rights and *require* revoking the liberty of those convicted for a *minimum* of 20

---

[173] Stanforth, E. T., Kostiuk, M., & Garriott, P. O. (2016). Correlates of engaging in drug distribution in a national sample. *Psychology of Addictive Behaviors, 30*(1), 138–146. https://doi.org/10.1037/adb0000124

[174] The Action Lab (2020). What's Behind Increased Attention to DIH Laws and Prosecutions? *Center for Health Policy and Law.* https://www.healthinjustice.org/drug-induced-homicide

[175] Crowley, R., Kirschner, N., Dunn, A. S., Bornstein, S. S., & Health and Public Policy Committee of the American College of Physicians. (2017). Health and public policy to facilitate effective prevention and treatment of substance use disorders involving illicit and prescription drugs: An American College of Physicians position paper. *Annals of Internal Medicine, 166*(10), 733-736. illicit and prescription drugs.

years. Twenty-plus years for a crime that at least fifty percent of those convicted:
1) are medically incapable of committing,
2) the deceased is the driving force in their death, and
3) the examination of motive is denied.

There are certainly cases in which almost everyone would agree that a loss of liberty for many years or life is warranted (e.g., serial killers, premeditated murder, etc.). However, when charges for 'drug dealing' are applied to those who *cannot* perform the task, serious questions are not only valid *but necessary*.

> **The National Center for Drug Abuse Statistics** (2023):
> *80% of prison inmates have abused drugs or alcohol.
> *244,000 people are sent to prison each year solely for drug-related crimes.
> *Opioids are a factor in 72% of overdose deaths

Motive Matters

Due Process

The concept of due process, which includes establishing the defendant's *mens rea* or motive, was first embraced by Anglo-American law in the 15th century, appearing in the 39th article of *Magna Carta* (1215), which provided a royal promise that *"No freeman shall be taken or (and) imprisoned or land taken or exiled or in any way destroyed...except by the legal judgment of his peers or (and) by the law of the land."* Due process is best defined by one word: *fairness*. Drafters of the US Constitution adopted the due process phraseology in the Fifth Amendment, ratified in 1791, which provides that *"No person shall...be deprived of life, liberty, or property, without due process of law."* The Fifth Amendment was inapplicable to state actions that might violate an individual's constitutional rights until the ratification of the Fourteenth Amendment in 1868. At that time, states became subject to federally enforceable due process constraints on their legislative and procedural activities.[176]

---

[176] https://www.britannica.com/topic/due-process

Due process of law covers two types of processes:
   a) Procedural due process – Are the government's actions fair?
   b) Substantive due process - Does the government have the right to act in the first place?

Due process does not guarantee that the result of the government's actions will be to a citizen's liking. Fair procedures help prevent arbitrary and unreasonable decisions, such as incarcerating someone for 20 years for a crime they *cannot* commit. Due process emphasizes two fundamental considerations:[177]

1) Was adequate notice given to the accused?
At a minimum, due process requires that a citizen affected by a government decision be given advance notice of what the government plans to do and how its actions may deprive them of life, liberty, or property.
Notice is the process by which a person is informed of a legal action involving their rights, obligations, or duties. An *adequate notice* gives the individual enough time to respond to the government's proposed actions.

2) Did the accused have an opportunity to be heard?
Having the *"opportunity to be heard"* means the defendant is entitled to a formal hearing before a judge, a jury, or an intermediary. This hearing allows the defendant to present evidence and arguments before judgment by the government. An opportunity to be heard ordinarily bestows the following rights:
- → The right to receive adequate notice of the hearing.
- → The right to secure the assistance of legal counsel.
- → The right to cross-examine witnesses and face one's accusers.
- → The right to testify in one's defense.
- → The right to receive a written decision, with reasons based on evidence.
- → The right to appeal the decision.

To summarize, due process protects citizens from government abuse. When the US government harms a person without following the exact

---

[177] https://www.investopedia.com/terms/d/due-process.asp.

course of the law, it violates due process, which offends the rule of law. Essentially, citizens charged with DIH crimes are denied constitutional protections from government abuse.

Addicts and Motive

Congress removed the constitutional right to be heard from those charged with DIH crimes with the passage of the *Anti-Drug Abuse Act of 1986* (ADAA), effectively ignoring the intent or motive of the defendant. Understanding an opioid addict's motive to share drugs with another person with an opioid addiction first requires some basic comprehension of opioid withdrawal. Scott described one of his withdrawal experiences when he was initially incarcerated.

"I hadn't slept in 3 or 4 days from smoking crack. On the day of my arrest, I shot up some fentanyl, smoked some meth, and then took some clonazepam and smoked some weed to help bring me down. By the time I was arrested in front of my house on Feb. 11, 2019, I barely knew my name. I only remember bits and pieces of the hours-long interrogation and the rejection of my request for a drug test. I was sitting on a bench in a hallway, handcuffed and passed out, when an officer awakened me. The next thing I remember, I was in a single man holding cell in Jennings [Missouri] eating spaghetti. I have no idea how I got there...I don't remember the ride, walk, or whatever brought me to this place. I only remember the enormous, inescapable pain of early withdrawal. Shortly, I was moved to Macoupin County Jail [Illinois], where I had a huge guy for a cellmate. That only lasted one day before he asked the guards to move me because I stank so badly. The guards asked me to take off everything at booking, so I didn't even have boxers for the first week. The withdrawal, mixed with grinding fear, then started in earnest. I couldn't eat and had horrible gas, heavy sweats, and gut-wrenching pain. I cried out as it got worse. I was shaking, trembling, and could not sleep at night. I could not separate reality from my hallucinations, which were frightening in their intensity. I once thought we [inmates] were watching a movie about a space academy where people learned to fly spacecraft. I believed that other inmates who were taken from the common area were on the spaceship and could drop off weed on the side of the jail."

The Criminalization of Addiction

"I believed there were cases of Mountain Dew (my favorite) under the bed, and I was under there drinking the soda. I thought my mom had ordered Domino's pizza delivered to the jail, and we were eating pizza and drinking Mountain Dew. I thought the guards let me go up front to get my oversized black jacket, and I got real cigarettes out of the pockets and gave them to people in the common area. But then I ran out of cigarettes, and I had to go and ask for some back.

I must have looked insane talking about something I didn't have, giving something that wasn't real to someone who was not there. I remember banging on the doors and telling the guards I was not supposed to be there. I thought I had one job to do for the guards before they would let me leave. Hallucinations continued to plague me for almost a year. I thought I was working for a female FBI agent and helped bust a massive load of cocaine in the hidden compartments of a car. While we were searching, the cartel drove by and shot me 16 times. In real-time, one of the guards opened my cell, and I popped up as if I had a gun in my hand, old Western style. I had a shoot-out with the guard, using my hands as a gun...unfortunately, many people in the common area at the jail saw this, and it wasn't until enough people left that the story stopped being told.

The daily physical gut-wrenching pain was masked by total lunacy; the world was blurred, and there was no clear line between truth and fantasy. I begged for relief.

I could not separate the physical pain from the world around me, and I lived and I suffered. I would not wish this level of torment on my worst enemy, much less a friend or family member. How could trying to help someone avoid this be so wrong? I believed it [giving TG five pills] was an act of kindness."

As with all people with an opioid addiction, Scott learned the severe pain that comes from withdrawal each time he could not obtain drugs promptly. Even the withdrawals under medical watch in the rehabilitation centers were unbearable. He described one withdrawal episode that started with being *"...naked, covered in sweat and vomit, curled in a ball in the corner of my room. The odor was rancid, and the pain was constant for days with no relief. It was like I simultaneously had food poisoning, the flu, a cold, and vertigo. I never imagined that this type of suffering was possible while still having a heartbeat. Even then, I didn't realize the craving would be with me for the rest of my life."*

Many times, Scott wished he could just die because he did not have the strength to fight his addiction any longer. In his words, *"The thing about withdrawal is that addicts spend 100% of their time trying to avoid it. Always searching for drugs gets intense and exhausting after a while, and sometimes you just want to get off the merry-go-round and say, 'I give up. Take me.'"*

Scott surrounded himself with other addicts, and drug sharing was the norm. When one addict was out of heroin or fentanyl, another addict in the group would supply them, with the expectation that the favor would be returned when the need arose, which it always did. This type of sharing among people with an addiction is a common way of reducing the risk of withdrawal. When the circle of 'friends' is large, there is a lower probability of running out of sources for drugs.[178]

Ignoring due process means that information, like Scott's motive, does not have the *"opportunity to be heard,"* and the defendant is held 100% liable for the accidental overdose death despite their intent to help rather than harm. Scott's feelings of obligation to KT and the knowledge of the pain TG would go through if she did not obtain fentanyl motivated him to obtain drugs for her. Advanced opioid addicts have a vastly different view of the consequences of sharing drugs with fellow addicts than society or drug dealers have. Society, through the DOJ, expresses its view that drug sharing can be an act of homicide. Drug dealers do not have a view on drug sharing, only on the quantity of drugs sold. People with an addiction view drug sharing as a necessary part of their existence, but they do not *want* to be separated from their drugs. However, if there is an emergency among friends, people with opioid addiction will reluctantly sell some of their drugs. The addict's motive generally falls into one or both of the following categories:

---

[178] Scott Hancock, *"When you are a heroin addict all your 'friends' are heroin addicts because no one else wants to be around you."*

1) Empathy- stemming from excruciating withdrawal experiences, and
2) Goodwill- among the people in their inner circle.

While not altruistic, the second reason does not indicate any murderous intent, only the desire to build goodwill among friends so that when the time comes, drugs can be obtained promptly. Scott's accounts of his withdrawal experiences explain why a motive of empathy or kindness is much closer to accurate than homicidal intent. Unlike dealers, when addicts share drugs with other addicts, profit is not a motive; drugs are generally shared at cost.

Varner (2019) argues that even when considering real drug dealers, DIH statutes are inappropriately holding them responsible under a strictly liable charge for homicide. *"Even though the accused has no intent to harm, they still receive sentences that far exceed any considered permissible under a traditional public welfare analysis and appear too severe to pass constitutional muster."*[179] Logic dictates that the motive of the drug dealer is not to murder his clients but to make money from their mutually agreeable deals. Similarly, friends, addicts, or family members are not ordinarily intent on murdering each other either. The only one intent on death is the addict taking the drug.

Buikema (2015) puts it like this, *"An accidental overdose death has occurred, and the deployment of harsh criminal penalties are used as retribution for the surviving addict. These facts alone raise serious constitutional questions that are repeatedly ignored by the judicial system. For example, it ignores the intentions of the addict, which are never considered in sentencing, thereby denying a fully vetted due process for the defendant."*[180]

Mandatory Minimum Sentences

A *mandatory minimum sentence* is created by Congress or a state legislature to establish the number of years a court *must* impose on a

---

[179] Varner, H. (2019). Chasing the Deadly Dragon: How the Opioid Crisis in the United States Is Impacting the Enforcement of Drug-Induced Homicide Statutes. *University of Illinois Law Review*, 1799.

[180] Buikema, J. (2015). Punishing the Wrong Criminal for Over Three Decades: Illinois' Drug-Induced Homicide Statute. *Available at SSRN 2662312*.

person convicted of a crime, no matter the unique circumstances of the offender or the offense. Typically, mandatory minimums only apply to those crimes where guilt is assumed from the moment of arrest, gun and drug crimes. Once guilt is established (i.e., assumed), the only additional pieces of information needed to determine sentencing are:

1) the type and weight of the drug involved, or
2) the possession or presence of a gun.

If a death occurred, whether accidentally or intentionally, then a mandatory minimum number of years will be imposed during sentencing. More than 60 federal laws include mandatory minimum penalties. However, the four covering drug and weapon offenses account for 94% of all compulsory federal minimum cases.[181]

Purpose of Mandatory Minimums

Legislators enacted mandatory minimum sentences believing that such penalties would bring greater consistency to the sentencing process and *"send a message"* to potential offenders that specified behaviors will be met with harsh and certain punishment. Mandatory minimum sentences require judges to impose a sentence of imprisonment for at least the time specified in a statute; more time can be added to the sentence, but none can be removed (not by the judge).

Mandatory minimums have existed throughout American history, with examples from as early as 1790.[182] The relationship between federal mandatory minimum sentences and a judge's discretion to impose appropriate sentences has fluctuated.[183] Pitzer (2013), a retired warden, gave his thoughts on sentencing:

> *"The 1980s "get tough on crime" and war on drugs agendas resulted in substantial changes to sentencing and correctional structures. From the abolition of parole to mandatory minimum sentences, these initiatives resulted in prison*

---

[181] https://famm.org/wp-content/uploads/FS-MMs-in-a-Nutshell.pdf
[182] Congressional Research Service (2023). When is a Mandatory Minimum Sentence Not Mandatory Under the First Step Act? *Congressional Research Service*, Feb. 2.
[183] Hofer, P. (2015). After ten years of advisory guidelines, and thirty years of mandatory minimums, federal sentencing still needs reform. *University of Toledo Law Review, 47*, 649.

populations larger than anyone could have ever anticipated. I entered the Bureau of Prisons in 1973. By 1980, the federal prison system had 24,000 prisoners; today [2013] federal prisoners total 156,428. Each year, we lock up more individuals than we release. How long can this continue? How long can the American taxpayer foot the bill for increased incarceration? And more importantly, is it necessary? We have removed common sense from the federal judge's arsenal and determined that one prescription fits all, more and longer terms of incarceration. We spend more money as a country incarcerating individuals than educating our kids. I am not saying that some people don't need to go to prison. I am saying that long prison sentences without the benefit of common sense and real investment in reentry programs create a bigger problem than we had to start."[184]

The warden makes several vital points, including the forfeiture of common sense in sentencing and the cost burden to the American taxpayer. Now, one in two adults in the US has experienced an incarceration in their families.[185]

Figure 6.1.   The Magnitude of US Incarceration

___

[184] Pitzer, P. (2013). Federal Overincarceration and Its Impact on Correctional Practices: A Warden's Perspective. *Criminal Justice, 28*, 41.
[185] Home screen *Families Against Mandatory Minimums* (FAMM.org), 6/24/24.

At the end of 2023, the total number of people incarcerated in the US was 1.9 *million*. Total incarceration consists of 550,000 people in local jails, 1,071,000 in state prisons, and 208,000 federal prisoners. In addition, there are 25,000 in juvenile facilities, 7,000 in territorial prisons, 46,000 in immigration detention, 25,000 are involuntarily committed, 2,000 are incarcerated in Indian territory, and 1,000 are detained in military facilities.[186]

Mandatory minimums increase the length of time society must support inmates. The original goals of mandatory minimum sentencing were to ensure that,
    1) all persons committing the same crime did the same time, and
    2) an ominous message was sent to other potential offenders.

The goals sounded reasonable but entirely failed in practice because no two crimes or two offenders are *precisely* the same. When it comes to drug offenders, the language used by Congress and the DOJ does not distinguish between people with an addiction, drug dealers, and recreational users. However, each has a very different set of circumstances and motives.

Predictably, neither dealers nor users have received the intended DOJ message. To send an effective message to a *healthy brain*, the message must be:
    i) Clear,
    ii) consistent, *and*
    iii) repetitious.

State DIH laws lack all three elements of an effective message because each state has its own set of rules, guidelines, and mandatory minimums. Additionally, the federal government's DIH laws differ from most state laws, providing zero opportunity for a clear, consistent, repetitive message. Offenders cannot know in advance whether the state or the federal government will prosecute them. Further, out of every 10,000 cases, only two go to public trial; the remaining 9,998 cases are settled by plea agreements conducted in private behind closed doors. Prosecutors

---

[186] Sawyer, Wendy and Wagner, Peter (2024). Mass Incarceration: The Whole Pie 2024. *The Prison Policy Initiative*, March 14.

make capricious decisions regarding specific charges and can add or subtract time from a given defendant's sentence, leaving little room for predictable outcomes.[187]

Therefore, it is virtually impossible for potential offenders to receive a meaningful message. More importantly, opioid addicts *do not* have a healthy brain that can receive or interpret consistent messaging because, as detailed in Chapter 4, the neural circuits needed to process that information have been disrupted or destroyed.[188]

Levy (2011) argues that *"neural circuit damage results in addicted individuals making poor choices despite awareness of the negative consequences; it explains why previously rewarding life situations and the threat of judicial punishment cannot stop the addict from taking drugs and why a medical, rather than a criminal, approach would be more effective in curtailing drug use."*[189]

Previous chapters discussed how the threat of severe punishment for advanced opioid addicts is meaningless. Heroin and fentanyl addicts are keenly aware of the risk of death with every 'high' attempt; there is no punishment more severe than death. When death is an accepted outcome, punishment loses its meaning.

When I asked Scott about the deadly consequences of fentanyl, he explained as follows:

"Hahaha, I'm sorry to laugh at the question, but the answer is probably the craziest thing you have ever heard. What if the fentanyl or heroin starts killing people you know? The first thing you do is ask where they got it

---

[187] Prosecutors can reduce sentences below the mandatory minimum, but judges cannot. For example, the prosecutor in Scott's case offered 15 years, five years below the mandatory minimum. The judge, however, would not have been allowed to reduce the sentence below the mandatory minimum.

[188] i) Health in Justice (2021). Drug Induced Homicides. *Health in Justice*, Sept 13. https://www.healthinjustice.org/drug-induced-homicide.

   ii) National Institute on Drug Abuse (2020). The Science of Drug Use and Addiction: The Basics. *NIDA,* June 25. https://www.drugabuse.gov/publications/media-guide/science-drug-use-addiction-basics

[189] Levy, N. (2011). Addiction, responsibility, and ego-depletion. *Addiction and responsibility*, 89-111.

from because that's the good shit. Any heroin or fentanyl addict will tell you the same thing because if it's killing people... that's the good shit...."

When he shared this insight, Scott knew of three people who had overdosed and died from fentanyl. His words are from an unhealthy, drug-damaged mind that has rationalized taking a deadly poison. Trying to rationalize life-threatening behavior would never occur to someone with a healthy brain. The attempts at rationalization highlight the true INSANITY of opioid addiction.

At the *American Bar Association* Spring Conference, Gill (2009) presented a paper arguing that mandatory minimum sentences violate two fundamental human rights principles.[190]

"First, lengthy mandatory minimum sentences are cruel, inhumane, and degrading because they obliterate individualized justice, the bedrock of any fair sentencing system. Instead of considering all the circumstances of the crime and the individual offender, the court **must** *impose a lengthy, predetermined sentence created by a legislature that knows nothing about the particulars of the offense or the defendant. Offenders go to sentencing hearings justifiably expecting to be treated like individuals. Mandatory minimums replace the individual in the sentencing equation with drug type and weight or whether the crime is a third strike. They fail to account for the nature of the crime or the offender's mental state, criminal history, or role in the offense, which are essential factors in determining how much punishment is deserved. The inevitable result is cruel, inhumane, degrading, and undeserved over-punishment."*

"Second, mandatory minimums produce sentences that are disproportionate to the crime. There are indeed times when the compulsory sentence best fits the crime. If an offender has two prior armed robberies, a fifty-year-to-life sentence may be perfectly appropriate for a third strike involving premeditated murder. But what if it isn't?

Mandatory minimums make getting a proportionate sentence a matter of luck, not justice."

---

[190] Gill, M. M. (2009). Let's Abolish Mandatory Minimums: The Punishment Must Fit the Crime. *Human Rights, 36*, 4.

The Law

In 1984, the *Sentencing Reform Act* (SRA) created the *United States Sentencing Commission* (USSC) and the *Federal Sentencing Guidelines* (FSG), under which all federal crimes have been prosecuted since 1987. In 1983, Senator Charles Mathias (MD) was alone in opposing the SRA and mandatory minimums. He stated, "Hardly anyone disagrees that there is too much disparity in criminal sentences and that prison sentences are too uncertain in duration. While mandatory minimum sentences may increase severity, the data suggest that the uneven application of the law also dramatically increases uncertainty."[191]

Before the SRA and FSG were authorized, the sentencing of convicted criminals was entirely up to the judge. Inconsistent sentences were the result of giving such power to a singular opinion. There was no way to predict the accused's length of imprisonment; it depended on the judge. These indeterminate sentencing practices were predominant for many decades, leading to the significant reform efforts undertaken by many states and the federal government in the 1970s and 1980s. The perceived failure of the inconsistent system to *"cure"* criminals, coupled with renewed concern about rising crime rates during the mid-1970s, resulted in broad experimentation with sentencing systems at the state level. The SRA abolished indeterminate sentencing at the federal level and created a *determinate*, consistent sentencing structure through the FSG. The SRA of 1984 reformed the federal sentencing system by:

1) dropping rehabilitation as one of the goals,

2) creating the USSC and charging it with establishing sentencing guidelines,

3) making all federal sentences determinate by using mandatory minimum sentences and

4) authorizing appellate reviews of sentences.[192]

According to Wallace (2020), the simultaneous existence of the FSG and mandatory minimum sentences poses a significant danger to sentencing

---

[191] Wallace, H. S. (2020). Mandatory minimums and the betrayal of sentencing reform: A legislative Dr. Jekyll and Mr. Hyde. *The American Court System* (pp. 391-401). Routledge.

[192] Congressional Research Service Report (2009). Federal Sentencing FSG: Background, Legal Analysis, and Policy Options. *CRSR*, March 16.

reform and society because the two approaches are in opposition. They both aim to achieve more certainty in sentencing by reducing judicial discretion and arbitrary, unpredictable sentencing disparities. However, the FSG attempts to reduce disparity by applying specific guidelines to each type of crime while still allowing the sentence to be individualized. Alternatively, mandatory minimums attempt to reduce disparity by treating everyone equally regardless of individual circumstances.

Unintentionally, implementing mandatory minimums has effectively transferred sentencing power from a single judge to a single prosecutor. Prosecutors, like judges, are human and have recreated the same indeterminate system through arbitrary applications of the law and plea deals that allow some offenders to serve significantly less time. Unlike judges, prosecutors succeed by increasing the number of convicts and the time they must serve. Prosecutors have personal and professional incentives to *win*. Mandatory minimum sentences have proven counterproductive and serve no purpose that the FSG does not serve better.[193]

Effectiveness of Mandatory Minimums

Transfer of Power

Mandatory minimums conflict with the notion that a judge should ensure that the punishment fits the crime *and* the criminal, a precept *"deeply rooted and frequently repeated in common-law jurisprudence."* [194] Mandatory minimums go to the extreme by eliminating the ability of judges to use case-specific information about the offense and the defendant to impose a prison term. Mandatory minimums have done little to eliminate punishment discrepancies among similarly situated defendants but have pushed sentences to absurd lengths. The inconsistent application of mandatory minimums has only exacerbated disparities, expanding the sentencing differentials in analogous cases. According to most critics, the problem is the transfer of sentencing power from *neutral* judges to *biased* prosecutors, who often pre-set punishment through creative investigations and selective charging practices, producing

---

[193] Wallace, H. S. (2020). Mandatory minimums and the betrayal of sentencing reform: A legislative Dr. Jekyll and Mr. Hyde. *The American Court System* (pp. 391-401). Routledge.

[194] John S. Martin, Jr. (2004). Why Mandatory Minimums Make No Sense. *Notre Dame J.L. Ethics & Public Policy,* 18, 311.

troubling punishment differentials among offenders with similar culpability.[195]

> It took a very long time for our family to *fully* understand that the judge was irrelevant in Scott's sentencing. I kept believing the judge could do *something* to reduce his sentence because he had no previous convictions; I was wrong.

For example, if charge 'X' has a 10-year mandatory minimum and charge 'Y' has a 20-year, the prosecutor has the power to choose which charge applies.

Figure 6.2A shows the original sentencing structure with the defense counsel on the side of the accused and the prosecutor on the side of the state or federal government. In the middle is a neutral judge listening to each side's evidence. The judge can use the facts presented in the case from both sides and the jury's judgment to determine the appropriate sentence for the defendant. The constitutionality of plea deals was established in 1970 by the Supreme Court ruling on *Brady vs. US*.[196] Robert Brady was indicted under 18 USC § 1201(a) in 1959 for kidnapping and failing to release the hostage without harm. The prosecutor threatened the death penalty if he did not plead guilty, even though such a penalty was not possible without a jury recommendation. In 1967, Brady sought post-conviction relief, arguing that 18 USC § 1201(a) was coercive and impermissible under *US v. Jackson*, which was decided after his conviction.[197] The court concluded that a guilty plea is *not* coerced even if the only reason the plea is entered is to avoid the death penalty.

After the 1970s, the justice system reconfigured itself into **Figure 6.2B.**, as plea bargaining grew. The role of the judge is completely removed for the 98% of cases settled by plea deals. The judge is bound to the mandatory minimum sentence in the 2% of cases that go to trial. There are two sides with no role for a neutral judge except to rubber-stamp the prosecutor's decision. Now, two sides are battling for the outcome, but one side has the power to establish both the crime and the sentence. This power dynamic

---

[195] Luna, E. (2017). Mandatory minimums. *Reforming criminal justice: A report of the Academy for Justice on bridging the gap between scholarship and reform*, 4, 117-146.
[196] Supreme Court (1970). *Brady v. US*, 397 U.S. 742.
[197] Supreme Court (1968). US vs. Jackson, 390 U.S. 570.

would be like playing a football game where the offense is also the referee! Not exactly a 'fair' game.

The USSC found that prosecutors selectively bring charges that carry mandatory minimum penalties. As a result, in the words of the USSC, mandatory minimums *"transfer sentencing power from the judge to the prosecution,"* producing severe sentencing disparities. These disparities diminish the retributive, deterrent, and communicative goals of sentencing. Some in the judicial community have also expressed concern that mandatory minimums restrict sentencing discretion from judges and frustrate their ability to impose individualized terms. Scholars and others have observed that the threat of mandatory minimums can coerce defendants into pleading guilty to one charge to avoid another that comes with a mandatory minimum sentence—a guilty plea results in forgoing constitutionally protected rights that are only available when the accused has a jury trial.[198]

Figure 6.2A.   Original Configuration

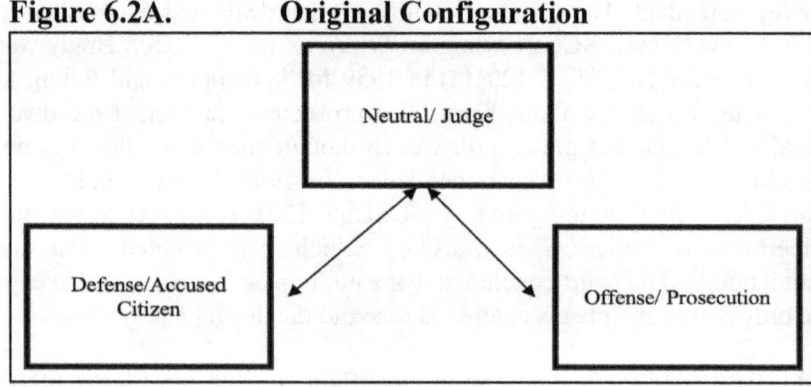

---

[198] *Congressional Research Service* (2023). When Is a Mandatory Minimum Sentence Not Mandatory Under the First Step Act? *CRS*, Feb. 2.
https://crsreports.congress.gov/product/pdf/LSB/LSB10910#:~:text=As%20a%20result%2C%20in%20the,and%20communicative%20goals%20of%20sentencing.

Figure 6.2B.   Current Configuration

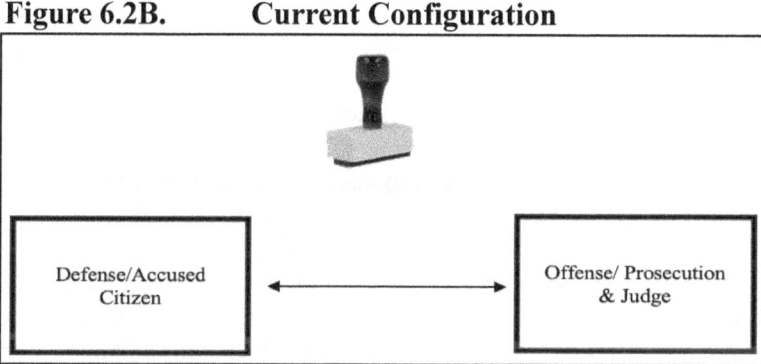

The inconsistent sentencing produced by prosecutors' actions is motivated by the desire to win against the defense. The desire to win against the defense creates a hostile dynamic that is not apparent when judges rule. Additionally, their wins in court improve prosecutors' positions and prospects.

The assigned role of the judge is neutral, and they do not 'win or lose' based on their sentencing decisions. The inconsistent sentencing produced by judges was the result of differing opinions and personal biases rather than improving their position.

Even theories of retribution require that the punishment be *proportionate to the gravity of the offense*, and any decent retributive theory demands a sentencing maximum. The idea of proportionality reverberates throughout criminal law theory as the ideal, but agreement on what that means remains elusive. The Eighth Amendment to the US Constitution states, in part, *"Excessive bail shall not be required, nor excessive fines imposed, nor cruel and unusual punishments inflicted."* In 1976, the US Supreme Court interpreted the Eighth Amendment as the *"...punishment must not be out of proportion to the crime committed."*[199]

Mandatory minimums ignore proportionality and push the boundaries of punishment with overly harsh consequences. For example, twenty years or more in prison for an accidental overdose is far from proportionate to the so-called 'crime.'

---

[199] Gregg v. Georgia, 428 U.S. 153, 173 (1976).

Logic dictates that incarceration will only be effective at stopping the crime if:
1) The accused would continue committing the crime(s), were not imprisoned.
2) The accused is not easily replaced by others who can commit the same crime.

The argument for incarceration as public protection is moot if the imprisoned person would not be committing a crime. Consider that offenders typically' age out' of a criminal lifestyle, making long sentences redundant. Requiring the continued incarceration of individuals who present little to no danger of further crimes is costly, unnecessary, and harmful.

Similarly, if those incarcerated are quickly replaced by others who will commit the same crime, then there is no valid argument for incarcerating the first individuals or their replacements. The drug market is an excellent example of easily replaced individuals who commit the same crime as the ones in prison. Imprisoning drug crime offenders does nothing to disrupt the vast supply of, or insatiable demand for, drugs.[200] Public safety remains unchanged.

Even though *violent* offenders have inspired some mandatory minimum legislation, the statutes themselves are not tailored to those criminals alone. Instead, these laws give federal prosecutors the power to apply the laws to minor participants in non-violent offenses, such as overdose deaths. If an accidental overdose is, in fact, a homicide, then the perpetrator of this crime is the deceased, not the drug provider.[201] Once drugs are obtained, the deceased uses their own free will to determine how to dispose of or consume them. Under the current regime, mandatory minimum sentences are applied equally to a person with an addiction, a low-level drug courier, or a narcotics kingpin.[202] Worse, prosecutors

---

[200] i) Farrington, David P. (1986). Age and Crime, *Crime &Justice*, 7, 189.
  ii) Hirschi, Travis and Gottfredson, Michael (1983). Age and the Explanation of Crime. *American Journal of Sociology*, 89, 552.
[201] William J. Stuntz (2001). The Pathological Politics of Criminal Law, *Michigan Law Review*, 505, 519-20.
[202] *US vs. Brigham*, 977 F.2d 317 (7th Cir. 1992).

resolve most cases by entering plea deals with the accused. When the accused has valuable information for the prosecutor, they can easily 'buy down' their time or serve no time at all. However, low-level offenders, and indeed people with an addiction, typically lack the type of valuable information that can be used as a bargaining chip with prosecutors. This results in longer sentences for the *least* culpable individuals. [203]

Congress

The 1984 SRA contained guideline development procedures that could have produced fair and effective sentences. However, Congress frequently overrode the guidelines, or the USSC did not fully implement them. The same year it enacted the SRA, Congress began passing mandatory minimums, which superseded the FSG, hindered development efforts, and ultimately doomed sentencing reform. Two years later, Congress enacted the ADAA (1986), establishing mandatory minimum penalties based on drug type and quantity that remain operative today. As a result of these Acts and others, average sentences levied by prosecutors are much longer than judges had previously imposed. The different motives of the prosecutor and the judge can explain the progression to longer sentences. The prosecutor's motive is to give longer sentences to improve their record, and the law gives them the power to win *every time*. Alternatively, the judge's motive is to ensure justice is served; sometimes, this means shorter sentences. Unsurprisingly, the average prison time given to federal defendants has more than doubled after the FSG became effective. On Nov. 1, 1987, the SRA eliminated parole for federal sentences and gave the *US Parole Commission* authority to supervise state offenders transferred to federal supervision under the witness protection program.[204] Since the US has a higher incarceration rate than any other country, it is not surprising that the *Federal Bureau of Prisons* is the most extensive prison system in the world.

---

[203] Luna, E., & Cassell, P. G. (2010). Mandatory minimalism. *Cardozo Law Review, 32*, 1.
[204] DOJ. United States Parole Commission. *Organization, Mission, and Functions Manual.* https://www.justice.gov/doj/organization-mission-and-functions-manual-united-states-parole-commission

Legal and medical scholars widely recognize the failure of the SRA.[205] Even the USSC's fifteen-year evaluation noted that *"the goals of sentencing reform have been only partially achieved."*[206] Practitioners and medical specialists declared the federal system a *"disaster,"* a *"mess,"* and *"a cure worse than the disease."*[207] Others were more moderate, but very few found anything to like about the federal judicial system. Some who initially defended the FSG grew disillusioned. Judge Frankel, often recognized as the *"father of sentencing reform,"* called upon the USSC to identify *"what we mean to achieve, and what we may in fact achieve, as we continue to mete out long prison sentences."* An inescapable conclusion emerged: *"Twenty-five years have produced a strong and informed consensus that the first bold and hopeful round of federal sentencing reform has largely failed."*[208]

In the 2005 *US vs. Booker* case, the US Supreme Court determined that the FSG, as it had been applied since 1987, violated the Sixth Amendment right to trial by jury.[209] Even so, the court returned and authorized the FSG as an advisory resource. The transformation of the FSG from a binding system to a purely advisory system has unquestionably altered thousands of individual sentencing outcomes.[210]

During a 2009 congressional hearing, former US Attorney Michael J. Sullivan asked, *"Has the role that Congress played in sentencing, including the passage of mandatory minimum sentences, had an impact on*

---

[205] Bowman III, Frank O. (2005). The Failure of the Federal Sentencing System: A Structural Analysis. *University of Missouri School of Law Scholarship Repository*, Spring.

[206] https://www.ussc.gov/research/research-and-publications/research-projects-and-surveys/fifteen-years-guidelines-sentencing

[207] Prison Policy Initiative (2004). Fifteen Years of FSG Sentencing. An Assessment of How Well the Federal Criminal Justice System is Achieving the Goals of Sentencing Reform, *Prison Policy Initiative*, November.

[208] i) Hofer, P. (2015). After ten years of advisory guidelines, and thirty years of mandatory minimums, federal sentencing still needs reform. *University of Toledo Law Review*, 47, 649.

ii) Howell, R. (2003). Sentencing reform lessons: From the sentencing reform Act of 1984 to the Feeney amendment. *Journal of Criminal Law & Criminology*, 94, 1069.

iii) Oleson, J. C. (2010). Blowing Out All the Candles: A Few Thoughts on the Twenty-Fifth Birthday of the Sentencing Reform Act of 1984. *University of Richmond Law Review*, 45, 693.

[209] *U.S. v. Booker* (2005). 125 S. Ct. 738.

[210] Bowman III, F. O. (2013). Dead Law Walking: The Surprising Tenacity of the Federal Sentencing Guidelines. *Houston Law Review*, 51, 1227.

public safety and crime?" He continued, *"What, then, do we know about the extent to which federal penalties have been responsible for declines in crime? To date, virtually no data can demonstrate a direct link between federal mandatory penalties and declines in crime."*[211] When examining the effect of federal mandatory penalties, note that the federal court system handles less than 10% of all criminal cases. Therefore, attempting to draw any conclusions about the specific impact of *federal* mandatory penalties on US crime rates is not possible.

The *First Step Act* (FSA), passed by Congress in 2018, returns some power to federal judges by allowing them to impose sentences shorter than the mandatory minimum for certain drug offenses. The FSA provides that a defendant is eligible for this *"safety valve,"* or relief from the mandatory minimum, depending, in part, on the defendant's criminal history. Note that the FSA does NOT cover those charged with a DIH crime because a death occurred. One of the many tragic consequences of a DIH conviction is that the defendant is classified as 'violent' even when no aggression, coercion, or weapons were involved.

> For example, Scott was 25 miles away when T.G. took the drugs and overdosed, but by statute, Scott is considered violent, so the FSA does not apply.

Indeterminate Sentences

Predictably, replacing a neutral judge with an incentivized prosecutor has proven to be a nightmare for defendants. When the opposing team has the power to determine the outcome, it is no surprise that defendants are prosecuted and sentenced to the most extended term of imprisonment allowed.

The situation of variable sentencing remains, but with prosecutors in control, the length of sentences has risen 124% since the 1980s. The average sentence for federal drug offenses in the 1980s was 3.25 years; by 2016, the average had grown to 5.00 years and 7.25 years by 2022, representing an average sentence increase of 124%.[212]

---

[211] Mauer, M. (2010). The impact of mandatory minimum penalties in federal sentencing. *Judicature*, 94, 1.

[212] Special Report (2015). Drug Offenders in Federal Prison Estimates of Characteristics Based on Linked Data. *U.S. Department of Justice, Bureau of Justice Statistics*, October.

Drug offenses have proven to be predominately immune to more and longer prison terms. At the macro level, this happens because of the easy replacement of those who leave the market due to imprisonment. As previously discussed, 50% of drug offenders charged with DIH crimes are not even part of the selling apparatus of the drug market; they are friends, family, or co-addicts. The other 50% are mainly from the lowest ranks of the drug trade, with only a few middle-ranking individuals. Their imprisonment, in effect, creates a job opportunity for someone else seeking to earn quick money. There is always someone else willing to step forward, as evidenced by the fact that drug use has expanded exponentially over the years. The increased criminalization of drug use since 1980 can also be seen in the 1442% increase in the total number of persons incarcerated for drugs since that time. This story is not one of success. As long as there is a demand for illegal drugs, there will be a large pool of potential sellers.

At the micro level, users and addicts alike are undeterred by longer prison terms. As mentioned previously, this is not surprising since these are people who risk overdose death every day. If the threat of death cannot prevent drug use, then the danger of a more significant punishment will not do so either.

DIH laws and the associated mandatory minimums appear to have no socially redeeming value beyond serving the dual purposes of satisfying the punishment needs of society and the revenge desires of the families of the deceased. Unfortunately, those suffering from addiction are punished despite being incapable of being a 'drug dealer.' Americans have become *addicted to punishment* even when evidence shows (see Chapter 3) that it is to society's detriment.

Unintended Consequences

Evidence shows that mandatory penalties adversely affect recidivism and reduce 911 calls for help. Whatever one may think about the wisdom of mandatory sentencing, it is undeniable that such penalties serve to increase the length of time that offenders serve in prison by restricting the discretion of judges and corrections/parole officials. By doing so, these penalties may have a *criminogenic effect*, increasing the likelihood of criminal behavior. A 2002 review by leading Canadian criminologists entailed a meta-analysis of 117 studies measuring various aspects of recidivism. The researchers concluded that extended periods in prison were *"associated with an increase in recidivism."* Research also shows that maintaining close ties to families and communities during incarceration is one of the keys to successful reentry, which reduces recidivism. Yet extended mandatory penalties increase the challenges for successful reentry because federal prisoners are often housed in prisons far from their homes. Such long distances lessen the ability of friends and family to visit their loved ones, isolating the inmates. Combining extended sentences and long distances erodes family ties and reduces the likelihood of successful reentry.[213]

New research suggests there are reasons to believe harsh sentencing laws have resulted in *additional* overdose deaths. Studies, such as Jakubowski et al. (2018), Koester et al. (2017), Wagner et al. (2019), and Banta-Green et al. (2013), show that strict DIH laws have resulted in a decline in 911 emergency calls for overdoses because people are afraid they will be charged with a DIH.[214] To the extent this holds, it increases the risk of overdose deaths and is in direct conflict with one of the DOJ's stated goals of reducing overdose deaths.

One primary reason people do not call 911 for help during an overdose is fear of retribution.[215] Some states have implemented *Good Samaritan*

---

[213] Mauer, M. (2010). The impact of mandatory minimum penalties in federal sentencing. *Judicature, 94,* 6.

[214] i) Banta-Green, C. J., Beletsky, L., Schoeppe, J. A., Coffin, P. O., & Kuszler, P. C. (2013). Police officers' and paramedics' experiences with overdose and their knowledge and opinions of Washington State's drug overdose–naloxone–Good Samaritan law. *Journal of Urban Health, 90*(6) 1102-1111.

ii) Jakubowski, Andrea MD, Kunins, Hillary V. MD, Huxley-Reicher, Zina and Siegler, Anne (2018). Knowledge of the 911 Good Samaritan Law and 911-calling behavior of overdose witnesses. *Substance Abuse*, 39:2, 233-238, DOI: 10.1080/08897077.2017.1387213

iii) Koester, S., Mueller, S. R., Raville, L., Langegger, S., & Binswanger, I. A. (2017). Why are some people who have received overdose education and naloxone reticent to call Emergency Medical Services in the event of overdose? *International Journal of Drug Policy, 48,* 115-124.

iv) Wagner, K. D., Harding, R. W., Kelley, R., Labus, B., Verdugo, S. R., Copulsky, E., & Davidson, P. J. (2019). Post-overdose interventions triggered by calling 911: Centering the perspectives of people who use drugs. *Plos One Journal,* 14(10), e0223823.

[215] LaSalle, L. (2017). An overdose death is not murder: why drug-induced homicide laws are counterproductive and inhumane. *The Drug Policy Alliance.*

Laws to shield an individual from prosecution if they call for help during an overdose. But DIH charges have been leveled against such people anyway, so it is not surprising that the *Good Samaritan* exemption is not working. *"Ultimately, rather than reduce fatalities, drug-induced homicide laws only result in additional overdose deaths due to people failing to summon medical help for overdoses out of fear of prosecution."*[216] Thus, DIH laws do not decrease overdose deaths but, instead, cause more overdose deaths. Is justice or retribution that results in additional deaths worth the cost? The answer is *no*, not if *your* child or loved one died from lack of emergency care.

Another unintended consequence of mandatory minimum sentences is the cases are settled mainly by plea deals that function to release high-level drug dealers and imprison low-level dealers. Prosecutors reduce or dismiss the charges depending on the information the accused can share. Typically, high-level dealers have information to trade, while low-level dealers do not. The use of plea deals by prosecutors allows high-level offenders to go free while low-level offenders go to prison for decades. Former Chief Justice Rehnquist commented in 2000 that *"...these measures* [mandatory minimum sentences] *are perhaps a good example of the law of unintended consequences."*[217]

Phillips (2020) questions whether DIH laws have any functional use at all. His *Duke Law Journal* article discussing DIH laws says: *"...considering these laws have limited deterrent effect, do not reduce the rate of overdose deaths, and contravene other legislative initiatives enacted to protect the public, justifying their utility is difficult. Perhaps the only valid rationale for DIH laws is retributive—to punish those whose actions, however indirectly, lead to a death."*[218] Retribution to one person can be seen as justice by another.

---

[216] Jakubowski, Andrea MD, Kunins, Hillary V. MD, Huxley-Reicher, Zina and Siegler, Anne (2018). Knowledge of the 911 Good Samaritan Law and 911-calling behavior of overdose witnesses. *Substance Abuse*, 39:2, 233-

[217] House Hearing 106th Congress (2000). Drug Mandatory Minimums: Are They Working? *Subcommittee on Criminal Justice, Drug Policy and Human Resources*, May 11.

[218] Phillips, K. S. (2020). From overdose to crime scene: The incompatibility of drug-induced homicide statutes with due process. *Duke LJ*, 70, 659.

Another unintended consequence of mandatory minimums is the overpopulation of both federal and state prisons. Without adding one more inmate, the BOP does not have sufficient staff or correctional officers to manage the day-to-day lives of the current inmates. Inmates are locked in cells for weeks and months at a time because no one is there to manage their movements.[219] Families are denied visits because of staffing shortages, leaving inmates isolated from their loved ones.

Staffing shortages typically indicate insufficient compensation for the job requirements. The low compensation may motivate many correctional officers to make business deals with inmates. During COVID-19, when the prisons closed to outside visitors, the prisons were still full of drugs, suggesting that those working on the inside, not those visiting from the outside, were the suppliers.

Upon entering prison, inmates are thoroughly searched visually and technologically, but prison staff is not vetted as meticulously. Inside the prison, the proliferation of synthetic drugs has intensified the overdose problem.[220] The small size of these drugs allows supply shipments to be easily concealed, making them a perfect form of contraband to smuggle inside. According to *Bureau of Justice* data, overdose deaths in state prisons have surged by more than 600% over the last two decades. During the same time frame, overdose deaths in county jails have escalated by more than 200%.

Interestingly, obtaining information from the federal BOP is exceedingly difficult because they do not follow their own reporting policies.[221] **Figure 6.3** shows an estimate of federal inmate deaths from 2014 to 2021, as *The Office of the Inspector General reported.*[222] The *'Accident'* and *'Unknown'* categories are commonly where overdose victims are listed, but some also appear in the *'Suicide'* data. Overall, the data suggests that federal inmate deaths have risen by 50% from 2014 to 2021.

---

[219] FIRST-Network data.
[220] E. Ann Carson (2021). Mortality in State and Federal Prisons, 2001-2018. *The Bureau of Justice Statistics,* April. https://bjs.ojp.gov/content/pub/pdf/msfp0118st.pdf
[221] Department of Justice (2024). Evaluation of Issues Surrounding Inmate Deaths in Federal Bureau of Prisons Institutions. *Office of the Inspector General*, Feb.
[222] DOJ (2024). Evaluation of Issues Surrounding Inmate Deaths in Federal BOP Institutions. *The Office of the Inspector General*, Feb. https://oig.justice.gov/sites/default/files/reports/24-041.pdf

Due in part to low compensation rates, prisons experience high turnover rates among correctional officers, denoting an undesirable work environment. If the work environment is unpleasant and the pay is poor, there will always be a shortage of qualified applicants. Those who do apply are more desperate and are often underqualified to manage the population humanely. The BOP expenses have increased more than 98% in the last 20 years; it is unknown how much of that goes to incarcerating the mentally ill.[223]

Figure 6.3   Federal Inmate Deaths by Year and Type

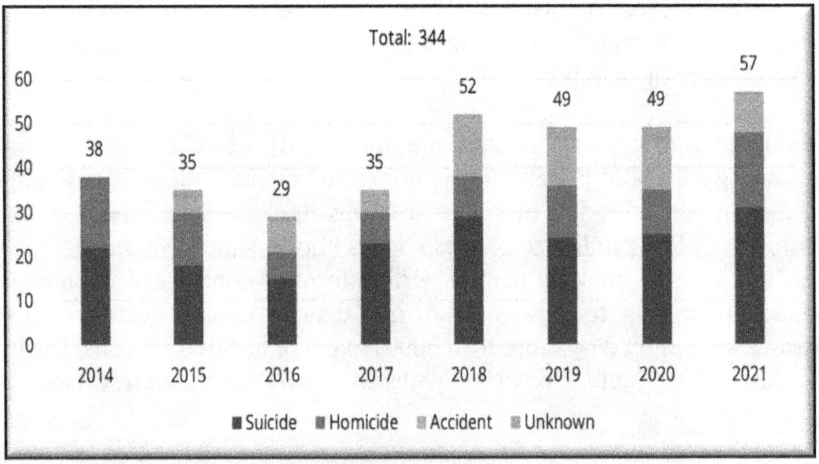

Year	Total
2014	38
2015	35
2016	29
2017	35
2018	52
2019	49
2020	49
2021	57

Total: 344

Legend: Suicide, Homicide, Accident, Unknown

Source: OIG Analysis of BOP Data

The final unintended consequence is the exacerbation of the conditions that lead to addiction. The prison environment, the intrusive correctional officers, the distance from family, and the lack of normal human relations all serve to exacerbate the agitators of addiction by maximizing stress. Sending those with addictions to prison rather than a mental health facility has condemned many inmates to death upon their release from prison. Recent findings from *Oregon Health & Science University* indicate that

---

[223] Department of Justice FY2004 Budget Summary (4.4 billion)
Department of Justice FY2024 Budget Summary (8.7 billion)

the risk of overdose death for newly released inmates is 10X greater than for the population.[224]

Borschmann et al. (2024) studied mortality outcomes in eight countries (Australia, Brazil, Canada, New Zealand, Norway, Scotland, Sweden, and the USA) from 1980 to 2018 for 1,471,526 inmates released from incarceration, creating 10,534,441 *person-years* of follow-up (range 0–24 years per person).[225,226] During just the first week of freedom, 75,427 died, and most deaths were due to alcohol and other drug poisoning. In the weeks and years that followed, deaths due to drug overdoses continued to dominate the outcomes in each period measured.

Evidence in this section shows that mandatory minimum sentences serve to impose the unintended consequences of:
- → increased recidivism rates,
- → reduced 911 calls for help (increased overdose deaths)
- → long sentences for low-level dealers and reduced sentences for high-level drug dealers,
- → over-populating prisons beyond manageability
- → exacerbation of known agitators of addiction, and
- → high death rates among released inmates.

Fifty DIH Convictions

During the fall of 2020, I began researching the US federal judicial system and DIH laws to find a way to help Scott. As it turns out, there is no help or hope for Scott to reduce his sentence; it would take an act of Congress.

To better understand whether mandatory minimum sentences have created the intended consistency of sentencing, a sample was drawn to study sentencing disparities.

---

[224] Rideout, Nicole (2023). Opioid Overdose Risk is 10X Greater for those Recently Release from Prison. *Oregon Health & Science University* and *Oregon State University*, March 10.

[225] Borschmann, R., Keen, C., Spittal, M. J., Preen, D., Pirkis, J., Larney, S., & Kinner, S. A. (2024). Rates and causes of death after release from incarceration among 1 471 526 people in eight high-income and middle-income countries: an individual participant data meta-analysis. *The Lancet*, 403(10438), 1779-1788.

[226] A *person-year* is calculated by multiplying the number of people in a study by the time each person spends in the study. For example, if there were 1,000 people in a study that lasted 2 years, the study would have collected 2,000 person-years of data.

Sample

The sample consists of fifty DIH convictions over the six years from the beginning of 2015 through the end of 2020. A final sample of 25 state and 25 federal convictions was compiled from newspaper articles, FBI releases, and DEA commentaries.[227] The goal was to obtain sample cases that mirrored my son's case and compare the differences in the sentences. Predictably, there were no defendants with the exact same background as Scott, so those with the closest characteristics were selected. Even so, the range of criminal backgrounds spanned from no prior crimes to long records with prior drug and gun convictions.

Despite the effort to find similar cases, the motives, circumstances, and sentences varied widely, as shown by four examples from the fifty DIH convictions studied. The summaries are quoted from local newspapers reporting on the deaths.

1. *"ST. LOUIS – United States District Judge Henry E. Autrey sentenced Travis Broeker to **23 years** in prison today. On Sept. 17, 2020, after a four-day jury trial, the 36-year-old Clayton, Missouri resident was found guilty of distribution of fentanyl resulting in death and conspiracy to distribute fentanyl. The evidence at trial established on Feb. 28, 2018, Broeker met the victim in the parking lot of a convenience store and sold him six fentanyl capsules. The victim returned to his residence in the 2800 block of Telegraph, ingested fentanyl, and overdosed. The victim's roommate called 911 at 7:27 p.m. The victim was successfully treated with NARCAN and released from the hospital late in the evening of Feb. 28. While the victim was in the hospital, his roommate confiscated what he believed to be the victim's remaining fentanyl and his cell phone for the victim's safety. Unfortunately, the victim's roommate was unaware that the victim had concealed some of the remaining fentanyl in a hollowed-out rubber ball. The victim returned home around midnight, and he and his roommate spoke before the roommate went to sleep. During the early morning hours of Mar. 1, the victim's roommate found him unresponsive, in a fetal position. The same paramedics who treated the victim the previous night responded a second time and determined he was "beyond help." The victim was pronounced dead at 6:08 a.m. on Mar. 1. St. Louis County Police investigators obtained the victim's remaining fentanyl and cell phone from his roommate. The police used an undercover detective purporting to be*

---

[227] One of the federal cases is *US* vs. *Gary Scott Hancock.*

the victim's friend to contact Broeker, who agreed to distribute additional fentanyl to the victim and the undercover detective. Broeker enlisted co-defendant Pamela Barton to deliver 20 capsules of fentanyl to the undercover detective. Barton unwittingly contacted the police to make the fentanyl delivery and was arrested. Investigators later arrested Broeker, who admitted distributing fentanyl to the victim."

2. "In May 2016, 26-year-old Caleb Smith was prepping for medical school entry exams and ordered what he thought was Adderall off the internet to help him study. After the package arrived at his home in Williamsport, Pennsylvania, his girlfriend, 26-year-old Amanda Leach, asked to try some. Smith obliged, and days later, Leach was found dead from an overdose in her apartment. The stimulant Smith thought he ordered online turned out to be illicitly manufactured fentanyl, a synthetic opioid responsible for tens of thousands of deaths across the country.

Prosecutors with the US Attorney's Office for the Middle District of Pennsylvania charged Smith with "drug-induced homicide" for giving Leach the deadly dose, triggering a **20-year** mandatory minimum sentence. With the federal government bearing down on him, a guilt-stricken Smith killed himself. He was an aspiring doctor who had no criminal record and no intention of killing his girlfriend. But none of that mattered to federal prosecutors who, amid one of the worst drug crises in America's history, have been directed to get tough on dealers as part of an aggressive nationwide response."

Smith's story highlights the trend among prosecutors to extend the law to ridiculous extremes while claiming to fight the opioid epidemic. Known as "drug-induced homicide," prosecutions like Smith's are on the rise. According to a report by the Drug Policy Alliance, news articles about individuals charged with or prosecuted for drug-induced homicide increased by over 300 percent in just six years, to 1,178 in 2016 from 363 in 2011. Cases like these are difficult to track, and the numbers are likely much higher. A New York Times investigation documented over 1,000 such prosecutions since 2015 in only 15 states."
In the end, Smith's sentence was his life.

3. "Seattle – A former US Navy sailor was sentenced today in US District Court in Seattle to **4 years** in prison and three years of supervised release *for distribution of fentanyl, announced Acting US Attorney Tessa M. Gorman. Ivan Armenta, 21, was separated from the Navy and taken into federal custody on Aug. 7, 2020. Armenta provided pills tainted with fentanyl to another sailor who died of a drug overdose. At the sentencing hearing, US District Judge Robert S. Lasnik noted that Armenta had been warned the pills could be deadly but still shared them with his friends. Prosecutors have also charged those who distributed the pills to Armenta. Chase Friedrich, 29, supplied the pills to Armenta. He was arrested on Apr. 21, 2020, at his Des Moines, Washington, apartment. A search of Friedrich's apartment revealed cocaine, a handgun, and a bag of approximately 100 counterfeit pills. His drug supplier, Raoul V. Normandia, Jr., 29, was arrested on Apr. 24, 2020, near his Federal Way, Washington, residence. In his vehicle was cocaine. During a court-authorized search of Normandia's residence, law enforcement recovered cocaine, MDMA, firearms, ammunition, body armor, narcotics, and various signs of the drug trade, including scales, baggies, heat sealers, MoneyGram receipts, and twenty cell phones."*

4. *"Cathy Seibel, a US District Court judge for the Southern District of New York, sounded ambivalent on Oct. 8, 2015, as she sentenced Dennis Sica in a courtroom in downtown White Plains. "I think the one thing we can all agree on is that this whole case is a tragedy of immense proportion," she said. "The defendant is not a high-level drug dealer. He's by no means a kingpin or a dealer living a life of luxury off his profits. He's a small-time, small-town drug dealer." Sica, then 35, had struggled with heroin use for nearly 15 years when the Dutchess County Drug Task Force arrested him on Feb. 2, 2014. He'd been living in a modest condo in Hopewell Junction, a semi-rural community in the Hudson Valley, and selling heroin to friends and acquaintances. Federal prosecutors alleged that in just over one month in late 2013 and early 2014, Sica sold heroin to three customers who overdosed and died. Later, law enforcement claimed that text messages and informant testimony linked Sica to the three deaths. Sica pleaded guilty. Bharara's office had chosen to prosecute him under a special sentencing enhancement that allows for severe penalties for even low-level drug trafficking when death results. He was sentenced to **35 years**."*

Despite the intention of mandatory minimums to bring about consistent sentences, the four above defendants were sentenced to 23, 20, 4, and 35 years.

Findings

The data indicates that the most critical factor in lessening the sentence of a DIH charge, whether state or federal, is having information of interest to the prosecutor. Prosecutors significantly reduced or eliminated the sentences if the defendant provided helpful information. Unfortunately, only some mid-to-upper-level dealers tend to have the information prosecutors seek. People with an addiction, such as Scott, operate on the *demand side* of the market and have nothing to offer prosecutors who are looking for information on the *supply side* of the drug market. There is substantially more variation and leniency among state sentences than in federal, but the harshest punishments fall on those who do not have information to share.

Table 6.1 summarizes the findings on the frequency of various prison sentences in the 25 state and 25 federal cases reviewed. As expected, in all 50 cases, the state and federal judicial systems ignored the defendant's motive. Of the 25 state cases, 24 (96%) ended in a plea agreement with the prosecutor; 100% of the federal cases ended in a plea deal. Only one (2%) of the 50 cases went to trial.

Of the 25 state convictions reviewed, 5 (20%) resulted in a sentence of 20 years or more. The remaining 20 cases (80%) received 15 years or less. One state case was dismissed entirely through a plea deal, and in another, the sentence was one year in prison plus 1-year probation. Inexplicably, one state case sentenced the accused to 124 years!

Of the 25 federal DIH cases reviewed, 22 (88%) resulted in a sentence of 20 years or more. The three remaining cases (12%) were sentenced to 15 years. Most cases (80%) received the mandatory minimum 20-year sentence, but one case resulted in a 45-year sentence, and another imposed a life sentence.

Table 6.1. DIH State and Federal Sentencing		
Sentence	State DIH	Federal DIH
Years	# Cases	# Cases
0	1[a]	0
1-5	7	0
6-10	7	0
11-15	5	3
16-20	2[b]	13[c]
More than 20 years	3	9
Total	25	25

[a] Case ended in a plea deal with no prison time.
[b] One case was 16 years, and the other was 20.
[c] All 13 are 20-year sentences.

Four messages come through:
1) It is better to be arrested by state authorities than the federal DEA.

2) The distribution of sentences offers no consistent messaging to users, addicts, or dealers.

3) Using mandatory minimums to improve consistent sentencing has not worked.

4) The prosecutor alone can reduce a mandatory sentence through a plea deal and will do so if the accused has information of interest.

The results of this study confirm that the same crime and the same criminal do not exist, and even if they did, the law is not evenly applied. The range of sentences in the sample is an unbelievable 0-124 years!

The results show mandatory minimum sentences do not result in consistent sentencing but create long average sentences for federal inmates.

Recommendations
The following are recommended solutions to the problems discussed in this chapter.
1) Congress should repeal mandatory minimum sentences. There are never two crimes, never two criminals that are *precisely* the same.

Guidelines for judges, rather than mandatory minimums, would be a better approach for reducing sentencing variability.

2) Congress must remove prosecutors entirely from any part in the sentencing decision. After each side has presented their evidence, the judge should decide sentencing according to FSG.

3) Plea deals harm the goal of 'justice' and should be eliminated. Too often, plea deals are harmful to those who should be shown the most mercy and beneficial to those who are high-level dealers.

Regardless of the goals for minimum sentencing, the policy has had an overall negative impact on the country's battle with drug abuse. Instead, overdose death rates, addiction rates, and prison costs have mushroomed to astonishing levels.

A Word from Scott

Three days after my arrest, the prosecutor issued an indictment for Fentanyl Distribution, Resulting in Death. *The indictment also listed the criteria the government needed to prove to convict. To be guilty of a DIH, the government needed to show:*

1. *The defendant distributed a controlled substance.*
2. *The defendant engaged in distribution on two or more occasions.*
3. *The defendant did so knowingly and intentionally.*
4. *The victim ingested said controlled substance.*
5. *The victim died because of the use of said controlled substance.*

Initially, I thought, "You're going to be okay; they can't prove two of those five things." At the time, I did not realize that proof was not necessary. The DEA arrested one of my roommates, KR, for possessing a loaded syringe of fentanyl. KR could be looking at a sentence between 1 and 5 years, maybe more, since he had a previous felony drug conviction. For opioid addicts, one to five years without drugs is an insanely long time, plus the excruciating withdrawal makes it worth anything *to escape. To avoid prosecution, he signed a written statement saying I sold drugs to him and other people. KR was the prosecution's only witness against me, and he disappeared shortly after being questioned.*

The government completely ignored the motive behind my drug sharing and sentenced me to the mandatory minimum of 20 years. The strangest part of this experience is having fewer rights than those who commit first-degree murder. In murder cases, one of the most crucial parts of the defense is the defendant's motive, which is fully vetted and researched. Yet, in DIH cases, it is legally ignored.
It is not just ignoring motive and imposing mandatory minimum sentences; the laws are written to give the prosecution the ability to determine the defendant's charge, and the sentence imposed. Power in the hands of one side will never *result in a fair game outcome. A 99.98%-win rate for the prosecution sounds like loaded dice to me!*

An illustration of how sentencing goes wrong can be shown with a simple example. Let's say friend A asks friend B to drive him to pick up something at friend C's house. B does not ask A what he picks up, and A does not volunteer the information. A and C put something in the trunk of B's car and start the drive home. On the way, B gets pulled over, the vehicle is searched, and 10 kilos of heroin are found in the trunk. All three friends are indicted on a Conspiracy to distribute *heroin charge. A tells the police all about C's involvement with drugs and receives a sentence of eight rather than the mandatory minimum sentence of ten years. C happens to be a mid-level dealer, and he gives the prosecutor some valuable information, resulting in a sentence of 3 years. Having no knowledge to share with the prosecutor, B is sentenced to 10 years. B was an unknowing participant, had no previous criminal record, and was just doing a favor for a friend. Yet, B must serve seven more years than the mid-level dealer. This judgment is not justice.*

In my case, I wasn't dealing drugs at all; I was trying to help a dope-sick friend obtain fentanyl from my drug dealer. She texted me early in the morning, asking me to contact 'my dude' because she needed some fentanyl; she was starting to go through early withdrawal. I had just run out of dope myself and was already in the process of getting more. I had already contacted my dope dealer, BZ, so it wasn't going to be a problem to get a little bit more from him. BZ finally shows up after what seemed like forever; it seems like forever when waiting for a fix. BZ headed to my *kitchen and got the blender out to whip up the fentanyl. When he was finished, he filled capsules with the drug using a miniature pill press. BZ gave me three beans to try; I shot up all three and nodded off for a while. About 25 to 30 minutes later, TG arrived at my house with $20. She was in front of my house calling me on the phone to get my attention. Finally, I asked BZ to give me five beans for TG and walked out to her car. I got in her car, and she gave me $20 in exchange for the five beans. I asked TG to drive around to the back side of my house so things wouldn't look sketchy to my neighbors. I got out of the car, walked into the back door of my home, and gave BZ the $20. Four months later, I learned TG had died. TG's father found text messages between us in her iCloud and called the DEA. He was adamant that I be convicted and sent away for a long time. Her family believes I was 100% responsible. Ultimately, I received 20 years in prison for doing what I thought was a good deed.*

The difference between the motive of drug dealers and the motive of addicts who share drugs is enormous. Dealers trade drugs for profit; they seek out new customers to grow their business. Addicts do not have such lofty goals; they just want to keep friends happy as future sources of drugs. I did not need TG as a source of drugs; I was simply trying to help a friend avoid the pain of being dope sick.

Summary

Mandatory minimum sentencing was intended to ensure that all persons committing the same crime did the same time. The goal sounds reasonable, but in practice, the policy fails because no two crimes or two criminals are *precisely* the same. Additionally, the law does not distinguish between an addict or user and a dealer; the sentence is the same regardless. Harsh sentencing is used to signal to those selling and using drugs that they will be severely punished. However, the message must be clear, consistent, *and* repetitious to signal a healthy brain. As discussed, not only do advanced opioid addicts *not* have a healthy brain, but the messages sent by the DOJ and the states are unclear and inconsistent.

Mandatory minimum sentences have ushered in a world of illogical punitive justice where more and more time is added to sentences, well beyond what can be considered rational or productive. Prosecutors appear to disregard the cost to taxpayers or the impact on society. One thing is certain: 20 years in prison for an accidental overdose, plus the denial of Constitutional rights, goes far beyond a proportional judgment.

Not surprisingly, the transfer of sentencing power from the judge to the prosecutor is to blame for the dramatic sentencing disparities and the increased average time spent in prison. The significant sentencing disparities result from prosecutors making plea deals for short sentences with those holding important information. Unfortunately, those who do not have any information for the prosecutor are low-level dealers or addicts. The result is that mid to top-level drug dealers get away with a slap on the hand, and people with an addiction and low-level dealers are imprisoned for decades.

Due process is one of the Constitutional rights denied to those charged with a DIH. This government denial of due process is paradoxical because the right is designed to prevent the unfair use of governmental power against citizens. When a government harms a person without following the exact course of the law, this constitutes a due process violation, which offends the rule of law. Yet the government has waived the laws that hold it accountable to its citizens. No entity or person should be able to waive the laws that apply to their immoral actions against a significantly disadvantaged group.

The importance of due process in DIH cases cannot be overstated because advanced opioid addicts have a vastly different view of sharing drugs with fellow addicts than does society or drug dealers. Society views drug sharing as illegal, immoral, and dangerous. Dealers view drug sharing as necessary to introduce people to their product. Alternatively, people with an addiction view drug sharing as essential to solidifying sources for future needs. Addicts share drugs with other addicts; profit is not one of the motives because, generally, drugs are shared at cost.

People with opioid dependence are motivated to share drugs by the dual desires to help a fellow addict avoid the pain of withdrawal and to secure a source for future drugs.

CHAPTER 7: PROSECUTORIAL MISCONDUCT

"Power tends to corrupt, and absolute power corrupts absolutely. Great men are almost always bad men, even when they exercise influence and not authority, still more when you super-add the tendency or the certainty of corruption by authority. There is no worse heresy than that the office sanctifies the holder of it. That is the point at which . . . the ends learn to justify the means. You would hang a man of no position, but if what one hears is true, then [Queen] *Elizabeth I asked the gaoler* [prison guard] *to murder Mary, and William III ordered his scots minister to destroy an entire clan. Here are the greater names coupled with the greater crimes. You would spare these criminals for some mysterious reason. I would hang them, higher than Haman* [evil persecutor of Jews], *for reasons of quite obvious justice; still more, still higher . . ."*[228]

Introduction

Lord Emerick Acton's (1887) characterization of unchecked power in his letter to Bishop Mandell Creighton strongly resonates when applied to today's prosecutors, even though it is 135 years old. Human nature does not change.

In the 1935 *United States v. Berger* ruling, the US Supreme Court broadly defined how a prosecutor should behave: *"He may prosecute with earnestness and vigor — indeed, he should do so. But, while he may strike hard blows, he is not at liberty to strike foul ones. It is as much his duty to refrain from improper methods calculated to produce a wrongful conviction as it is to use every legitimate means to bring about a just one."* Since then, the Supreme Court has said that the twofold aim of a prosecutor is that *the guilty shall not escape and the innocent will not suffer*. Even so, this same court has also ruled that prosecutors are *absolutely* immune from liability, which means that they cannot be sued for their decisions as prosecutors, no matter how outrageous their conduct.

---

[228] Lord Emerick Acton's Letter to Bishop Mandell Creighton (April 5, 1887). *Historical Essays and Studies*, edited by J. N. Figgis and R. V. Laurence (London: Macmillan, 1907). https://history.hanover.edu/courses/excerpts/165acton.html.

The Supreme Court has held that absolute immunity holds even when prosecutors knowingly use false testimony and suppress evidence in murder trials that lead to a conviction.[229]

According to legal ethics rules, prosecutors are *supposed* to act as "ministers of justice." However, long sentences are a valued reputational achievement for prosecutors, reinforcing the need to seek higher prosecution rates and longer sentences.[230] A more comprehensive method of incentivizing prosecutors is needed to change the current focus from punishment to justice. Justice requires weighing both sides of the story and, when appropriate, dismissing a case or reducing a sentence. Justice requires a system that either rewards prosecutors for such decisions or limits the power of the office.

Prosecutorial Power
According to the *US Supreme Court*, prosecutors cannot be removed from office for misconduct of any kind; they are not subject to civil liability for misconduct, they are not subject to professional condemnation, and they are rarely subjected to dismissal by the US AG for federal crimes, or state AG for state crimes.[231] Therefore, there are no incentives for prosecutors to restrain their behavior. When it comes to state and local prosecutors, they hold significant power and influence over local criminal justice communities. According to Henning (1999) and Jalain (2021), judges and defense counsel do not report prosecutor misconduct due to fear of backlash. In certain situations, prosecutors can challenge judges' ability to sit on criminal cases.[232] At the federal level, prosecutors face very few limits. Prosecutors can and do bring charges on real or imagined offenses, change charges at random, threaten those charged, threaten family members of those arrested, coerce guilty pleas, ignore evidence,

---

[229] Imbler v. Pachtman (1976), 424 US 409.
[230] i) Henning, P. J. (1999). Prosecutorial misconduct and constitutional remedies. *Washington University Law Quarterly*, 77, 713.
ii) Jalain, C. (2021). Punishing the Powerful: A Study of Prosecutorial Misconduct in the Era of Ethics Reforms. *Scholarly Open Access Repository*. https://soar.usi.edu/handle/20.500.12419/8.
[231] Oppel, Richard A., Jr. (2011). Sentencing Shift Gives New Leverage to Prosecutors. *New York Times*, Sept. 25. https://www.nytimes.com/2011/09/26/us/tough-sentences-help-prosecutors-push-for-plea-
[232] Gershowitz, A. M. (2008). Prosecutorial shaming: Naming attorneys to reduce prosecutorial misconduct. *University of California-Davis Law Review*, 42, 1059.

silence judges, intimidate defense attorneys, and deny the accused their constitutional rights.

According to Davis (2005), prosecutors are the most powerful officials in the American criminal justice system. Their decisions, particularly charging and plea bargaining, control the system's operations and often predetermine the outcome of criminal cases.[233] Prosecutorial power is vast and unrestrained, while the mechanisms that purport to hold prosecutors accountable are weak and ineffective. In addition, the most critical prosecutorial decisions are made behind closed doors – away from public scrutiny and thus immune to public accountability.

The most remarkable feature of these critical, sometimes life-and-death decisions is that they are totally discretionary. The deficiency of prosecutorial discretion lies not in its existence but in its random and arbitrary application. Even in prosecution offices that promulgate general policies for prosecuting criminal cases, there are no effective mechanisms for enforcement or public accountability for prosecutors. Self-regulation by prosecution offices is nonexistent, and the US Supreme Court has protected prosecutors from public and judicial scrutiny.

In 1940, Jackson published an article that provided a simple, accurate description of prosecutors. He said:

"The prosecutor has more control over life, liberty, and reputation than any other person in America. His discretion is tremendous. He can have citizens investigated, and if he is that kind of person, he can have this done to the tune of public statements and veiled or unveiled intimidations. Or the prosecutor may choose a more subtle course and simply have a citizen's friends interviewed. The prosecutor can order arrests, present cases to the grand jury in secret sessions, and, based on his one-sided presentation of the facts, cause the citizen to be indicted and held for trial. He may dismiss the case before trial, in which case the defense never has a chance to be heard. Or he may go on with a public trial. If he obtains a conviction, the prosecutor can still make recommendations as to the sentence, as to whether the prisoner should get probation or a suspended

---

[233] Davis, A. J. (2005). The power and discretion of the American prosecutor. *Droit et cultures. Revue internationale interdisciplinaire*, (49), 55-66.

sentence, and after he is put away, as to whether he is a fit subject for parole. While the prosecutor at his best is one of the most beneficent forces in our society, when he acts from malice or other base motives, he is one of the worst."[234]

Through the decades of new laws to toughen sentencing for criminals, prosecutors have gained greater leverage to extract guilty pleas from defendants and reduce the number of cases that go to trial, often by using the threat of more serious charges with mandatory sentences or other harsh penalties. Some experts say the process has become coercive in many state and federal jurisdictions, forcing defendants to weigh their options based on the relative risks of facing a judge and jury rather than simple matters of guilt or innocence.[235] In effect, prosecutors give defendants more reasons to avoid having their day in court.[236]

"We now have an incredible concentration of power in the hands of prosecutors," said Richard E. Myers II, a former Assistant US Attorney, and an Associate Professor of law at the *University of North Carolina*. He stated that so much influence and power currently reside with prosecutors that *"in the wrong hands, the criminal justice system can be held hostage."* Growing prosecutorial power is a significant reason that the percentage of felony cases that go to trial has dropped sharply. Plea bargains have been standard for more than a century but are now so prevalent that the trial system of justice does not apply. Fewer than two percent of all federal drug cases make it to trial, according to Pew Research.[237]

---

[234] Jackson, Robert H. (1940). The Federal Prosecutor. *Journal of Criminal Law*, 31, 3.
[235] Oppel, Richard A., Jr. (2011). Sentencing Shift Gives New Leverage to Prosecutors. *New York Times*, Sept. 25. https://www.nytimes.com/2011/09/26/us/tough-sentences-help-prosecutors-push-for-plea-bargains.html#:~:text=25%2C%202011-,GAINESVILLE%2C%20Fla.,sentences%20or%20other%20harsher%20penalties.
[236] See, for example,
i) Viano, E. C. (2012). Plea bargaining in the United States: A perversion of Justice. *Revue internationale de droit pénal*, 83(1), 109-145.
ii) Caldwell, H. M. (2011). Coercive plea bargaining: The unrecognized scourge of the justice system. *Catholic University Law Review*, 61, 63.
iii) Klein, R. (2003). Due process denied: Judicial coercion in the plea-bargaining process. *Hofstra Law Review*, 32, 1349.
[237] Gramlich, John (2019). Only 2% of federal criminal defendants go to trial, and most who do are found guilty. *Pew Research Center*, June 11. https://www.pewresearch.org/fact-tank/2019/06/11/only-2-of-federal-criminal-defendants-go-to-trial-and-most-who-do-are-found-guilty/.

The Criminalization of Addiction

Cases like *United States v. Nunez* help explain why. Mr. Nunez, 22, was arrested for conspiracy to deliver counterfeit oxycodone pills to Rosaliana Lopez-Rodriguez. The pills were designed to look like oxycodone 30-milligram pills, with 'M' and '30' stamped on them. But they were fakes tainted with fentanyl. To pit the two against one another, the prosecutor lied to each, saying the other would testify against them. The sad part is that neither Nunez nor Lopez-Rodriguez was aware that the oxycodone pills were laced with fentanyl. The ruse worked, and both pleaded guilty to the charges of drug-induced homicide and conspiracy.

The decrease in trials has also resulted from underfinanced public defender offices and the rise of drug courts and other alternative resolutions.[238] In many jurisdictions, overloaded court systems have also seen comparatively little expansion, making a massive increase in plea bargains a cheap and easy way to handle the tripling of felony cases over the past generation. The tripling of felony cases is not due to more committed felonies but because Congress has defined more behaviors and actions as felonies.

The drug laws passed in the 1970s and 1980s defined an extensive range of drug behaviors as illegal. With more activities defined as unlawful, more arrests were made, and the prison population of the US began to outstrip the rest of the world. Stricter sentencing penalties for drug crimes meant more people stayed in prison for more extended periods. Drug laws have increased the number of activities considered criminal, and convicted users have enlarged prison populations to levels that lawmakers in some states say they can no longer afford.

Prosecutors seem oblivious to the costs of incarceration and take billions of taxpayer dollars each year without any thought to the social financial burden. Judge Kozinski wrote:[239]

---

[238] Drug courts are specialized court docket programs that target criminal defendants, juveniles who have been convicted of a drug offense, and parents with pending child welfare cases who have alcohol and other drug dependency problems. There are approximately 2,500 drug courts in the US, serving less than half (47%) of all US counties.

[239] Volokh, Eugene (2015). Judge Kozinski on Prosecutorial Misconduct. *The Washington Post*, July 17.

"Prosecutors hold tremendous power, more than anyone other than the jurors. However, most cases do not go to trial, so jurors are irrelevant in at least 98% of the cases. Prosecutors and their investigators have unparalleled access to the evidence, both inculpatory [indicating guilt] *and exculpatory* [indicating innocence] *evidence, and while they are required to provide exculpatory evidence to the defense, it is very difficult for the defense to find out whether the prosecution is complying with this obligation. Prosecutors also have tremendous control over witnesses and, thus, jurors: They can offer incentives — often highly compelling — for suspects to testify, including sweetheart plea deals to alleged co-conspirators and engineering jailhouse encounters between the defendant and known informants. Sometimes, they feed snitches non-public information about the crime so that the statements they attribute to the defendant will sound authentic. And, of course, prosecutors can pile on charges to make it exceedingly risky for a defendant to go to trial. There are countless ways in which prosecutors can prejudice the fact-finding process and undermine a defendant's right to a fair trial. This, of course, is not their job."*

According to Redlich (2017), research has shown some rather disturbing indications that numerous prosecutors, and sometimes entire prosecutorial offices, engage in misconduct that seriously undermines the fairness of criminal trials. The misconduct ranges from misleading the jury to outright lying in court and tacitly acquiescing or actively participating in the presentation of false evidence by police.[240] Resolving prosecutorial misconduct is overcomplicated by a veil of secrecy that surrounds their work. Who would know when a prosecutor fails to disclose exculpatory evidence to the defense? Who would know when a prosecutor delays revealing evidence helpful to the defense until after the defendant has accepted an unfavorable plea bargain? Who would know when prosecutors rely on the testimony of police officers they know to be untruthful? It would take extraordinary luck and persistence for anyone to discover the full extent of prosecutorial misconduct — and in most cases, no one would ever find out.[241]

---

[240] Kreag, Jason (2019). Disclosing Prosecutorial Misconduct. *Vanderbilt Law Review*, Vol. 72, 1, pp. 297.
[241] Redlich, A. D., Bibas, S., Edkins, V. A., & Madon, S. (2017). The psychology of defendant plea decision making. *American Psychologist*, 72(4), 339.

Even though academic and law journals have documented many cases of prosecutorial misconduct, the exact number is unknown due to the absence of a safe reporting method. I reviewed over 125 random federal cases for this chapter to understand the scope of the problem. One high-profile case stood out because it involved a powerful, wealthy white man charged with corruption. The 2008 case, *US v. Stevens*, details the prosecution of Ted Stevens, then the longest-serving Republican Senator in US history.[242] The prosecutor charged Senator Stevens with corruption for accepting the services of a building contractor and paying him far below market price — essentially a bribe. The prosecutor's case hinged on the testimony of the contractor. Still, the prosecutor failed to disclose the contractor's initial statement to the FBI that he was probably overpaid for the services. The prosecutor also failed to announce that the contractor was under investigation for unrelated crimes and thus had good reason to curry favor with the FBI.

Stevens was convicted one week before he stood for re-election. Not surprisingly, Stevens lost his re-election bid, which changed the balance of power in the Senate. The prosecutor's deceit came to light when an FBI agent named Chad Joy blew the whistle on the prosecutor's knowing concealment of exculpatory evidence. The prosecutor argued strenuously that his ill-gotten conviction should stand because *"boys will be boys* [referring to the agents who concealed exculpatory evidence], *and the evidence probably wasn't material to the case anyway."* When prosecutors can engage in such behavior with a sitting US Senator and experience no repercussions, imagine the danger to the average citizen.

It was only with the extraordinary persistence and intervention of District Judge Emmet Sullivan that an investigation into the prosecutor's misconduct was launched. Judge Sullivan made it clear that he would dismiss the *Stevens* case due to the prosecutor's misconduct. The investigation results forced the DOJ to admit wrongdoing and vacate the former senator's conviction. Instead of contrition, the high-ranking justice

---

[242] He now ranks the tenth longest serving Senator.

department officials patted themselves on the back for *"doing the right thing."* [243]

Assistant Federal Public Defender Scott Graham (2019) writes of a prosecutor's experience: *"Up to that point in my career, I was certainly aware of the vast power and discretion prosecutors possess in the United States criminal justice system. This phenomenon has been well-documented in books and scholarly articles over the years. But it had not occurred to me that prosecutors could manipulate charges in response to political "hot button" issues, such as fentanyl, in a way that created mandatory prison time for even the lowest, most impuissant players in the drug trade."* [244]

According to the *Human Rights Watch* organization, Federal prosecutors routinely threaten extraordinarily severe prison sentences to coerce drug defendants into waiving their right to trial and pleading guilty. In the rare cases where defendants insist on going to trial, prosecutors often win longer sentences. Federal drug offenders convicted by trial receive sentences that average three times longer than those who accept a plea bargain, according to new statistics developed by *Human Rights Watch*.[245] Prosecutors also pressure drug defendants to plead guilty by threatening increased mandatory sentencing enhancements and penalties that are applicable if the defendant has one or more prior drug convictions or possessed a gun at the time of the offense; prosecutors make good on their threats by adding decades to the defendant's time behind bars.

Across the country, prosecutors have violated their oaths and the law with impunity, committing the worst types of deception in the most severe cases. They have prosecuted a man, knowing the police planted the evidence. They have prosecuted a woman, knowing she was only

---

[243] The Trial of Ted Stevens (2007-2009). *Wikipedia*, https://en.wikipedia.org/wiki/Trial_of_Ted_Stevens#:~:text=United%20States%20v.,the%20Alaska%20political%20corruption%20probe.

[244] Turner, J. I. (2020). Transparency in plea bargaining. *Notre Dame Law Review*, 96, 973.

[245] Human Rights Watch (2013). US: Forced Guilty Pleas in Drug Cases, Threat of Draconian Sentencings Means Few Willing to Risk Trial. *Human Rights Watch*, Dec. 5. https://www.hrw.org/news/2013/12/05/us-forced-guilty-pleas-drug-cases#:~:text=(New%20York)%20–%20Federal%20prosecutors,in%20a%20report%20released%20today.

protecting her husband. They have prosecuted a single mother, knowing she was innocent of the drug charge. They have prosecuted a single father, knowing he was driving a friend's car with drugs in the glove compartment.[246] Why do prosecutors do this?

They do it to win. They do it because they can. They do it because they won't get punished.

Zottoli et al. (2016) studied people who pleaded guilty to felonies in New York City.[247] They found that prosecutors offered substantial sentence reductions to those who pleaded guilty. Twenty-seven percent (27%) of the participants claimed they were wholly innocent of the charge, 41% said they were not guilty *as charged*, and 32% said they were guilty as charged. The 41% who claimed they were not guilty as charged admitted to involvement in a separate crime. Participants also reported infrequent contact with their attorneys before accepting their plea deals, with little time to make decisions.

Discretionary power plays a role throughout the US criminal justice system. Police exercise discretionary power upon arrest; they decide who to arrest and what crime(s) to charge. Prosecutors wield an unlimited amount of discretionary power. Prosecutors subjectively decide whether to file charges, which charges to file and how many counts to charge. They choose whether to divert cases entirely by referring the accused to a treatment program. They offer lenience in exchange for guilty pleas or pursue more aggressive charges when defendants do not "cooperate." In conjunction with mandatory minimum laws, they actively shape sentences through the charges they bring.[248]

Consider for a moment a justice system that grants the defense all discretionary powers of the law. President S has just taken office and announced that all advice on criminal justice matters will come from the

---

[246] Joy, P. A. (2006). Relationship between Prosecutorial Misconduct and Wrongful Convictions: Shaping Remedies for a Broken System. *Wisconsin Law Review*, 399.

[247] Zottoli, T. M., Daftary-Kapur, T., Winters, G. M., & Hogan, C. (2016). Plea discounts, time pressures, and false-guilty pleas in youth and adults who pleaded guilty to felonies in New York City. *Psychology, Public Policy, and Law*, *22*(3), 250.

[248] Frederick, Bruce and Stemen, Don (2012). The Anatomy of Discretion: An Analysis of Prosecutorial Decision Making-Technical Report. *National Institute of Justice*.

Federal Defender's Office (FDO). Moreover, President S puts the FDO in charge of all federal prisons, forensic science, and the clemency process. After pushback, President S argues the FDO best understands federal criminal law from the ground up and has a rich understanding of the social conditions that lead to criminal behavior. President S believes that since FDO attorneys are responsible for protecting individuals' Constitutional rights, they are the obvious choice for determining the charges, sentencing, and oversight of the accused.[249]

People would be outraged. Critics would complain that the defense counsel represents only one part of the justice system and is inherently biased towards defendants because their work in the courts is always on behalf of the accused.

Yet, the mirror image of that situation exists unchallenged. Despite an obvious conflict of interest, the DOJ evaluates clemency petitions, runs federal prisons, decides what forensic evidence to introduce in federal cases, and advises the president on criminal justice reform. Prosecutors dominate the DOJ; its 93 *United States Attorney's Offices* set policies across various issues and run most divisions. The dominance of prosecutors matters since they instinctively oppose reforms that could make criminal law less punitive and more effective.

Applied to DIH Charges

Drug-induced homicide laws are an additional powerful tool that expands prosecutors' already sweeping discretion. Unfortunately, prosecutors have abused this discretion by pursuing cases against those who are less culpable than the deceased and are not capable of being dealers. Many of the DIH laws already in place, as well as those currently being proposed, are touted as targeting so-called "professional" drug sellers who profit from their drug-using clients' addictions. However, the distinction between *seller*, *user*, and *addict* is determined by prosecutors who do not hesitate to prosecute friends, family, and co-addicts of the deceased.

A 2004 *Bureau of Justice* report found that 70% of people incarcerated in state prisons for drug trafficking used drugs themselves in the month

---

[249] Osler, Mark (2017). The Problem with the Justice Department. *The Marshal Project*, May 30. https://www.themarshallproject.org/2017/05/30/the-problem-with-the-justice-department

before the offense.[250] A 2017 report by the *Bureau of Justice Statistics* similarly found that nearly 75% of people in state prisons and local jails had regularly used drugs. Additionally, more than half of people serving time for drug crimes were on drugs at the time of the offense, and more than 20% of state prisoners were incarcerated for crimes committed to get money for drugs.[251] Drug market experts find that many sufferers of substance use disorder sell drugs to support their habit. As a result, the current climate of approval for arresting addicts is a windfall for medium- and high-level drug dealers because the prosecutor has someone to arrest in place of the dealers who avoid punishment. The people who get the harshest punishments are the very ones that the DIH laws were intended to protect – people at risk of death due to a substance use disorder.

A New Jersey law proves illustrative. The legislature designed the law to apply to major drug dealers or "kingpins" in the organized drug trade. In practice, prosecutors have used the law to incarcerate minor drug dealers, many with no record, without presenting evidence. In fact, of the 32 New Jersey DIH prosecutions identified by Knight (2003), 25 involved prosecutions of decedents' friends who did not deal drugs in any significant manner.[252]

After analyzing 100 recent DIH cases in southeastern Wisconsin, *Fox 6 Milwaukee* reported in 2017 that 11% of defendants were at least one step removed from the direct sale or delivery of drugs to a victim. The other 89% of those charged were friends or relatives of the person who died or were people low in the supply chain who often sold to support their drug use.[253] A *Chicago Tribune* review of DIH cases between 2011 and 2014 in six Chicago-area counties showed that the person most often charged in

---

[250] Mumola, C. J., & Karberg, J. C. (2007). Drug use and dependence, state and federal prisoners, 2004. Washington, DC: US Department of Justice, Office of Justice Programs, *Bureau of Justice Statistics*.
[251] Bronson, J., Stroop, J., Zimmer, S., & Berzofsky, M. (2017). Drug use, dependence, and abuse among state prisoners and jail inmates, 2007–2009. *Washington, DC: United States Department of Justice, Office of Juvenile Justice and Delinquency Prevention*.
[252] Knight, J. H. (2003). The First Hit's Free... or Is It-Criminal Liability for Drug-Induced Death in New Jersey. *Seton Hall Law Review*, *34*, 1327.
[253] Polcyn, Bryan (2017). High Level Drug Dealers are Rarely Charged with Drug Related Homicides as Wisconsin's Death Toll Reaches 10k. *Fox 6 Milwaukee*, Feb. 10.

these cases was typically the last person who was with the overdose victim.[254]

Moreover, because prosecutors misuse their discretionary power and because the potential penalties are so harsh (minimum of life in prison in six states), many people resort to pleading guilty to a lesser offense to avoid risking a DIH murder conviction, even if there is little proof and weak causation. Politicians are also introducing legislation to establish more extreme sentences for fentanyl sellers and users. For example, in 2023, lawmakers in Virginia designated fentanyl as a *"weapon of terrorism."*

Prosecutors and other law enforcement officials have also explicitly broadcast their intentions to use DIH laws more aggressively against fentanyl users; any user can be accused of selling. For example, Sheriff Peyton Grinnell, Lake County, Florida, recorded a viral video aimed at people who sell and use drugs in which he warned, *"We're coming for you."* Throughout the country, law enforcement officials have increasingly spoken about their commitment to using these laws whenever they can connect a seller or provider to a specific overdose death. In New York, Erie County District Attorney John Flynn said, *"If I can prove it, I will charge a drug dealer with murder."* At the same time, Sue Burggraf of the *Minnesota Bureau of Criminal Apprehension* told a local newspaper, *"We're treating these overdose deaths as homicide investigations...When we find those drug dealers, we intend to charge them with third-degree murder."*

Regulation

Congress recognized a potential problem with the 1980s SRA that threatened to frustrate the entire endeavor. The FSG gave prosecutors tools to control sentences more precisely than they could in the indeterminate sentencing era. Prosecutors had control over information used to establish guideline ranges. They also had control over most mechanisms available for leniency, such as sentence reduction for cooperating against others. Mandatory minimum statutes gave prosecutors even more power to set absolute floors, which judges could not override, regardless of other

---

[254] An Overdose Death is Not Murder: Why Drug Induced Homicide Laws are Counterproductive & Inhumane. *The Drug Policy Alliance*. Nov 2017 booklet copyright owned by DPA. https://drugpolicy.org/sites

considerations. Without attention to charging and plea bargaining, *"sentencing reform could actually increase disparities in the federal sentencing process."*[255] With the benefit of hindsight, this has proven all too true.

Several provisions of the SRA addressed the concern of prosecutorial overreach. Most significantly, Congress directed the US Sentencing Commission (USSC) to issue policy statements regarding the appropriate use of *"the authority granted to accept or reject a plea agreement."* The intention was for judges to participate in regulating plea bargaining to advance the goals of the SRA and protect their sentencing prerogatives. *"The legislative history illustrates that both the House and Senate viewed this provision as crucial to the success of the sentencing reform effort."*[256]

The USSC has responded to concerns about prosecutorial discretion and sentencing disparity, acknowledging that the system has deviated from the intended actions of the SRA in several novel ways. In addition to policy statements governing acceptance of plea agreements, the USSC developed the *"multiple counts"* and *"relevant conduct"* rules to help ensure that sentences for most types of crimes would reflect defendants' *"real offense conduct,"* regardless of charging and plea-bargaining decisions.[257]

The USSC knew prosecutors wanted sentencing incentives to induce defendants to plead guilty and cooperate with the government in prosecuting other persons, for example, by acting as confidential informants or government witnesses. Incentives for pleading guilty would be helpful to the government, but constitutional and policy concerns clouded any explicit 'discount' for waiving the right to trial. When almost everyone pleads guilty, the discount becomes the norm, perversely creating penalties for exercising constitutional rights. Penalties for

---

[255] USSC. Chapter 1: Introduction to the Sentencing Reform Act.
https://www.ussc.gov/sites/default/files/pdf/research-and-publications/research-projects-and-surveys/miscellaneous/15-year-study/chap1.pdf
[256] Freed, D. J. (1992). Federal Sentencing in the Wake of Guidelines: Unacceptable Limits on the Discretion of Sentencers. *The Yale Law Journal*, 101(8), 1681–1754.
https://doi.org/10.2307/796945
[257] Frederick, Bruce and Stemen, Don (2012). The Anatomy of Discretion: An Analysis of Prosecutorial Decision Making-Technical Report. *National Institute of Justice*.

exercising constitutional rights raise the issue of a *trial penalty* that, in effect, punishes offenders for exercising their rights to a trial.[258]

The USSC ultimately decided to provide a fixed and explicit incentive for defendants to plead guilty while addressing the constitutional and policy concerns in two ways. First, it limited the sentencing reduction to two offense levels, equivalent to an average of about 25%. Second, to counter perceptions of reductions as a reward for pleading guilty, judges were given discretion, and plea deals were framed as merely a mitigating factor. Reductions would not apply automatically or be precluded if defendants went to trial.

Almost forty years later, the alarm over penalizing defendants for asserting their constitutional rights or declining to cooperate with prosecutors can seem antiquated; the alarm began to fade even before the implementation of the FSG. Congress amended the SRA at the urging of the DOJ and made mandatory minimum sentences for drug offenses part of the *Anti-Drug Abuse Act of 1986* (ADAA). Judges would be permitted to impose a sentence less than the stated minimum, but *only* upon the prosecutor's motion *"to reflect a defendant's substantial assistance in the investigation or prosecution of another person who has committed an offense."* The *"substantial assistance"* motion could prompt defendants to testify against accomplices, work as confidential informants, or assist law enforcement in various other ways. Congress also directed the USSC to amend the FSG to permit sentencing below the guideline range for the same reason. The USSC endorsed the FSG policy statement and made a *plea reduction* contingent on a motion by the prosecutor.

Having successfully persuaded Congress to give them control over sentence reductions for cooperation, prosecutors made an additional request that proved too much even for the USSC. Rather than merely reducing sentences for those who cooperated, prosecutors urged the USSC to require judges to punish defendants who refused to cooperate. The unseemly prospect of punishing defendants for failing to accede to prosecutors' demands led the USSC to reject this proposal and add policy statement 5K1.2: *"A defendant's refusal to assist authorities in the*

---

[258] USSC (2020). Federal Sentencing, The Basics. United States Sentencing Commission. https://www.ussc.gov/sites/default/files/pdf/research-and-publications/research-publications/2020/202009_fed-sentencing-basics.pdf

investigation of other persons may not be considered as an aggravating sentencing factor."

Nonetheless, the prosecutor's desire to use sentencing to reward or punish defendants for reasons unrelated to the seriousness of their crimes was now explicit. Prosecutors soon learned they had tools, especially mandatory minimum sentences, to circumvent the USSC's policies and punish uncooperative defendants. A climate of crime politics, congressional micromanagement, and prosecutorial power was emerging that would betray the promise of the SRA. The SRA was a reform intended to ensure that sentences were sufficient but not greater than necessary to advance the purposes of incarceration. Still, it soon devolved into an unbalanced system that shifted power from judges, the defense, and even the USSC toward the interests of prosecutors.[259]

Scott's Prosecution

On Feb 11, 2019, Scott was criminally charged with one felony count of *drug-induced homicide* in the case of TG's accidental overdose death in October 2018. Guilt was already established in the minds of the DEA agents upon arrest, as evidenced by their words to Scott and, separately, his family that he would be *"going away for a long, long time."*

Despite that dire prediction, the family was optimistic because we knew Scott was not a dealer, so naturally, he would be acquitted. Plus, he had not forced drugs on TG, so we thought everything would be fine, eventually. I imagined a jury trial where the prosecutor could not produce any evidence, and the defense attorney would exonerate him. The text messages the prosecutor would use to show Scott's guilt actually demonstrated his innocence by identifying BZ as Scott's dealer. Scott lived in a crummy house I purchased, had no car, and had a low-paying job at a local restaurant. If he was a dealer, then he was a remarkably unsuccessful one. But all those ruminations came before we knew about the plea deal; naively, we still believed there would be an investigation, and that proof would be required to convict. Little did we know that none of that was relevant.

---

[259] Hofer, P. (2015). After Ten Years of Advisory Guidelines, and Thirty Years of Mandatory Minimums, Federal Sentencing Still Needs Reform. *University of Toledo Law Review*, 47, 649.

The story of CP (introduced in Chapter 2) needs to be told to comprehend Scott's plea deal fully. Scott and CP met in eighth grade and became good buddies. After high school, they stayed in touch, probably because both were on a path to opioid addiction. At one point, CP and Scott were roommates until the police arrested CP for possession of heroin. A few years later, in March 2018, CP was released from prison and contacted Scott to celebrate his freedom by buying what he thought was heroin from an old dealer friend, JR. Unfortunately, the heroin was laced with fentanyl, and CP's tolerance was low. Scott landed in the emergency room, and CP was found dead the following morning. Our whole family grieved the loss of CP, or at least the CP we knew as a young boy, before drugs took over his life. The St. Louis County police investigated CP's death, JR was arrested, and the investigation was closed.

During the first few months of Scott's time in county jail, there seemed to be a lot of motions and actions. One action I remember well. I had prepared to go to court to argue on my son's behalf at a detention hearing. The detention hearing is all about what to do with a prisoner while awaiting trial. I wanted Scott to come home, but the prosecutor had a different idea. She told Scott's attorney that if I testified, she would charge me with *"owning my son's drug house."* I'm not sure what kind of crime that is, but that was the threat. She also told Scott's attorney that she felt like *"...the whole family are criminals."* Prosecutors with the mindset that the accused is a criminal and so is their family do not belong anywhere near the word 'justice.'

The family had no idea that legal authorities were now viewing accidental overdoses as homicides. Nor did we fully comprehend the meaning of a mandatory minimum sentence of 20 years or understand the prosecutor's power. We walked into a lion's den unarmed. We *thought* we knew what was *supposed* to be going on, but that never happened. We believed that a federal manslaughter charge might be applied, which would be a 6–7-year sentence. When the prosecutor offered 15 years for a guilty plea, it seemed like an insane number of years for an accident; Scott was given only 24 hours to respond. Naively, he declined her offer. Her response of charging two additional felonies was like a vicious slap in the face that woke us up; *now* we understood who we were dealing with and what she was capable of – we were frightened to our core. There was no way out.

Within 48 hours of declining the offer, the prosecutor indicted Scott on two additional felony charges related to CP's death, each carrying a mandatory minimum 20-year sentence, and a second defense attorney was appointed to take the two new cases. Scott faced a potential 60 years in prison versus 15 years if he agreed to plead guilty and waive a jury trial. We had to learn to wrap our heads around the fact that no one, not the defense, not the prosecution, and not the judge, cared about guilt, innocence, or the facts of the case. What a strange system of justice.

The newly appointed defense attorney explained the two fundamental rules of the US criminal justice system:

> **Rule #1**: Guilt or innocence is irrelevant.
> **Rule#2**: Someone *is* going to prison.

Our heads were swirling! How is it possible that the 'rules' sound illegal? Are prosecutors allowed to charge defendants with contrived crimes? How could any of this be happening over an accidental overdose? It was as if the entire world had lost its mind, and my son was alone in the center. What happened to the need for proof? Wasn't there going to be an investigation first? What happened to the assumption of innocence?

With a 0.02% chance of winning one acquittal, Scott had a zero percent chance of escaping all three charges, regardless of his innocence.

During the first year of his incarceration, Scott was in a confused cognitive state due to his withdrawal from fentanyl. As a result, he was often bewildered and could not process the information he received from his attorneys. Learning for the first time that he could be imprisoned for 15-20 years seemed like another hallucination, not reality.

I forced myself to do what I thought I would never do: I advised my son to accept the 15-year deal. There was no other way out. The prosecutor immediately dropped the additional charges after Scott pleaded guilty to the first charge for *"lack of evidence."* But the prosecutor changed the plea deal from 15 to 20 years because *"I did not like the number of motions filed by the defense attorney...they wasted my time."* Five more years of Scott's life because his attorney was trying to do his job.

The power the prosecutor held over his precarious situation belatedly sank in for Scott and the family, as did the powerlessness of the judge. We had entered an alternate reality that we did not understand. What *choice* did Scott have but to plead guilty? *He* knew he was not a dealer but now knew the prosecutor would stop at nothing to win at trial, regardless of the lack of evidence. Scott felt betrayed by a system that was uninterested in the truth.

Scott: *"I had an idea from the beginning that the DEA wasn't interested in justice because they told my mom after my arrest that I was going away for a long, long time. I first learned I could be facing 20 years in prison, about 2-3 months after being arrested, at the height of my insanity. When I received the plea deal, I wasn't clear on what was real and what another hallucination was, but I felt sure that there was no way that this could be real, that there must be some sort of mistake. I'd never been in legal trouble before. I felt for the first time that I might end up in prison for TG's overdose. It was so strange that the prosecutor didn't ask me anything about my case. I kept expecting someone to dig deeper into my case to find BZ. When I realized no one, including my worthless defense attorney, was doing anything and no one was interested in learning the facts... that's when I felt genuine fear for the first time in my life. Knowing the prosecutor was not interested in justice scared the shit out of me because I knew for sure she could convict me of anything, and I would be helpless to fight back."*

Selecting an Attorney

After Scott was arrested, we found a criminal attorney and explained Scott's situation, asking if he had experience working on federal cases. He assured us he had federal expertise and knowledge; later, we learned he did not. For the first two years after the DEA arrested Scott, I railed against his attorney's incompetence. But the truth is, it does not matter who the attorney is; you will lose a federal criminal case regardless.

In the fall of 2023, Paul and I attended the *Rewriting the Sentencing Project II*, held in Washington, DC. Most of the 500 attendees were judges, prosecutors, advocates, and federal defenders. After speaking with several federal defenders, I deeply regret hiring a private attorney. Accepting a federal defender is the best choice because they know the prosecutor and how to play the game. They do not seek to win; they seek the best deal possible for their clients and are well-versed in accomplishing that goal. If we could restart this process, we would have sought a federal defender for Scott.

Losing is to be expected; mitigating the loss is the only victory.

Consequences of Plea Deal

Plea deals relegate the accused to a horrible long-term situation. Reading from Scott's plea deal: *"... in exchange for a 'voluntary' plea of guilty to 1 count of drug-induced homicide, the defendant 'fully understands' he forgoes the following protections:*

1. *The defendant waives all rights to appeal any sentencing issue.*

2. *The defendant waives all rights to appeal any non-sentencing issues.*

3. *The defendant agrees to waive all rights to contest the conviction or sentence in any post-conviction proceeding, including Title 28, US Code, and Section 2255.*

4. *The defendant waives all rights to request any records from any US agency pertaining to the investigation or prosecution of this case. This includes any information sought under the* Freedom of Information Act.

5. *The defendant understands that there is no right to parole.*

6. *The defendant can never say he is not guilty."*

Scott's guilty plea was not *voluntary,* and he did not *fully understand.* The six statements are predicated on the notion that *"the defendant fully understands..."* The plea-bargaining process was completed during Scott's first ten months of opioid withdrawal in county jail when he could not fully understand anything.

Another consequence of Scott's plea deal was the actual perpetrator, the *dealer* BZ, walked away free. Weintraub (2020) argues that this outcome is the norm when prosecutors engage in misconduct. Increased prosecutorial misconduct is associated with decreased odds of identifying the actual perpetrators because prosecutors waste resources framing the wrong people for crimes.[260] Society rewards prosecutors for high conviction rates and lengthy sentences, <u>not for getting it right</u>. Upon reflection, Scott said:

"This was my and my family's first exposure to the criminal justice system; we didn't even know there was a big difference between the state and federal legal systems and ended up hiring a 'state' attorney for a federal case. It didn't help that he failed to explain the difference and misrepresented his experience. That's how naïve we were of the situation that I was in. I always believed that in the US legal system, you were innocent until proven guilty; I found out that you are assumed guilty until you can be proven guiltier. For example, when I wouldn't cooperate and plead guilty to a 15-year sentence, they [the prosecutor] *decided to indict me on two additional random felonies in which I was, according to a St. Louis County police investigation, a victim. How is that even possible to be charged like that...is that even legal? Once I was indicted on the additional counts, instead of 15 years, I was looking at a minimum of 60 years and a maximum of 3 life sentences, which was absolutely the most insane thing I had ever heard since I had never been in serious trouble before. I can't think of anyone who wouldn't plead guilty with that much time on the line and the deck stacked against them. I felt I had no choice but to say I was guilty. After pleading guilty, the other charges were dropped for lack of evidence. For me to get acquitted, I would have to go to two different trials and win on all three counts-- and all this over an accident?? I naively believed that a prosecutor's job was to find the truth. I didn't know prosecutors force* guilty pleas *to make themselves look good; it has nothing to do with guilt or innocence. It has nothing to do with justice. The more cases a prosecutor wins, the greater the chance they can be considered for a higher position or office. The system encourages prosecutors to win by <u>any</u> means necessary...and they do that by making up the rules as they go. It seems no one in the system cares about justice, nor do they care when prosecutors take even worse actions than the defendants. Who is the real criminal here?*

---

[260] Weintraub, J. N. (2020). Obstructing Justice: The Association Between Prosecutorial Misconduct and the Identification of True Perpetrators. *Crime & Delinquency, 66*(9), 1195-1216.

Plea Deals

Plea bargaining as a systematic alternative to trials did not emerge until the 20th century. From 1900 to 1925, the guilty plea rate rose from 50% to 90%.[261] Throughout the 20th century, plea bargaining became increasingly prevalent.[262] Numerous concerns have been raised about the coercive nature of plea bargaining, its role in encouraging the forfeiture of procedural protections, and its role in fueling mass incarceration.

The main benefit of plea bargaining is that it allows prosecutors to avoid costly, unpredictable trials. But at what cost to justice?

According to Turner (2020), one problem with plea deals is that they are negotiated in private and off the record, resulting in a lack of transparency.[263] Victims, the public, and the defendant are typically excluded from the negotiations, which makes studying plea deals virtually impossible--the First and Sixth Amendments, which establish the rights of public access, do not apply to plea negotiations.

Fixing the significant failings of America's justice system is much more difficult when common and fundamental court operations, such as plea bargaining, are concealed. As a result, plea bargaining is primarily shielded from outside scrutiny, which blocks oversight of coercive plea bargains, untruthful guilty pleas, and unequal treatment of defendants. It can hinder defense attorneys from providing fully informed advice to their clients. It can also potentially impair *victims'* rights and interests. Finally, the absence of transparency leaves judges with few guideposts to evaluate plea deals and inhibits informed public debate about criminal justice reform.

---

[261] Dervan, Luciant (2024). Fourteen Principles and a Path Forward for Plea Bargaining Reform. *American Bar Association*, Jan. 22.
https://www.americanbar.org/groups/criminal_justice/publications/criminal-justice-magazine/2024/winter/fourteen-principles-path-forward-plea-bargaining-reform/#:~:text=Although%20little%20data%20are%20available,50%20percent%20to%2090%20percent.

[262] Dervan, L. E. (2018). Bargained justice: The history and psychology of plea bargaining and the trial penalty. *Federal Sentencing Report, 31*, 239.

[263] Turner, J. I. (2020). Transparency in Plea Bargaining. *Notre Dame Law Review, 96*, 973.

Neily (2019) says, *"...plea deals are often made quickly, and given the lack of transparency, lies by the prosecutor are the norm."*[264] When the accused has an opioid use disorder, plea deals become much more complicated, at least morally, if not legally. During the period when a plea is usually negotiated, the opioid addict is embroiled in the excruciating pain of withdrawal, is cognitively confused, and possibly experiencing hallucinations. It is implausible that these individuals are legally capable of entering into such an important, life-changing contract until at least a year has passed with no opioids. Once a deal is secured, the defendant forfeits all the protections of a trial, such as the right to an appeal, and can never declare they are not guilty. The implication is that those individuals forced to plead guilty can never bring the information of coercion to light. Crespo (2018) argues that plea bargaining operates in secrecy and incorporates a third body of law, the *sub-constitutional law* of criminal procedure, that establishes the mechanisms by which prosecutorial plea-bargaining power is generated and deployed.[265] When Congress awarded prosecutors the power to create plea bargains, they inadvertently allowed for a new, unwritten sub-constitutional law, the law according to prosecutors.

According to some researchers, plea bargaining evolved in the unregulated gaps of our criminal justice system and is driven not by law but by prosecutorial power.[266] As plea-bargaining scholars have long recounted, prosecutors' ability to threaten inflated sentences and their power to trade those sentences for pleas of guilt allows them to control *"who goes to prison and for how long."*[267] The justice system has abandoned efforts to

---

[264] Neily, C. (2019). Jury Empowerment as an Antidote to Coercive Plea Bargaining. *Federal Sentencing Report, 31*, 284-286.

[265] Crespo, A. M. (2018). The Hidden Law of Plea Bargaining. *Columbia Law Review, 118*(5), 1303-1424.

[266] i) Kipnis, K. Criminal Justice and the Negotiated Plea (1976). *Ethics, 86*, 93.

ii) Ortman, W. (2016). Probable Cause Revisited. *Stanford Law Review, 68*, 511.

iii) Sklansky, D. A. (2016). The Nature and Function of Prosecutorial Power. *Journal of Criminal Law & Criminology, 106,* 473.

iv) Luna, E., & Wade, M. (2010). Prosecutors as Judges. *Washington & Lee Law Review, 67*, 1413.

v) Miller, M. L. (2003). Domination & Dissatisfaction: Prosecutors as Sentencers. *Stanford Law Review., 56*, 1211.

[267] Stuntz, W. J. (2004). Plea Bargaining and Criminal Law's Disappearing Shadow. *Harvard Law Review*, 2548-2569.

impose legal restraints on prosecutors through regulation. Substantive criminal law now penalizes so much conduct so severely and regularly that it merely delegates power to prosecutors. This delegation of power has transformed prosecutors into administrators of an *"unwritten criminal 'law' that consists only of their own discretionary decisions"* to charge certain offenses or to offer specific deals.[268]

Meanwhile, the constitutional law of criminal procedure supposedly regulates government power but imposes virtually no constraints on prosecutors' plea-bargaining practices. Thus, plea bargaining operates *"outside the law's shadow,"* governed only by brute prosecutorial power exercised in ways not written anywhere, let alone governed by formal legal standards.[269] Crespo (2018) contends that plea bargaining is lawless according to substantive and constitutional criminal law. The prosecutor *alone* determines the charge(s) and the appropriate sentencing range. For example, in Scott's case, the prosecutor decided to file a DIH charge, which carries a mandatory minimum of 20 years. The prosecutor could have just as easily decided to charge Scott with manslaughter, often a seven-year sentence, or with any other charge, or with no charge at all. It is easy to see how allowing prosecutors to control the charge(s) empowers them to control the sentence length.

Mallgrave (2020) argues that the *Commerce Clause* limits the federal government's authority to prosecute co-users who share the drugs that ultimately cause an overdose.[270] Furthermore, by charging co-users with drug-induced homicide, federal prosecutors threaten to derail local efforts to mitigate the overdose crisis. As my son's case highlights, federal prosecutors can and do bring charges for real or imagined offenses, change sentences at random, threaten those charged, threaten family members of those arrested, force guilty pleas, ignore evidence, silence judges,

---

[268] Stuntz, W. J. (2001). The Pathological Politics of Criminal Law. *Michigan Law Review, 100*, 505.

[269] **i)** Lanni, A., & Steiker, C. (2015). A Thematic Approach to Teaching Criminal Adjudication. *St. Louis University Law Journal, 60,* 463.

ii) Crespo, A. M. (2015). Systemic facts: Toward institutional awareness in criminal courts. *Harvard Law Review, 129*, 2049.

[270] Mallgrave, A. (2020). Purely Local Tragedies: How Prosecuting Drug-Induced Homicide in Federal Court Exacerbates the Overdose Crisis. *Drexel Law Review, 13*, 233.

intimidate defense attorneys, and deny constitutional rights. These were all part of our experience with the US criminal justice system.

Take, for example, how Scott dared to refuse the prosecutor's invitation to plead guilty in exchange for 15 years, even though she knew BZ was the dealer. At that point, none of us had any idea what we were up against because we had little to no understanding of the *actual* administration of so-called justice. Within two days, he was indicted on two additional contrived felonies, exposing him to 60 years in prison. Tactics like this have been long criticized as illicit coercion but are also seen as an inevitable feature of the administration of criminal law.[271] Since defendants lose 99.98% of their cases, going to trial hoping to win is illogical. Knowledgeable defendants will often go to trial despite knowing they will lose. They do it to retain all the rights foregone in a plea agreement.

Academics and practitioners studying the problems with punishing prosecutorial misconduct agreed that the disciplinary measures in place are grossly inadequate.[272] Most recognize that, although misconduct should not be tolerated, the lack of accountability results in an implicit acceptance of wrongdoing. Caldwell (2013, 2017) argues that "...*to deter further misconduct and abuses of power, prosecutors must be punished*

---

[271] **i)** Barkow, R. E. (2005). Separation of powers and the criminal law. *Stanford Law Review, 58,* 989.

ii) Stuntz, W. J. (2001). The pathological politics of criminal law. *Michigan Law Review, 100,* 505.

iii) Easterbrook, F. H. (1991). Plea bargaining as compromise. *Yale Law Journal, 101,* 1969.

[272] **i)** Gershowitz, A. M. (2008). Prosecutorial shaming: Naming attorneys to reduce prosecutorial misconduct. *University of California- Davis Law Journal. Rev., 42,* 1059.

ii) Henning, P. J. (1999). Prosecutorial misconduct and constitutional remedies. *Washington University Law Quarterly, 77,* 713.

iii) Jalain, C. (2021). Punishing the Powerful: A Study of Prosecutorial Misconduct in the Era of Ethics Reforms. *Scholarly Open Access Repository.* https://soar.usi.edu/handle/20.500.12419/8.

iv) Joy, P. A. (2006). Relationship between Prosecutorial Misconduct and Wrongful Convictions: Shaping Remedies for a Broken System. *Wisconsin Law Review,* 399.

v) Schoenfeld, H. (2005). Violated trust: Conceptualizing prosecutorial misconduct. *Journal of Contemporary Criminal Justice, 21*(3), 250-271.

vi) Weintraub, J. N. (2020). Obstructing Justice: The Association Between Prosecutorial Misconduct and the Identification of True Perpetrators. *Crime & delinquency, 66*(9), 1195-1216.

more severely than attorneys who hold less distinguished and privileged positions."[273] For example, prosecutors guilty of misconduct could be punished as willful perjurers and levied heavy penalties. Punishing prosecutors may help, but it could produce unintended consequences, just as it has with drug sentencing. A 2018 *Brennan Center for Justice* Report provided specific examples of common-sense legislation, including eliminating imprisonment for low-level crimes, reforming prosecutor incentives, and making sentences proportional to crimes.[274] Unfortunately, without a significant change in the justice system's attitude, neither punishment nor changing incentives for prosecutors will be sufficient to bring about meaningful, lasting change.

Consider a coin toss with both sides equally weighted by guilt and innocence; there is a 50% chance it will be heads and the same for tails. In an ideal world, we could reasonably expect the defense and prosecuting attorneys to be equally matched so that the defense wins 50% of the time. However, it is not reasonable to believe that the pool of defendants is 50% guilty and 50% innocent, so this expectation must be adjusted to account for sufficiently well-qualified police and DEA agents. Assuming the police are correct 'most' of the time, the pool of defendants will be weighted toward the guilty. Therefore, a conviction rate of 70%-75% would seem about normal. But a 99.98% conviction rate implies the 'game' is indisputably unfair. Something is wrong with the way the US practices 'justice.'

Secretive plea deals are neither theoretical nor abstract—they are used in practice every day. As US District Judge John Gleason observed in a 2013 ruling, *"The government's use of certain draconian sentencing provisions during plea bargaining coerces guilty pleas and produces sentences so excessively severe they take your breath away."*[275]

---

[273] i) Caldwell, H. M. (2013). The Prosecutor Prince: Misconduct, Accountability, and a Modest Proposal. *Catholic University Law Review.*, *63*, 51.
  ii) Caldwell, H. M. (2017). Everybody talks about prosecutorial conduct, but nobody does anything about it: A 25-year survey of prosecutorial misconduct and a viable solution. *University of Illinois Law Review,* 1455.
[274] *Brennan Center for Justice* (2018). Prosecutorial Reform. https://www.brennancenter.org/issues/end-mass-incarceration/changing-incentives/prosecutorial-reform
[275] US vs Lulzim Kupa (2013). United States District Court, *Eastern District of New York.*

The Criminalization of Addiction

As mentioned on the first page of this book, drug addiction is a progressive disease that is best handled as a *medical* problem. By criminalizing drugs, we have moved the person with a substance use disorder from the medical arena to the legal one. Rather than regulating drugs, instituting fines, or making drug use a misdemeanor punishable by going to a licensed rehabilitation facility, the US solution is to imprison everyone accused for a long time. If that does not work, then make the sentences even longer. The harsh US policies around drugs mark users as criminals and thus contribute to the overwhelming disdain directed toward people contending with a debilitating and often fatal *medical* disorder.

The criminalization of addiction has fueled a rise in prosecutorial power and misconduct. It was effortless for the prosecutor to sentence Scott aggressively because the case involved fentanyl. Just the word *fentanyl* elicits such fear in society that it makes it easy for prosecutors to get away with anything in those cases.

There is growing support for legislative efforts to address the harms of fentanyl via DIH prosecutions. In late 2016, US Representative Tom Reed of New York introduced the *Help Ensure Lives are Protected Act* to specifically allow federal prosecutors to seek capital punishment or life imprisonment for people linked to an overdose death caused by heroin laced with fentanyl. Florida, for instance, expanded its DIH law to include fentanyl in 2017. Underlying such efforts are fundamental misperceptions about fentanyl distribution, namely, that the people selling it are aware their drugs are laced and are purposefully poisoning their unwitting customers. The justice system has not yet caught on to the fact that advanced opioid addicts are actively seeking fentanyl as their drug of choice; Scott and TG are two examples.

During the 2023 legislative sessions, 46 states introduced hundreds of fentanyl crime bills, according to the *National Conference on State Legislatures*. An Iowa law makes the sale or manufacture of less than five grams of fentanyl — roughly the weight of five paper clips — punishable by up to 10 years in prison. Currently, 12 states do not have specific DIH laws, but legislation is pending in several of them.[276] The remaining 38 states have enacted DIH laws, with penalties ranging from manslaughter to first-degree murder.

For example, Arkansas, Florida, Illinois, Indiana, Nevada, New Jersey, Oklahoma, Pennsylvania, and the District of Columbia have DIH statutes that allow first-degree murder prosecutions of people who socially share drugs that contain lethal fentanyl doses. Several states passed legislation to enhance criminal penalties relating to fentanyl, including establishing mandatory minimums. Arkansas and Texas recently passed legislation creating the offense of drug-induced homicide, which includes a criminal penalty for an individual who delivers fentanyl that causes death. North Carolina also passed legislation to enhance sentences for drug-induced homicide and increased the fines imposed on people convicted of trafficking certain substances. Pending legislation in Pennsylvania would provide similar penalties, as well as creating the specific offense of fentanyl delivery resulting in death.

The BOP perpetrates the criminalization of addiction inside prisons where drug use is considered as serious as murder and rape. People with an addiction are forced into the system and further tortured by frequent and extended stays in the SHU for their drug abuse.[277] The US is on the wrong path to solving the country's addiction problems. If incarceration could cure addiction, then the solution to all drug problems would be obvious, and the US would be the most drug-free country in the world since we have the highest incarceration rate. Instead, without help, the person with an addiction becomes worse and, when imprisoned, is unmanageable by the system. The cycle of abuse continues with the participation of the prison system. Once released, the person with an addiction will too often either die from an overdose or be reincarcerated.

Recommendations
The criminal penalty enhancements (including execution) enacted for fentanyl, combined with the social fear surrounding the drug, have

---

[276] *Prescription Drug Abuse Policy System* (2019). Drug Induced Homicide Laws. No DIH laws in: Alabama, California, Hawaii, Idaho, Kentucky, Maine, Maryland, Montana, New Mexico, Ohio, South Dakota, and Utah. Alabama and Kentucky are considering proposed DIH legislation.

[277] SHU-Special Housing Unit. Known publicly as *'the hole.'*

empowered prosecutors to use their offices in any way they see fit, with no concerns about community reprisals. Researching prosecutorial misconduct can quickly lead to discouragement because many articles from 50 years ago discussed the same problems experienced today. Yet, nothing has changed. Many types of prosecutor punishments have been tried, such as appeal court reversals, professional sanctions, judicial reprimands, civil penalties, and criminal prosecution. None of these have worked because the parties involved in the punishment refuse to act.

The *Office of Professional Responsibility* (OPR) already oversees the conduct of lawyers, including prosecutors. While the OPR has done a more than adequate job of policing defense lawyers, it has accomplished next to nothing regarding prosecutors.

Several innovative approaches have been suggested, but further research revealed that they had already been considered and discarded. For example, the idea of creating another position for a person to oversee *"justice"* was discarded because that is a fundamental responsibility of judges, despite the challenges created by mandatory minimum sentences. A proposal from the *Fair Justice Agency* outlined a similar oversight proposal, but the USSC rejected it as redundant to the OPR.

The only thing that has not been tried is rewarding prosecutors for 'getting it right.' Theoretically, two existing mechanisms could curtail prosecutorial misconduct or overreach:

1) **Lawyer Ethics** and **Disciplinary Boards**. State prosecutors (OPR applies to federal prosecutors) often sit on state ethics boards for attorneys, significantly influencing the proceedings and hearings. No evidence has been found that state ethics boards have disciplined a prosecutor. Therefore, these control mechanisms exist in theory only, as they are never used in practice.

2) **Adjudicatory Remedies** through the **Courts**. Court remedies can take the form of judges punishing prosecutors who fail to follow the law and punishing those who have harmed the other party. In theory, both options seem reasonable. However, judges do not impose penalties on prosecutors, and the Supreme Court has provided prosecutors with complete immunity from civil damages. One of the most significant ironies of the judicial system is that prosecutors, like many defendants, are guilty of breaking the law. No one charges the prosecutor, so they are not at risk of

being punished for having *wrongly imprisoned thousands of people and ruined countless lives.*

Why have all the tools designed to maintain the balance of power failed to hold prosecutors accountable? In the language of psychologists, prosecutors are surrounded by fearful *co-dependents*. Many honorable lawyers have failed to speak about unethical prosecutors, thus enabling their breaches of behavior. The silent co-dependents include practicing defense lawyers, judges, ethics board members, attorney disciplinary bodies, and court employees who have observed prosecutorial misconduct yet have failed to act out of fear of reprisals.

Sullivan (2015) offers some workable suggestions for reducing abuses of power:

1) **Require Open-File Discovery**: The *Brady rule* (1963) grants prosecutors too much leeway in sharing information with the defense.[278] One solution is to mandate a verifiable *'pretrial open-file discovery'* requirement for all cases. Under open-file discovery, a defendant can access the prosecutor's files to avoid trial surprises.

2) **Revoke the Harmless Error rule**: Often, when prosecutors are accused of misconduct, they invoke the *'harmless error'* rule. The harmless error rule allows a conviction to stand even if prosecutorial misconduct occurred. Congress must revoke the *'harmless error rule,'* and any convictions must be reviewed when prosecutorial misconduct exists.

3) **Publish Names**: The names of prosecutors who engage in misconduct must be identified in trial and appellate opinions.

4) **Change to Qualified Immunity**: Currently, prosecutors enjoy absolute immunity from civil damages for misconduct. Congress must change this to *qualified* immunity instead of *absolute* immunity.

---

[278] The *Brady rule*, named after Maryland vs Brady (1963), requires prosecutors to disclose material, exculpatory information in the government's possession to the defense. However, it sets no specific timeframe for providing the information.

5) **Appoint the DOJ's *Office of Inspector General*** to investigate alleged misconduct by federal prosecutors.[279]

Schoenfeld (2005) argues that trial judges should use their inherent authority to forbid prosecutors from handling cases until they have completed training on *Brady v. Maryland, Batson v. Kentucky*, and other examples of prosecutorial misconduct.[280] He also argues that trial judges have the inherent authority to impose a training requirement on prosecutors to ensure the orderly administration of justice. Knowing that a respected trial judge in a sizable jurisdiction is enforcing a training prerequisite for prosecutors would likely encourage other judges to adopt similar (or perhaps even more rigorous) training requirements. Prosecutors receiving mandated ethics training before handling cases is comparable to some state legislatures' enhanced training requirements for indigent defense lawyers. If a judge demands adequate training before prosecutors can handle cases in her courtroom, the district attorney's office will then have two options to comply:

1) Assign better-trained prosecutors (who already have completed the judge's training requirements) to that judge's courtroom or

2) Provide the necessary training to more of the office's prosecutors.

Suppose judges oppose prosecutorial misconduct, do not like having their decisions reversed, and do not like less-qualified lawyers. What would they do if a colleague who imposed training prerequisites was only assigned the best-trained prosecutors?

Schoenfeld posits that the other trial judges will insist on the same (or better) training and competency required by the first judge, saying,[281]
"In the past decade, investigations into wrongful convictions have uncovered multiple incidents of prosecutorial misconduct during trial. To the public, prosecutors are agents of trust, and prosecutorial misconduct is viewed as a violation of the norms of trust. We explain how the structure of the trust relationship creates motivation and opportunities for

---

[279] Sullivan, T. P., & Possley, M. (2015). The chronic failure to discipline prosecutors for misconduct: Proposals for reform. *J. Criminal Law & Criminology, 105*, 881.
[280] Schoenfeld, H. (2005). Violated trust: Conceptualizing prosecutorial misconduct. *Journal of Contemporary Criminal Justice, 21*(3), 250-271.
[281] Schoenfeld, H. (2005). Violated trust: Conceptualizing prosecutorial misconduct. *Journal of Contemporary Criminal Justice, 21*(3), 250-271.

misconduct. Motivation to engage in misconduct stems from prosecutors' definitions of success, which are influenced by the reward structure of the system. Opportunities for misconduct arise because of the organization of the prosecutorial role and weak sanctions for prosecutors' misbehavior. Given the motivation and opportunity, prosecutors' decisions to engage in misconduct depends on their evaluations of existing opportunities, which is influenced by their workplace subculture and their values and beliefs."
"Current remedies for prosecutorial misconduct, such as reversal of conviction or dismissal of charges, are rarely granted by courts and thus do not deter prosecutors effectively. Further, such all-or-nothing remedial schemes are often problematic from corrective and expressive perspectives, especially when misconduct has not affected the trial verdict. When granted, these remedies produce windfalls to guilty defendants and provoke public resentment, undermining their expressive value in condemning misconduct. To avoid these windfalls, courts refuse to grant any remedy at all, either refusing to recognize violations or deeming them harmless. This often leaves significant non-conviction related harms unremedied and egregious prosecutorial misconduct un-condemned and undeterred."

The irony is that when the justice system overlooks misconduct, prosecutors often disregard the law to the same extent as those sent to prison. The implication is that criminals, or misbehaving prosecutors, are running the DOJ. Prosecutors are well aware that their conduct violates the law but are unconcerned that it will result in removal from their position. When the wrong person goes to prison, prosecutors such consequences would force a system of checks and balances on prosecutorial power and refocus their energy on finding the truth.

Starr (2009) suggests a less extreme approach where sentence reductions could be prescribed by a legislature (or sentencing commission) as a remedy for prosecutorial misconduct.[282] Oversimplifying, Starr's article explains how judges could be empowered to reduce a defendant's sentence incrementally in response to prosecutorial misconduct. Departures from the original sentence could be required or recommended. The magnitude of the allowed reduction to the original sentence could be indeterminate or be determinant within a range of specified reductions. Congress would

---

[282] Starr, S. B. (2008). Sentence reduction as a remedy for prosecutorial misconduct. *George Mason Law Journal*, 97, 1509.

need to pass a law allowing judges to reduce the mandatory minimum sentence by increments in response to prosecutorial misconduct.

Joy (2006) recommends reinvigorating the state bar associations to perform their primary function: licensing and governing conduct by attorneys in their jurisdictions.[283] While they supposedly hold attorneys accountable for violating legal and ethical obligations, state bars rarely reprimand prosecutors.

Prosecutors are rewarded for longer sentences and higher conviction rates, so it is no surprise that data shows more prosecutions and longer prison stays. Humans tend to act in their own best interests, so the incentive system for prosecutors must change. The question is: How does society incentivize prosecutors to become agents of justice who delve into the case facts and make a fair determination? Perhaps prosecutors cannot fill that role, and a reimagined justice system needs to be established.

A Word from Scott

It was not a coincidence that rampant prosecutorial misconduct was present in my first experience with the justice system. It happened because it is common practice. Many others before and after me will experience the same. The knowledge that prosecutors do not have to follow the law and there are no consequences made the whole process terrifying. I was petrified because I could not base my expectations on the law; instead, a biased and vindictive prosecutor would determine everything.

While in county jail waiting for trial, I had 2 or 3 face-to-face interactions with the prosecutor. Mostly, my attorney relayed communication from her to me, and most of it was bullshit stuff designed to make my life even more miserable. For example, my mom owned the house that I lived in at the time of my arrest. One week before the detention hearing, the prosecutor threatened to indict my mom for "owning and operating a drug house." The prosecutor made this threat in response to my mom saying she would like to speak on my behalf at the detention hearing. The prosecutor did not like this, so she issued the threat.

---

[283] Joy, P. A. (2006). Relationship between Prosecutorial Misconduct and Wrongful Convictions: Shaping Remedies for a Broken System. *Wisconsin Law Review*, 399.

Initially, we believed my chances of being able to stay at my parent's home while the case progressed through the system were promising because I had strong family ties and no previous arrests. Multiple people wrote to the judge in support of home confinement. At the hearing, the judge denied my request, and I spent 2.5 years in a county jail from the time I was arrested until the time I was sentenced.

Perhaps the most telling misconduct was when I declined the prosecutor's 15-year offer in exchange for a guilty plea. Within 24 hours, the prosecutor created two new felony charges against me:

<u>Charge #1</u>: A second DIH charge in the death of my friend CP. The St. Louis County police had already solved this case and were holding the dealer, making it clear this was a made-up charge.
<u>Charge #2</u>: Conspiracy to ... not sure. The prosecutor charged me with some conspiracy related to CP's death, but I do not remember the wording. At this point, I was laughing (it's better than crying) in my head, thinking this is so insane. Does anyone take this show seriously? How can someone with no criminal history, no weapons, and no violence face 60 years to life in prison?

The prosecutor told me, "...we plan to try you on TG's case first, and we will win. You will then have a history of fentanyl distribution resulting in death, and it will be easy to convict you on the other charges."

As it happened, the prosecutor made it crystal clear she was manipulating me when both charges were immediately dropped after I pleaded guilty to the initial charge. When guilty pleas are coerced, the whole process becomes a farce.

From this experience, we knew the prosecutor could and would do anything to imprison me. I chafed for a long time about the threat to my mom; I thought, who is going to believe that a tenured professor owns and operates a drug house? Then I remembered reality and knew it didn't matter; the prosecutor always wins. If the prosecutor wants it to be a crime, then it is.

After I was arrested, the agents interrogated me while I was under the influence of multiple drugs. I do not remember what I said, but they had it on videotape. Later, after I sobered up, I told my story again, and the prosecutor called me a liar. That accusation cut deep because I was trying to be careful and precise when relaying the series of events. To be summarily dismissed as a liar was so demoralizing. Yet, there is nothing to say or do to have your word accepted unless you lie to confess guilt. The word 'justice' is a misnomer when applied to people with addiction issues.

I was stunned by the prosecutor's response when I asked about the third party at my house (my dealer, BZ). The prosecutor responded, "Why didn't you bring this up during the initial interrogation? And why is this the first time I have heard of this?" I explained it was in my text messages, and I thought she had read them. The prosecutor simply said, "I don't believe you." Regardless of the facts, the prosecutor chooses the events that best fit her narrative.

It was not only me they coerced into making statements, but also their so-called 'witness,' KN, who was one of my roommates. When the DEA agents came to my house on 2/11/2019 to arrest me, they found KN passed out on the couch with a loaded fentanyl syringe right next to him. The agents took KN to an interrogation room and threatened to send him to prison for fentanyl possession if he did not tell them I was his dealer. Surprise, surprise, KN did just that. The fact that KN was already a convicted felon meant that he would be facing a long time in prison if convicted of fentanyl possession. The specific statements KN made about me were fed to him by the agents and were fabricated, but the prosecution did not care because his story fit her narrative of the 'crime.'

I naively believed that the prosecution sought justice and that the truth mattered; this is why I never thought they would sentence me to 20 years. Prosecutors have too much power, and you know what they say about power? "Power corrupts, and absolute power corrupts absolutely." In our judicial system, prosecutors are the closest to having absolute power; this is given to them by their immunity from prosecution for their 'mistakes.' If prosecutors had something to fear, it would go a long way toward correcting oversight of our judicial system. Another major problem with prosecutors is their reward structure. Prosecutors are rewarded based on the number of convictions and the length of sentences. In an environment where one has absolute power, this creates a strong incentive towards convicting many people and sentencing them to long incarcerations, regardless of guilt or innocence. Just think about it: in an environment where one has virtually endless power and controls all aspects of court negotiations to produce the desired outcome, would it not create the temptation towards corruption? Considering that there are zero consequences for a prosecutor's misbehavior and many rewards for keeping conviction rates high, their behavior is expected. Of course, prosecutors will do whatever is necessary to keep that conviction rate high.

The prosecutor threatened me and my family, coerced me into signing a ridiculous plea deal, and coerced lies from my roommate because it went with their predetermined narrative of the events that transpired that day. There is no 'justice' to be sought in an accidental death; my guess is that TG would never have wanted any of this to happen on her behalf. If there is some warped view of justice that needs to view some fentanyl addicts as innocent victims (the dead ones) and others as murderers, then there is nothing I can do about that.

As an addict who still practices, I can tell you that what I needed was to be forced into a long-term rehabilitation center for several years. I know professionals say that forcing someone into rehab does not work, but consider the alternative. I believe I would have died from an overdose within six months if I had not been arrested. Dead people cannot choose to go to rehab. There is NO CHOICE except to force rehab on advanced opioid addicts because the alternative is death. I don't know how many years I would need in rehabilitation to be safe from myself, but professionals in the field would be able to help me figure it out...if there was such a thing.

Summary

Prosecutorial misconduct represents a fundamental breakdown in the criminal justice system and undermines the legitimacy of the entire system. Legal scholars seem to agree that the disciplinary measures in place for prosecutors are grossly inadequate. Most recognize that, although misconduct should not be tolerated, the lack of accountability results in the implicit acceptance of wrongdoing. Prosecutorial misconduct flows from an environment that accepts, overlooks, and encourages it.

According to legal ethics rules, prosecutors are *supposed* to act as *"ministers of justice,"* but the system incentivizes them to seek higher conviction rates and longer sentences. A more comprehensive method for incentivizing prosecutors is needed to change the focus from "punishment" to "justice." Justice requires weighing both sides of the story and, when appropriate, dismissing the case or reducing the sentence. Genuine justice requires a system that either rewards prosecutors for getting it right or restricts the power of the office.

The most remarkable feature of these critical, sometimes life-and-death decisions made by prosecutors is that they are totally discretionary. The danger with prosecutorial discretion lies not in its existence but in its random and arbitrary application. Even in prosecution offices that promulgate general policies for the prosecution of criminal cases, there are no effective mechanisms for enforcement or public accountability. With the aggressive use of plea deals, prosecutor behavior has become almost impossible to manage, as evidenced by using sentencing to punish or reward defendants in matters unrelated to their crimes. A climate of crime politics, congressional micromanagement, and prosecutorial power have emerged, destroying the promise of the *Sentencing Reform Act*.

As scholars of plea-bargaining have long recounted, prosecutors' ability to threaten inflated sentences and their power to trade those sentences for guilty pleas allows them to control *"who goes to prison and for how long."*[284] The law has abandoned any legal restraints on prosecutors through regulation. When laws penalize so many behaviors so severely, it only delegates even more power to prosecutors, transforming them into administrators of an unwritten criminal 'law' that consists only of a prosecutor's discretionary decisions to charge certain offenses or offer specific deals.

With impunity, prosecutors across the country have violated their oaths and the law, committing the worst deception in the most severe cases.
They do it because they can.
They do it to win.
They do it because they won't get punished.

---

[284] Stuntz, W. J. (2004). Plea bargaining and criminal law's disappearing shadow. *Harvard Law Review*, 2548-2569.

CHAPTER 8: PRISON LIFE

By G. Scott Hancock

Introduction

A few months after my 29th birthday, my life drastically changed for the worse. However, that's somewhat debatable because when I was free, I wasn't doing much with my life except abusing drugs; fentanyl was my drug of choice. I was near death, with possibly three months left to live, when I was arrested on February 11th, 2019. My life forever changed that day when federal agents from the *Drug Enforcement Agency* (DEA) arrived at my home in St. Louis, MO, to *'talk'* to me. They didn't want to talk; they were beginning the process of my arrest. Before formally arresting me, they first wanted me to confess to a crime I did not know had been committed. I learned from them for the first time that a friend, TG, had died from a fentanyl overdose, and it was somehow my fault. At the time, I had no idea I was even being arrested, much less what for. I was so high on multiple drugs, including fentanyl, clonazepam, marijuana, methamphetamine, and crack cocaine, that I thought the agents wanted to help me get my roommates out of the house.

I thought they were there to help me evict them, but to my surprise, they were there for an entirely different purpose. The DEA agents took me downtown to the main office and put me in an interrogation room with multiple detectives. I remember very little of the hours of interrogation by the DEA agents. All I remember is that I was trying my hardest to appear sober because I didn't want them to arrest me for a drug charge. I soon realized the charge was for something much more severe: a *drug-induced homicide*.

My girlfriend in 2018, KT, used to get fentanyl for TG, but then KT left to go to rehab in Ohio sometime in the late summer of 2018. Before KT left, she asked me to help her friend TG obtain fentanyl if she ever needed it because TG didn't know where to get it except through KT, and she didn't want her to end up dope sick. So, for three months, I answered TG's phone calls and would get fentanyl for her when she asked. After that, I never heard from her again. I thought she had found another connection for drugs because I told her I did not want to keep doing this; it was too much trouble. I learned on February 11th, 2019, that the real reason I had not heard from her was that TG had died from a fentanyl overdose four months earlier.

I was not surprised to hear of TGs death because, during the past 18 months, three friends had died of fentanyl overdoses. Death is accepted as a natural outcome among fentanyl users. You almost become immune to the repercussions of using fentanyl.

In one of my texts to TG, I specifically stated I was not a drug dealer, made no money, and was tired of being inconvenienced at random times. Neither the DEA agents nor the prosecutor showed any interest in that particular text message nor the one specifying the drugs would come from my dealer, BZ. Instead, they focused only on the messages about when we would meet at my house for the exchange. Later, I learned that the laser focus on me was because TG's father wanted me held responsible for her death and told the prosecutor he wanted me to go away for a long time. TG's whole family vibrated with anger towards me, denying she had any part in her overdose and wanted me to pay with my life. I most likely *would* have paid with my life if I had been free for another month or two.

During the interrogation, I learned that I had been under surveillance for the past four months. This fact interested me because it seemed they were trying to catch me in the act of selling fentanyl. Of course, they never did, and, finally, they gave up trying and arrested me anyway. The prosecutor decided, before my arrest, that I would be charged as a dealer because I was the man TG's family wanted to punish. Once the prosecutor focuses on a desired outcome, that's how it is. Case closed.

The prosecutor had one 'witness,' my roommate, KN, also a fentanyl addict. He told the DEA that I got drugs for him, which I did, but he also got drugs for me. That's the way it works with opioid addicts. The bottom line is that it did not matter what KN said because he disappeared as soon as the police let him go and was no longer available to question or serve as a witness.

Anyway, the DEA took me from the interrogation room to a *municipal* jail that was used as a federal holding facility in St. Louis, MO. While in jail, I was kept in a cell with bars around it, like the old-school jails you see in the movies. I never learned much about that jail because I only stayed a few days before being transferred to a *county* jail in Illinois, about 90 miles from home.

County Jail

I began my 20-year federal sentence at the county jail in Illinois, another federal holding facility for St. Louis, during withdrawal from fentanyl. Opioid withdrawals have been the worst experiences of my life. It is hard to describe the disorientation and physical pain. Suffice it to say that all people with an opioid addiction spend 100% of their time trying to avoid withdrawal. I've told other stories in various chapters about my opioid withdrawal experiences, so I'll leave it at that.

At first, my mom came every weekend, but then we settled into a pattern of every other week until COVID-19 hit the jail in the fall of 2020. After COVID-19 infiltrated the small Illinois town, visitations were frequently canceled over the next two years, resulting in more loneliness and isolation from my family.

Over the next 28 months, while waiting for sentencing, I was introduced to an *entirely* new way of life. At the same time, I was trying to understand my case and fight for my freedom because of the severity of the charge. I had significant 'brain fog' and could not think straight for months. When I arrived at the county jail, the guards brought me in through the garage and photographed me. After the photo session, I dressed in the same clothes as the other inmates: scrubs. At the jail, five different blocks held inmates; it didn't seem like there was any natural order, except that one cell block was for 'protected' cases, and another was for people who were racist against blacks. Segregating a group for racism was a brand-new concept to me because I was not raised in a racist environment and had never experienced white people who hated that deeply—until I went to jail. I was initially held in cell block 4, the largest block, and was put into a cell with some guy; I don't remember his name. That only lasted about two days when the guards moved me to cell block 3, the second largest.

While in cell block 3, I saw that we could fill out commissary requests once a week and order phone cards and E-cigs daily. I always kept enough money in my account to order at least an E-cig a day, which made me very popular with the other inmates because they were ridiculously expensive.

It was $12 for a single E-cig, each having about 120 puffs. A cigarette doesn't last long when five other inmates are taking hits.

Figure 8.1.   **The County Jail, IL**

I was in block 3 for a few weeks when I got a new cellmate ('celly'), Jake, who was annoying. He had a strange sense of humor, and I didn't click with him. An example of dumb stuff: Jake had a tattoo of *State Farm* on his arm, as in Jake from *State Farm*. He thought it was so funny, but I am not sure why. I realized quickly that none of the other inmates were people I would have chosen as friends on the outside, but it is what it is. Within a month of being at the county jail, the prosecutor sent my first plea deal, offering 15 years in exchange for a guilty plea.

I could *NOT* believe it! 15 years? Why? Guilty of what? This arrest was my first time being in trouble with the law; I was *not* a dealer, no force or weapons were involved, and both of us knew we were taking fentanyl; each of us did so by choice. So, why the hell were they talking about so much time for an *accidental* overdose? At this time, I still held on to hope that justice was real and would prevail since I was not a dealer. The prosecutor charged me under *Title 21*, which requires the government to prove the 'drug dealer' claim and a few other things. I thought, *'Great, it's impossible to prove I am a dealer when I am not. Who are my customers? Where is all the money I supposedly make? Where are the drugs? Why didn't they see me selling while observing me for four months?'* I fully admit to being a drug addict, but I was never a drug dealer, although I tried once. That did not end well, and there was no going back for me. I had burned bridges and knew I could not stop using the product.

In TG's case, my dealer, BZ, arrived at my house about 15 minutes after I called to tell him I needed some fentanyl. He came in my back door, grabbed a blender, and started bagging up caps of fentanyl. After he had some caps made up, he gave 3 to me to try. I emptied all three caps into a spoon, put some fire to it, threw in a piece of cotton from the end of my cigarette, and drew the spoon's contents into a syringe. I then proceeded to inject the contents of the syringe into my arm and started nodding out. About 30 minutes had passed when I received a text from TG saying she was outside. I told BZ I would have $20 for him shortly, so he handed me another five caps. I took the five caps out of my front door to TG's car; I got in the car and handed the caps to her. She gave me the money and drove me around to the back of the house. I went in the back door and handed BZ $20. As was always the case, I received no compensation for the transaction. Now, I am in prison for 20 years for those actions despite not being a dealer. While fighting my case from county jail, I thought about this situation nonstop and felt sure someone would care about the truth. No one *ever* asked for my side of the story, not even my attorney.

While in county jail, my mom visited once a week, and my stepfather, Paul, frequently joined her. The visits were the only thing that gave me the strength and hope to hold on. All my 'friends' on the outside dropped me, except one, BR, but we had grown far apart. I met BR in middle school, and we hung out through high school, but he never became part of the drug crowd. He also never 'dropped' me. Apart from BR, I never saw or heard from any of my previous friends or acquaintances…it was as if I did not exist anymore. Even my dad would not come to visit me. In the five years I've been in prison so far, I have seen my dad only once. He flew from Albuquerque, NM, to Orlando, FL, rented a car, and drove to FCI Coleman prison; he lasted 2 hours and then left. If not for Mom and Paul, I would not have anyone.

Unfortunately, we all knew so little about the system because no one in our family had ever been to prison or gotten in legal trouble. Our naivete and our attorney's lack of knowledge resulted in an additional five years added to my 15-year plea offer. As mentioned earlier, I rejected the first plea deal mostly because I was pretty sure this whole thing was a hallucination. It did not seem real that no one in the system cared about justice; guilt or innocence did not matter. I had an exceedingly difficult time getting that through my head. I still have a hard time with that one. I can't believe it, even though I've lived it.

In due course, I pleaded guilty after the prosecutor intervened to indict me on two additional random charges. When the case entered the evidentiary hearing phase, I saw the prosecution's evidence against me. Not surprisingly, there wasn't much; there were only two things: the text messages and KN as a witness. I knew I did not have to worry about KN showing up to the trial because he had already disappeared. With hindsight, I laughed at how naïve I was--I actually believed it mattered what KN and the text messages said.

I am still somewhat angry with my private lawyer because of his dishonesty; I blame him for not counseling me on the prosecutor's 15-year offer. During their initial talk, my mom asked him whether he had experience in federal court. He said he did and implied he was very successful. But later, I learned that private attorneys are a waste of money because, at the federal level, ALL attorneys lose to the prosecutor. Don't waste your money. The only thing my attorney succeeded at was annoying the prosecutor; that's about it.

I experienced my first feelings of complete and total hopelessness when the prosecutor added two random charges to the DIH charge. I would face three federal charges, each carrying a mandatory minimum sentence of 20 years. I now understood the power of the prosecutor, and I was scared shitless. I knew there was no chance of winning despite being innocent of all the crimes for which I was charged. I am not saying I am innocent, period; I am saying I'm not guilty of being a *dealer*, a requirement for the DIH charge. I am guilty of being a fentanyl addict and guilty of facilitating TG's fentanyl purchase.

My hopes were crushed; I was going to spend my life in prison, and there was no way out. I pleaded guilty to the first DIH crime, and the prosecutor dropped the two made-up charges, but my life, as I once knew it, was over. The *Eastern District of Missouri Federal Court* scheduled my sentencing for March 2020, but COVID-19 closures hit, and a large backlog of court cases developed. No in-person court appearances were often allowed; instead, the courts held hearings via video conference. I moved from a double cell downstairs to a single upstairs, which was enjoyable because I didn't have to deal with a celly. I am an introvert, and one of the things I miss most is having alone time. I received many books from my family while in county jail, which helped me. I wasn't a reader on the outside, but on the inside, I grew very fond of it, especially in county jail, because it was an escape from reality. I didn't watch much TV, but I followed a couple of TV series to help pass the time. Things became more digital towards the end of my time in county jail. They got a texting device that we could use to text our family (if you had the money), and they made commissary ordering digital! We were able to have video visits on the commissary ordering screen.

Finally, the day of my sentencing arrived on April 9th, 2021. I was so nervous, still expecting that the judge would see that I was not a drug dealer and issue me less time than 20 years. Oh, how naive I was. Instead, I was ushered into the courtroom with chains around my legs and arms and was seated in the defendant's area. TG's family filled every seat in the courtroom; there was no room for my mom and stepdad--the only people there for me. Both my lawyer and the prosecutor tried their best to stop my parents from coming…but they did anyway. The judge eventually sat them in the jury box alone because there was no more room. I remember the prosecutor talking, and for a minute, I thought she was on my side. She spoke about how TG and I were both addicts; she mentioned my various stays in rehab. I was thinking, *"Yes, that's right!"* But we quickly moved from there to I should be locked up, and before I knew it, the judge brought the gavel down and sealed my fate. The guards transported me back to the county jail to wait for the signal to leave for prison. I had no idea what to expect from a prison relative to a jail, but I was getting ready to find out.

Racism Behind Bars

While growing up in St. Louis, race did not seem much of an issue. I never gave it much thought, probably because I was white living in the suburbs. I liked 'black' music; I listened to rap but never gave much thought to the artists' color. There was no segregation of races in my schools; the kids did everything together.

There is no doubt racism is still a significant problem in America, but it pales in comparison to racism in prison. The county jail was my first introduction to *real* racism. Once in prison, I experienced an entirely new level of racism: *segregation*. There are three main race groups in prison: whites, blacks, and Hispanics. Each group claims specific cells, and problems quickly arise when the guards put the wrong race in a cell. Racism runs in all directions, with whites being racist against blacks and Hispanics, blacks being racists against whites and Hispanics, and Hispanics being racist against blacks and whites. Hispanics are okay with being around whites, if necessary, but it is not their first preference. Although the blacks seem to hate whites the most, they argue they *cannot* be racist because they are black. I haven't figured that one out yet. In the dining hall, the races segregate themselves just as they do with the cell blocks. The guards do not try to force combining the races because it causes too much fighting and uproar. The guards want peace, not the 24/7 war that would result from mixing races. When races occasionally roll together, caution is necessary because, without a doubt, someone will try to get something over on somebody.

FCI Coleman Medium, FL

In June 2021, the BOP assigned me to the *Federal Correctional Institute* (FCI) Coleman medium-security prison in Florida with 38 points against me, 34 for my crime, and 4 for my age. The FCI-Medium security prison is on the *Federal Correctional Complex* (FCC) Coleman. The Complex consists of camp-level, low-, medium-, and high-security prisons plus an administrative level; it covers them all.

Interestingly, the BOP, not the judge, determines the prison security level. I thought the judge would assign a security level at sentencing, but the BOP determined that later by evaluating various factors. Each factor is assigned a point value: you want to get as few points as possible. The lower the number of points, the lower the assigned prison security level. I read a lot about the different federal prison levels while sitting in county jail, and a summary is included in **Appendix 8A** if you are interested.

FCC Coleman opened in 2001 and is in central Florida, approximately 50 miles northwest of Orlando, 60 miles northeast of Tampa, and 35 miles south of Ocala. One thing immediately stood out as different from county jail: everyone was laser-focused on how to make money. I quickly learned there was an underground economy in prison where services and products were available to those with money.

Additionally, once a week, we went to the commissary and could spend up to $90 (if you had it) on various stuff, such as food, clothing, shoes, personal hygiene products, and more. There is seldom enough to eat, so the commissary is a lifesaver. Like myself, many inmates relied on friends and family for commissary money; others had money before coming in, and then there were the forgotten guys who had nothing beyond their prison job money and money made on the side. Life is rough for those who cannot make money on the side. Everyone needs money in prison, even if only for personal hygiene.

The need for money creates a problem because most prison jobs pay meager wages while prices are astronomically high. This difference creates a gap between available resources and needs, requiring creative solutions. Guys do various jobs to make money, including tattooing, sewing, laundry, selling food, selling drugs, etc. I learned to make taffy from ingredients purchased at the commissary--it was easy and pretty popular! Everyone at Coleman was working or hustling, usually both. Aside from your prison job, the main problem with making money is that almost all the methods could result in a shot. For example, I could have gotten a 'shot' for making taffy because I used heat and sugar--both illegal. These types of shots are not usually serious unless they involve drugs.[285]

Drug shots are in the 100 series category, indicating the most severe infractions with the harshest sanctions. I never received a shot for anything during my stay at Coleman because I lucked out on the one drug test and never even went to the *Special Housing Unit* (SHU). On the outside and in movies, the SHU is called the 'hole'—it is where inmates are sent to solitary confinement as punishment for a shot.

As with the county jail, soon after I arrived at Coleman, I went to orientation, where the officers explained the rules of FCI Coleman-Medium in detail. I was assigned a counselor and case manager, my so-called '*team.*' A team meeting would be required every six months to review my progress in prison. At these meetings, your team can adjust your

---

[285] See Chapter 2 and Appendix 2A for more detail on shots.

The Criminalization of Addiction

points (up or down), adjust your record, and update your program status. My first team meeting was very close to the date I arrived, which was helpful because I learned several things not covered in orientation.

I learned about shots and random *urinary analysis* (UA) tests from my team. I was now officially terrified. My addiction had not disappeared just because I was in prison. The team can put almost any sanction they wish on a prisoner for drug use. For example, officers can send an inmate to the SHU indefinitely; they can withhold food; they can send an inmate to a higher security prison; they can increase an inmate's points, reduce *good time*, etc. All bad, bad stuff. Good time equals the length of your sentence times 15% since the BOP will release inmates after serving 85% of their sentence with good behavior. In my case, I started with three years of good time (0.15*20 years).

My first celly, DT, was a 300-pound sociopath with severe bipolar disorder who was exactly where he belonged: in prison. DT was manipulative and cared *nothing* about anyone but himself. I quickly learned that DT was lazy and frequently scammed people out of their money while laughing behind their backs. Unfortunately, he also had something I wanted: his skill as a tattoo artist.

The other inmates were all from other federal prisons, and I learned from them the different types of drugs available. It seemed you could get almost any drug you wanted if you had the money, but the most prevalent drugs were Duce and Suboxone. *Duce* is a prison name for K2 or spice, but it can be almost anything. K2 and spice are types of synthetic cannabinoids.

Synthetic cannabinoids are not organic but chemical compounds created in a laboratory. Duce is sold as a dot on a piece of paper that you can smoke. When I say it can be almost anything, I mean it--some say it is cockroach spray; others say it is some other sort of poison; who knows? Drugs in prison are far from pure. I can personally attest to the dangers of some of these drugs. I first tried Duce while in county jail; the doses were weak in the beginning, but they got stronger with each new batch coming into the jail. I noticed the more potent it was, the more paranoid I became.

Figure 8.2.   **Coleman Federal Correctional Complex
Medium Security**

As time passed, things got better as inmates came and went. There were always more inmates coming in than going out. Around July/August 2021, a bus arrived at Coleman to drop off some new inmates. One was named Vincent Ingino; we called him *Gino*. He and I hit it off immediately, first becoming card buddies. Spades were our game, and we beat pretty much everyone. Finding good competition in prison was difficult, so this was a nice break. We also found common ground personally, as we were in prison on the same charge of DIH.

In Gino's case, the prosecutor charged him with *two* deaths related to fentanyl-laced heroin. He had no idea the heroin was laced and still doubts it was his drugs that killed his two best friends. The reason for Gino's doubt was that he had also taken heroin and had no ill effects. He rejected the prosecutor's attempts to force him to plead guilty and opted to take his case to trial. Of course, he lost. The judge sentenced him to 50 years but allowed the sentences to be served concurrently, resulting in 25 years. We understood each other's pain. My mom included his case in her podcast because he took his case to trial but still lost and ended up with a 25-year sentence based on very suspicious evidence.

Gino was trying to get inked up by my celly, DT, and in doing so, he noticed that DT and I were not getting along living together. Even so, living with DT was the *only* way to compel him to do my arm and leg tattoos. That's how lazy he was. He couldn't even be bothered to go to someone else's cell...you had to live with him to get him to tattoo you. I also got part of my chest done but never finished because I couldn't take it anymore, so I moved out. Gino was ready to get his tattoos started, so we figured out a way for me to move out so Gino could move in with DT. I did my best to describe what it is like to live with a bipolar sociopath, but Gino was determined to get the tattoos. It took us a little while to organize the cell swap, but we did.

I moved in with Gino's celly, JS, from Seattle, Washington, and Gino moved in with DT. It was odd that JS was only sentenced to 10 years because he was a previously convicted felon who was caught in a hotel room with multiple firearms and drugs. He was a quiet, introverted individual who had attended some college but then dropped out, but he was damn smart for someone in federal prison. Like many others in prison, he was a junky, and one day he and I did Suboxone and Duce at the same time, which gave a heroin-like high. It felt incredible, like what I had been missing!

At least 80% of the inmates here have committed *intentional* crimes, far from anything resembling an *accidental* overdose. Yet, the system gives them far less than the 20 years I received for an accident. It seems the judicial system is blind to the entirely different personalities and mindsets of those who *intentionally* harm other people, which are absent in most drug addicts. People with an addiction spend most of their time trying to hurt themselves, not others. That's why finding friends in prison who are not drug addicts has been difficult—I stay far away from the type of people who intentionally hurt others; they're dangerous. But I agonized over their stories and wondered how an accident resulted in such severe punishment relative to these peculiar people who intentionally hurt others.

Society must not realize how different people with an addiction are from those who have no problem hurting other people, primarily sociopaths. Then there are the super sickos, psychopaths that enjoy hurting other people; you want to stay far, far away from these people. It was, and it is, hard not to become bitter. I am working on acceptance because there is no other choice. My favorite saying since I've been in prison is: *It is what it is.*

One night, at about 3 am, the guards came to take me for my first random UA test after being at Coleman for a year. I knew drugs were in my system, but I had no choice other than to comply. I urinated in the cup, the guard put my inmate number on it, and off it went to the lab. I started dreading what would happen to me. Would they take away visitation? Put me in the SHU? Take away commissary? A few days later, I learned a shipping delay combined with excessive heat had destroyed the integrity of the lab samples. I was incredibly lucky that time but began to get nervous about when it would happen next. It never did, at least not at Coleman.

By the fall of 2021, I had a job with the morning lawn crew to work the prison yards three days a week. Gino and another guy, Smiley, also got a job on the same crew, so it worked out well to have their moral support. Our job involved pulling out these old push lawnmowers and cutting the grass—man, it was exhausting! We were always covered in sweat from head to toe when we finished. It was a great job, though, because we were at pay grade one, which was $70 a week plus a $35 bonus, so I was getting paid $105 a week for three days' work. Each day, we only worked about an hour or two. There were even 2-3 months when I could only work one day a week, but I still got paid $105 each week!

'Lawn crew' was a great job, and I thought the extra money would help me, but I used it *all* to buy Suboxone. I started becoming obsessed with obtaining and using Suboxone, fearful of running out and not being able to get it. At one point, JS and I started using a needle to shoot it. We got the needles from a couple of diabetics and would use them until we couldn't use them anymore. We made a 'binkie' out of them by attaching the needle to a rubber suction tube at the end. We used the tube to suck up the drug. I have no idea how I didn't get Hepatitis C, but according to testing, I didn't.

I heard about a *Medically Assisted Treatment* (MAT) program that was supposed to be available to opioid addicts in federal prisons. I certainly qualify. MAT is a program that allows opioid addicts to use controlled amounts of Suboxone, administered by the staff, to help manage their addiction. I desperately needed such a program and searched Coleman for information. MAT had not yet made it to Coleman; it would be another nine months before I could apply to the program.

When MAT finally arrived at Coleman, JS was the first to apply. He showed me the MAT program paperwork, and I learned I needed to file a BP8 and a BP9 form, indicating sensitive documents that go to the warden or region to resolve an issue. After JS filed these documents and the appropriate people approved them, he became the first person at Coleman-Medium to be accepted into the MAT program. I had been trying to get on the enrollment list since arriving at Coleman but never passed the first step, requiring a visit with the psychologist because too much time remained on my sentence. So, the commanding officer put my case on the back burner regarding enrollment in the MAT program. Luckily, once I got to USP Atlanta, an advisor took me seriously and helped me get into the program by expediting my enrollment. Although the rejection at Coleman had been disappointing, it helped smooth the way for me to accelerate the MAT process at USP Atlanta.

It seemed the whole time I was at Coleman, I was broke. I needed a hustle. I noticed that some inmates resold their purchases from the commissary to make money, or they would create something from their purchases and sell it for *books*. 'Books' refers to *books of stamps*; one *book* is worth $10. In prison, the inmates use stamps as currency. I knew of a few inmates making good money selling cigarettes, which sounded like something I could do. There was just one tiny problem…I was addicted to nicotine, too. That wasn't the only problem. In this prison, ONE cigarette can cost $50!

After three-plus years in prison, I had saved all my birthday and Christmas money plus a refund from my car insurance, so my total savings were a little over $4,000. I took $500 to buy *one* pack of cigarettes, hoping to make $1,000. It did not work out that way. I underestimated how many I would smoke and overestimated the number of inmates that could afford $50 per cigarette! Even so, I kept it up because I was determined to get at least one hustle right! So far, I was failing big time. I spent all $4,000 in less than six months on drugs and attempting to do the cigarette hustle. Between the drugs and the failed hustles, I was flat broke. My adaptation to the prison environment was not going as well as I had hoped, but I was learning my way around better every day.

Repeated lockdowns characterized my days at Coleman due to the spread of the COVID-19 virus. COVID-19 resulted in many guards and administrators quitting or retiring, resulting in even longer, more stringent lockdowns. The guards did not needlessly harass the inmates, but they mainly did their jobs, according to the book. I worked out five days a week, was on lawns three days a week, and spent the remainder of the time trying to make money, and the time passed quickly.

There were gangs at Coleman-Medium, but I stayed far away from those people. Minor fights broke out regularly over stupid stuff, like card games or breaking in line. More serious fights would break out over turf and race issues, but everyone would get locked down when things got bad. I expected violence of some sort every day, maybe from the guards, maybe from other inmates. There was one incidence of significant violence when the guards put a gay guy in a cell with the wrong inmate; he ended up with his throat slit.

In November 2022, my case manager told me my points were low enough to qualify for a low-security prison. The move is typically handled within a few months when an inmate qualifies for a different security level. However, the manager said there was nowhere to move me right away, so she would have to put a *management variable* on my report so I could stay at Coleman. A *management variable* reflects the support of the BOP that a prisoner has the points necessary to go to a lower (or higher) security prison but must remain where they are for management reasons, which is almost always related to space availability. For me to stay at the medium-security prison with low points, they put a management variable in my file. I was expecting to be at Coleman for a while.

Less than ten days later, Coleman initiated a mass transfer of those inmates with management variables for a low-security prison. At first, I was elated, thinking I would never have to worry about being locked in a cell again because there would be no cells at a low-security prison! That is until I learned we were going to USP Atlanta, which had recently reopened as a low-security prison. I learned quite a bit about USP Atlanta from other inmates, guards, and articles my mom sent. The BOP opened USP Atlanta in 1902 to house high-security federal inmates. It was one of the three penitentiary facilities created by the *1891 Three Prisons Act*, which also created the federal prison system. It turns out that USP Atlanta has had a chilling recent history.

For many years, the federal penitentiary in Atlanta was a shelter for corruption and abuse. Staffers routinely helped traffic weapons and drugs. It had consistently operated as one of the most dangerous prisons in the federal system.

According to Senator Jon Ossoff, D-GA, *"These were stunning failures of federal prison administration that likely contributed to the loss of life. Conditions for inmates were abusive and inhumane and should concern all of us who believe in our country's constitutional traditions."*[286] A 2020 report written by a Senate panel formed to study USP Atlanta concluded that a constellation of security lapses contributed *"to a dangerous and chaotic environment of hopelessness and helplessness, leaving inmates to their own means to improve their quality of life."*[287] The findings revealed security breakdowns, staffing shortages, misconduct, and the rapid spread of the deadly COVID-19 virus. *"Interviews and records reveal a facility where inmates, including presumptively innocent pretrial detainees, were denied proper nutrition, access to clean drinking water, and hygiene products; lacked access to medical care; endured months of lockdowns with limited or no access to the outdoors or basic services; and had rats and roaches in their food and cells,"* Ossoff said.

As a result of the investigation into USP Atlanta, the BOP fired most of the staff and sent 1,100 prisoners to other federal prisons in different states. Only 134 inmates remained inside the prison. The prison closed for the summer and fall of 2021 and supposedly underwent a "security alignment" from medium to low. I'm not sure what that 'alignment' was supposed to be, but USP Atlanta still looks, feels, and operates like a high-security prison today. It still has barbed wire all over the buildings, roofs, and perimeter, and the guards keep inmates locked in cells.

FCI Coleman-Medium sent 3-4 busloads of inmates to USP Atlanta-Low, and I was in one of those. Several people I knew were transferred with me,

---

[286] Boone, Christian (2021). Atlanta Federal Pen Nearly Vacant Amid Corruption Investigation. *The Atlanta Journal-Constitution*, Aug. 20.
[287] Johnson, Kevin (2022). Atlanta Federal Prison 'Lacked Regard for Human Life'; Weapons, drugs Trafficked, Senate Panel Says. *USA Today*, July 26.

but not Gino. I wasn't expecting to be involved in the mass relocation, but one day, an officer called me to *Receiving & Delivery* (R&D) and told me to pack my stuff for transfer. No one told us where we were going, when we were leaving, or how far the ride would be--that's their way. The guards give inmates as little information as possible; they expect us to behave like cattle. We are not deserving of information in the eyes of the guards and are lucky to have food 'wasted' on us.

The inmates heard through the prison grapevine about USP Atlanta reopening, so we had some idea of where we were going. The guards told me to pack all my stuff, and I did, but it was not until four nights later that the buses came for us. Those four days living without anything, including a change of clothes and hygiene products, were miserable. Our *property* was all boxed up and sent via snail mail to Atlanta.[288]

Finally, the guards came for us in the middle of the night, took us to R&D, and put us into the 'tank.' The tank is a large holding cell where they can put a bunch of inmates; it has a bathroom and sink, and that is it.[289] While in the tank, the guards told us to pick our cellies and to choose someone with whom we could peacefully coexist. Pete, a Coleman buddy, and I chose each other to be USP Atlanta cellies.

Guards took us out of the tank individually, told us to strip naked, and then searched us. We then sat nude on a chair while the next inmate was searched. When finished, we were handcuffed and sent to a second tank to wait for the others to finish processing. In any other environment, this would be considered sexual assault, but the prison system has institutionalized this type of assault under the pretext of security. I have never heard of anything ever being found in a prisoner's butt; strip searches are mainly to denigrate the inmate.

The humiliating experience requires us to do a series of weird things buck naked. For example, open your mouth wide, run your hand through your hair, show your armpits, lift your ball sack and penis, turn around and show the bottoms of your feet, squat, spread your butt cheeks, and cough. It is incredibly degrading and humiliating. Being buck naked in front of guards

---

[288] In prison, 'property' includes your clothing and anything purchased at the commissary.
[289] The 'tank' is also called the 'bullpen.'

and prisoners while they inspect you reminds me of stories of enslaved people who were paraded naked and inspected by prospective slaveholders. The BOP should abolish strip searches, except for exceptional circumstances. Allowing guards to strip search anyone at any time for no reason beyond wanting to do so is inappropriate and ripe for abuse.

I remember it was freezing when we walked out of Coleman in handcuffs to board the bus that would take us to our new destination. Half asleep, we shuffled into the buses and began our journey to a hell I never thought I would experience. It wouldn't be long before I ached to be back in a medium-security prison.

We boarded the bus with no time to recover from the strip search. I sat near the back of the bus with Pete and was given a bagged lunch for the duration of the trip. The entire trip took about 7 or 8 hours. When we finally arrived, I was shocked by what I saw; it was like something out of a spooky movie. I noticed that the prison was surrounded by a 30-foot wall covered in double barbed-wire rolls. Even the roofs had rolls of wire covering the surface. We pulled into this strange garage-type area to unload the bus into USP Atlanta's R&D.

Once again, we were put in a holding tank to begin the same process we endured when we left Coleman. The guards asked if anyone had reasons to believe they couldn't *"walk this yard."* The guards asked this question so that people who are vulnerable to violence (e.g., gays, child molesters, etc.) can opt to go into a different tank. A few people indicated they couldn't *walk the yard* and were taken away, but I do not know what happened to them afterward. For the remaining people, they took us, one by one, for an initial medical exam. An officer, maybe a *Special Investigative Supervisor* (SIS), took us to get prison IDs, and the next day was orientation.

USP Atlanta-Low

On my first day at USP Atlanta, I jumped back into old habits right after moving into the cell with Pete.[290] Within 4 hours of arrival, someone offered me some Duce, and I said yes. Using drugs was a terrible way to start my time at a new location. I had not been doing Duce for at least a month before leaving Coleman, but I heard the quality of the substance in Atlanta was amazing. Naturally, my addict brain thought it was a good idea to try some, and I felt I could easily handle it. I took three hits, and the next thing I knew, I was paralyzed by paranoia. This time, the Duce was displayed on reddish wax paper; I had never seen this before. A previous inmate warned me that it may be highly potent when Duce is presented this way. Being a drug addict, I ignored all advice and proceeded to wrap the paper in a wire, put the wire ends to a battery to spark a flame, and inhaled the smoke with a type of crack straw. I had an acute reaction that resulted in repeatedly banging my head against a wall. My head and eyes were black and blue for weeks, and it left no doubt in anyone's mind that I was an incoming addict. It was this incident that convinced me to stay away from Duce. I remember thinking, surely this can't be any stronger than I had at Coleman. Wrong again!

Another thing I was wrong about was lockdowns. We were locked down the first night at 9:30 pm for a 10 pm count. The guards count all the inmates four times per day, and each time, we must be locked down in an assigned place, usually our cells, unless we are at work or in the visiting room. I took the three hits of Duce at about 9:15 pm and was experiencing extreme paranoia. I walked to the cell door to open it, but it wouldn't open. Terrified, I panicked! I started butting the door with my head as hard as possible to get out. What bad timing! The guards hadn't begun the count yet when they heard me banging my head as hard as I could into the door. They immediately called for backup, knowing they had a bad situation.

When bad situations arise, almost every guard on the compound will aid the other guards. One of the guards, a caring woman, was trying to count and paused to beg me to stop hitting my head on the steel door. But I *couldn't* stop. Shortly, backup arrived, and I was swat-tackled to the floor with what felt like 1,000 pounds of guards on me.

---

[290] The name *USP Atlanta* was changed to *FCI Atlanta* in April 2024.

Figure 8.3.   USP Atlanta

The guards dragged me up and carried me by my arms and legs out of my cell while I screamed, *"I can't breathe."*[291] In retrospect, that wasn't the best choice of words because George Floyd had recently been killed by the police while shouting those words. I was taken somewhere, and I don't remember where, but it was probably the SHU. I did not stay there long. I was taken back to my cell at about midnight. When I got back to my cell, I asked Pete where the rest of the Duce was, and he told me he flushed it because so many guards were coming into the room. That was the right decision, of course, but at the time I was pissed. The Atlanta Duce was the cheapest and best quality I had ever experienced, and rather than stay away, I continued using it for several months, even after this horrifying episode. I never had another episode, but I was hanging around with a bunch of addicts again, which leads to trouble in prison just like it does on the outside.

My buds were TW, Pete, and my two *homies*. In prison, when you are from the same place as another person, you are called their *homie*. RN was my homie from Pensacola, FL, where my family lives and where I will live when I leave prison. GR was my homie from St. Louis, where I grew up. GR was gay, which can be a dangerous thing in prison. In some prisons,

---

[291] Most of what happened that night, I have learned from inmate/witnesses. I have very few independent memories of that night.

gay people must be in a separate part of the prison for their protection. In the general population, gays are targets for violence. The three of us overlooked it because he kept it to himself and was careful around us.

Eventually, I gravitated away from Duce after the warden visited our unit for an inspection. I was lucky this time, but I started to be concerned about getting caught and was tired of worrying about it all the time. In this instance, the warden smelled weed in our unit and immediately locked us down for five days, from Thursday until Monday. The guards required everyone on the top floor to provide a UA; then, we were strip-searched, and our cells were tossed. If anything had been in my locker, I would have been sent to the SHU immediately.

The BOP claims they don't perform group punishments, yet here we all were, being punished for one person smoking weed. During the lockdown, we decided that this was bullshit because only one person did something wrong, not all of us. We went on a hunger strike to voice our grievances against the treatment we were receiving. Guards took pictures and filmed us refusing our meals—it was the first time I'd been a part of or even seen a group demonstration. Having all the inmates working together towards the same goal was liberating.

After four days, the warden came to our unit and held a meeting to tell everyone that we were off lockdown because he didn't find any drugs in the unit or our cells. About a week after that lockdown, the guards came into the unit and hit us with a bunch of random UAs again. Unfortunately, I was not so lucky this time and failed the UA. For the first time since coming to federal prison, I ended up in the SHU. It was not an experience I ever wanted to repeat. All your standard privileges, e.g., visits with family, commissary, etc., are revoked while in the SHU. It's lonely, boring, and mentally challenging to make it through. I was there for one month. Somehow, I made it through.

The SHU

The *Special Housing Unit* is where prisoners are put in solitary confinement. When the SHU is overcrowded, as it often is at USP Atlanta, then two inmates are placed in a cell. In the SHU, inmates have no access to the commissary, visitors, outside time, or communication with family. I don't think they care about punishing the inmates' families; the attitude is anyone hurt by what is going on in prison deserves it. In USP Atlanta, when an inmate receives a 'shot' for drugs, the first step in the punishment process is at least a 4-week stay in the SHU before the determination of the *real* consequences. I didn't get put in the SHU when I got popped at Coleman. The final punishments for a 100-series shot can be severe. I can't think of anything they *can't* do.

There are 15 possible punishments for 100-series shots, with multiple combinations because more than one sanction is usually selected, and all 15 can be chosen.[292] As previously mentioned, inmates in the federal prison system serve 85% of their original sentence if their behavior is 'good.' Getting a 100-series shot can reduce this *good time*, resulting in serving your entire sentence. Eighty-five percent of 20 years means I must serve 17 years, leaving three years of *good time* at stake. So far, I have been in SHU on three separate occasions, all for drugs, all 100-series shots. I spent three of my first nine months in the SHU, but through a series of unbelievable mistakes, I did not lose any 'good time.' Just when I thought I was safe, I was thrown into the SHU for the fourth time.

First Time

The first time I went to the SHU, it was for a violation of code 112, "*the use of any narcotics, marijuana, drugs, alcohol, intoxicants, or related paraphernalia not prescribed for the individual by the medical staff.*"[293] I failed a UA test, which indicated Suboxone in my system. The way testing works is a guard will call you out of the unit to the main corridor and have a drug test waiting for you in the hallway near the entrance to the building. The guard called my name, came into the bathroom with me, and watched me urinate into a cup. The lab administrator writes your inmate number on the cup and sends it to the lab; it usually takes two weeks to validate the sample. In the meantime, the inmate goes to the SHU to wait for the results. After about 14 days, the Lieutenant called me to his office and told me to read the results. It showed what had occurred and the consequence of a 112 shot.

A guard is always around to ensure you feel more confused and scared than you already are. Can this get any worse? I was reading the

---

[292] See Appendix 2B
[293] See Appendix 2A

consequences of my actions and rested my hand on the desk as I read. A guard immediately yelled at me to get my hand off the desk. I put the offending hand in my pocket, and the guard yelled again, this time for having my hand out of my pocket.

After reading the shot, I noticed something wrong with the amount of drugs listed in the report but chose not to point it out, at least not yet. A guard told me to wait outside for an officer to escort me to the SHU. The trek to the SHU was longer than I expected. The officer and I walked out of the main entrance, past the chow hall, through some fenced gates, and took a right to the R&D building. We made a left as we entered the building, followed the hallway until we passed *Detention Center Unit 2*, and then took a right. There were elevators, which we took down to a hallway that led to a giant sliding glass door. Behind the door was the SHU. Across from the sliding glass door was a large cell where inmates were waiting to enter the SHU. It did not take long for my turn; 15 minutes later, a guard took me to the SHU. I was put in a holding tank and strip-searched, and everything I was wearing was taken from me. Different uniforms must be worn in the SHU, and a guard directed me to change. I was put in a cell with a guy named Chase, my first SHU celly.

Chase came into the BOP during COVID-19, and the policy was to send everyone to the SHU for 15 days before they could go on the compound. The COVID-19 safety policy ensured newcomers were not COVID-positive; it was not meant as a punishment, even though it was. Chase only had three days before going into the general population. I talked with him about what I noticed was wrong with my shot. Namely, there were two different amounts of the same drug shown in my system, a physical impossibility. I started to feel like, maybe, I had a chance of beating this shot.

It took me a few days to get oriented with my surroundings and figure out how to live with new limits. I found it helpful to keep a schedule, and I learned how to *fish* to interact with my neighbors. *Fishing* is when inmates communicate by writing a note and attaching it to a weighted object with a string. The weighted object is thrown underneath the doors to another cell. When the other cell replies, you could pull the string back to your cell and read their response. Fishing is one of only two methods of obtaining information in the SHU.

The Criminalization of Addiction

After the first six days, I received some books and word puzzle games from my mom, so I knew she had received the message that I was in the SHU. I had told RN to call my mom, but I didn't know if he did. I found out that RN had called his mom, and his mom had called mine—the grapevine. I read a lot. I wrote letters to my mom almost every day. I explained what happened and what could happen; I knew it would upset my mom. Once again, I had let my family down and imposed more hardship on them. I apologized to my mom; she said it was okay, but it was not.

A few days later, I got a new SHU celly named MM. MM was unlike anyone I had ever seen or been around. He weighed at least 400 pounds, taking up a lot of space in the cell, and was mentally unstable. MM could not take being cooped up in the same room for so long and had a mental breakdown; he tried to hang himself in the cell after the guards did not give him dessert. Inmates are supposed to get out of their SHU cells at least every three days, but that rarely happens. We were kept in our SHU cells for 15 days with no break. It's not surprising this confinement pushed MM to the breaking point.

There isn't much to hang yourself with inside the SHU. He made a rope from his bed sheet and tied one end to the bunk and the other around his neck. He put all his weight on the sheet and let his body hang loose from the top bunk. I was freaking out and yelling at him that he was overreacting to not receiving dessert. I heard him shout, *"This is too slow!"* I ran over to the bunk and lifted his body as best I could, but his weight made it very difficult. I started yelling for the guards, and they shouted, *"Shut up and stop faking it!"* MM yelled that he was going to kill himself, and a guard yelled, *"Go Ahead!"*

When the guards finally decided to look, they realized this was no joking matter. They hit the radio button that signals all the guards on the compound, and at least ten guards immediately ran down to the SHU. When an inmate emergency occurs in the SHU, the celly (me in this case) must cuff themselves first so the guards can enter. I didn't know what to do...I held MM up to take the weight off his neck and could not risk letting go of him to cuff up. A guard opened the lid for the slot in the door and started pepper spraying the hell out of me and MM. The door opened, and a guard threw me against the wall while another guard threw MM on the ground. They took me to another cell and threw me in before it registered that there was actual shit on the floor. There was no getting out of there until they took care of MM. MM ended up getting beaten by the guards. Beating is the prison solution to life-threatening depression. I was finally let out of the shit-cell and taken back to the regular SHU cell with cleaning supplies to get rid of the pepper spray; it was almost impossible to get rid of the burn and the smell. Even after scrubbing the cell with bleach and washing my hands and face, if I rubbed my eyes, the burn would reignite, stinging me again. It was ridiculous; the smell lingered for days.

MM did not return to the SHU, and I was assigned a new celly, TW. I knew TW from the compound, and we were buds. His papers said he was in the SHU for attempting to steal a Suboxone strip, but TW said that is not what happened. According to TW, the medical attendant gave him another inmate's dose and did not want to admit her mistake, so she blamed him. TW was scheduled to be released in 30 days. It made no sense for him to do anything to break the rules, but the officers convicted him of the shot, and his release date was moved back. My anxiety about what would happen to me spiked. What if an officer took away some of my good time?

I had been in the SHU for 28 days, and it was finally time to see the *Disciplinary Hearing Officer* (DHO). The SHU is just the beginning of the punishment for a 100-series shot. The DHO decides what else will happen because of the shot you received. In the morning, Officer KP (a serious officer) escorted me to the DHO's office. I was so anxious that I was nauseous and weak-kneed and did not notice that a lieutenant standing outside the office door shook his head 'no' at KP. Suddenly, we turned around to go back down the stairs, and I asked what was happening. Officer KP informed me that the DHO had expunged my shot! I was elated. I did not even care why the shot had been expunged, only that it had. I later learned that since the test reported two different amounts of Suboxone in my system, it was ruled unreliable. I was released the same day, which rarely ever happens. I had narrowly escaped additional punishments beyond the SHU. I only wish my addiction had been listening because I would end up in the SHU again for the same reason: Suboxone.

I went back to the compound, and the guards returned most, but not all, of my property. Technically, the prison is not supposed to take the property you purchased at the commissary, but in practice, when you get back from the SHU, nothing is the same. Inmates stole an invaluable pair of scissors and my radio. Clothing and other miscellaneous property had permanently disappeared. Now, I needed more money to replace the missing and stolen property. Losing your property is considered part of your price for going to the SHU. The guards moved me to a different cell on the compound in the B2 wing.

The first time I saw my mom after the SHU, she was visibly shocked by my appearance; I had lost some weight, my eyes were sunken, and I was ghostly pale. The few hours a month I (possibly) get with my family are the only time I am treated like a human.

A couple of weeks after I left the SHU, I started working in the kitchen, thanks to Pete. Pete had a prized position working in the warehouse—where I wanted to work. Inmates like working in the warehouse because there is little oversight, and they can make a lot of money. The warehouse provides one of the very few quiet environments available in prison. Pete introduced me to Anderson, the kitchen boss at the time. I told Anderson about my experience working in restaurants on the outside, and he assigned me to the serving line--the worst position! BOP kitchens are mixed-race, so you must be extra careful about what you say and do because there is a lot of backstabbing and snitching among the workers. This lack of trust makes the kitchen a tense, uncomfortable, and competitive environment. As I mentioned, there is always trouble when the races are mixed.

The salary is meager in the kitchen, $18 a *month* (not per hour, day, or week) for 160 work hours. No one would work there except we are *encouraged* to steal as part of our compensation! There is unwritten approval for kitchen workers to steal food so that the workers can sell the food on the compound to make extra money. Some days, I made $80; others, I made $20 through approved stealing and selling. Warehouse workers can steal in bulk. However, as with most things in prison, stealing is not always easy. Sometimes, a guard will show off by pulling workers aside and removing all their 'approved' items. When a reward for inmates is built on an *unwritten* standard, that standard can be changed instantly based on a guard's personality or mood. It is an extraordinary and random approach to compensation that induces maximum anxiety, mistrust, and

The Criminalization of Addiction

pressure. Besides that, should they really teach prisoners to steal as part of their compensation? What happens to those released when they forget they're not supposed to steal as part of their compensation package?

Living in B2 and working from 4 am to noon five days a week made the time pass quickly. During the first few weeks out of the SHU, my new cellmate was BD, the only other white guy released from the SHU when I was. He was also gay and rich. BD had the prized bottom bunk, so, much to my dismay, I was relegated to the top bunk. Almost everyone wants the bottom bunk because it is easier to access than the top, but the combination of how much time you must still serve and how much each can contribute to the living arrangement determines the outcome.

Although BD had money and didn't care about spending it, he was too reckless. Being gay and loose with money is a recipe for getting your ass beat. BD and I lived together for about 2 to 3 weeks when he got to move back in with a friend of his. During the short period we lived together, BD started buying and smoking Duce. Naturally, I jumped on the bandwagon and smoked, too. This was the last time I smoked Duce, and it proved to be, once again, an abysmal idea. I failed a UA for the second time and was sent back to the SHU, where I stayed for about a month again. When I was first out of the SHU, I tried to be careful about what I put in my body, but I never stopped taking Suboxone. Combining Suboxone with Duce created a heroin-like high for me, which *felt* like just what I needed. It was just what I needed...to go back to the SHU. I was only four days away from being accepted into the MAT program when the medical staff would legally prescribe Suboxone for me.

Second Time

One day, Thursday, I think, I was sitting in my cell with BD and my friend, JS, smoking Duce. We attracted the attention of a guard, Lt. BK, who (apparently) walked past our room three separate times. We were passed out in the chairs each time she looked in. On her third time, she startled us out of our stupor, asking us to step out of the cell to be searched. We staggered out of the cell and were searched, but she found nothing until she searched the room. She started with the lockers and found nothing in mine, but when she searched my celly's locker, she found Suboxone. It's off to the SHU for both of us. When the guards find drugs in a cell, both people must go to the SHU. This time, my shot was a 113, *"Possession of any narcotics, marijuana, drugs, alcohol, intoxicants, or related paraphernalia, not prescribed for the individual by the staff.*"[294] As with the first time, I was subject to any or all possible sanctions.

BD and I went through the process previously described of going into the tank in the R&D building. The guards put us in the cage to get stripped, searched and assigned our SHU cells, but before we got separated, we talked about whose responsibility it was to own up to the shot. At the time, I believed it was BD's responsibility since the drugs were in his locker. However, now, I am convinced it was my responsibility. At the time, I believed my celly may have been using Suboxone, but he swore he wasn't, and I believed him. The most likely explanation is that the guards moved the Suboxone to my celly's locker by accident. When one of the guards recognized what it was, they wrote a shot for my celly, forgetting it was initially in my locker.

I was placed in a cell on the top floor of the SHU, and BD was on the bottom floor. The SHU was even more mentally challenging this time because my celly was Ecuadorian and spoke *no* English. I wondered how the guards could communicate his misdeeds to him or if he was utterly clueless as to why he was there. I'll never know. This time, I was able to let my mom know before I went to the SHU, and we implemented our *SHU Plan*. The *SHU Plan* was for Mom to send me books and word games ASAP. Luckily, I had those things to keep my mind busy, or I would have gone insane.

The SHU seemed to be experiencing a shortage of food. There was never enough to eat; I was always so hungry. I lost almost 40 lbs. in the month I was in the SHU. I later found out that the people who were supposed to be bringing us food were selling it to inmates on the compound instead.

I became eligible for the MAT program on my fourth day in the SHU. Every morning, the nurse gave me a 4 mg strip of Suboxone that saved me. Each day, I looked forward to getting the Suboxone strip, which made the day so much easier. After I got out of the SHU, the dose was gradually increased to 12 mg, and later, the nurse switched me to a once-a-month injection.

---

[294] See Appendix 2A and 2B

While the MAT program helps you avoid searching for opioids, it does nothing for other drug cravings or addictions. There is no demand in federal prison for opioids when Suboxone is available. At USP Atlanta, an excellent nurse practitioner oversees the program. She talks to me at least once a month, and those talks have helped me more than anything. I appreciate all she has done for me.

I slept and read most of the time in the SHU until I became desperate for communication. Then, BD and I started writing *kites* back and forth. *Kiting* is the second form of possible communication in the SHU and differs from fishing. Kites are notes passed around by the orderlies. The orderlies will take your note to another cell and drop it off. Shortly, our concerns about who should take the blame would no longer matter. After 29 days, we both went in front of the DHO, who said, *"This is going to be your one lucky shot, guys. They never tested the strip at medical to see what it was, and it was only identified visually, so there is no hard evidence to back up what it was."* The DHO dismissed the shot, and once again, I had narrowly escaped additional consequences. I couldn't believe it!

After the meeting with the DHO, we were put back in our SHU cells for a couple of days until there was a mass SHU kick-out. We were all put in the tank, and our property was released. The guards gave us a minute to ensure all our property was present before being released back onto the compound. As with the first time, I never found some of my property and valuables. I had lucked out at Coleman with the one UA being overheated; now, the two here were being dismissed. I wish I had stopped, but I did not.

I was assigned a new cell, which was on the B1 wing. I had now been in cells on every floor of building B. My new cell was in the back, where it was easy to hear the guards and anticipate their arrival. This location was perfect because I smoked cigarettes at the time. Cigarettes at USP Atlanta were only $10, rather than the $50 at Coleman, so I could afford to smoke a few.

My celly was a quiet, strange 70-year-old man named RO. We introduced ourselves and went through the usual, *"What are you in for? How much time did you get? etc., etc."* The story RO told me did not ring true at all. In prison, it is tough to hide your charges from other inmates. Someone may ask to see your documentation or use other means to find the truth. If you refuse to show your documents, that means there is something that you want to hide. His story was he was getting people high on his prescription oxycodone and having sex with younger women. One of the women he said he had sex with was 20 years old, which, he said, was considered a minor in the state of Kentucky. Nothing about his story made sense. First, we are in federal prison, not state prison, so Kentucky's laws do not matter. Second, having sex with a 20-year-old is not a federal offense. Later, my mom looked it up and found that the age of consent in Kentucky is 16, and adulthood is 18, so that part of the story was a lie. Lying is a big red flag that something 'bad' is going on with a person, and it's best to stay away.

While living in B1, Pete and I always hung out--he loved that I was in the unit with him. One day, a hefty Texan, about 34 years old, came to my cell and started messing with the old man and kicking his property around. When I say hefty, I mean 6'4 or 6'5 and 240+ pounds. The visits started happening regularly, and each time, the Texan was a little rougher and began calling RO names, such as child molester. Eventually, the Texan hurt RO, and the old man pulled a butter knife on him. Tex didn't like that and pushed the old man down. I calmed the situation, but RO was hurt, so Tex wasn't allowed back on our floor.

I felt sorry for the old man because Tex messed up his back, and now all he could do was lay around all day, and all I did was smoke cigarettes or think about smoking all day. Pete often hung out in our cell, but RO didn't like him because of his slick mouth. Pete doesn't know how to hold his tongue and thinks he is right about everything. It drove me crazy, too, at first, but I adjusted. Not surprisingly, Pete and RO eventually argued over some stupid bullshit. RO would *not* back down from a fight, but no one wants to beat up a 70-year-old man; that's chicken shit. You don't get any cred for beating up Grandpa. One night, we argued over something stupid enough that I cannot even recall the issue. Strangely, RO lay in his bed awake, with his shoes on, until I went to sleep. He was clearly worried that I would beat him during the night. Pete and I never hurt RO, but we never protected him either because there was something he had done that was no good.

One day, I came home from work and found RO had moved a few cells to a handicapped cell. He was likely tired of Pete always being in there and us smoking. I didn't blame him; I was getting tired of Pete, too. A few days later, I got another celly named GN. After asking about him, I learned he stole someone's MP3 player, a costly item. He was just coming out of the SHU, where he had requested to stay as protection from the guy from whom he had stolen the MP3. For better or worse, I could not live with a thief, so I moved out of a fantastic cell with a lower bunk to escape.

A new guy came into B1, MC, who seemed like a good dude at the time; he had a reputation for paying his bills on time. After being around RO, I figured it would be a good idea to check MC's paperwork to see if he ever hurt anyone; he was good because he was in for drugs.

People who are in for hurting kids are on the lowest rung of the prison social ladder. They are at the highest risk of random violence. People who are in for sex crimes are just above those who hurt kids.

On the other hand, people who are in for non-violent drug violations are primarily golden unless they are snitches. An inmate's paperwork shows whether they received a lesser sentence by informing on someone else. Everyone in prison hates a snitch, and it can lead to violence. MC was golden, so I started hanging out with him all the time. I introduced MC to some people in B1 and a few *plugs* on the compound so that he could start making money. A *plug* is someone who can supply you with a mass quantity of whatever you are looking for: drugs, cigarettes, food, whatever it is; the *plug* has connections to it.

MC was initially assigned to B1, but he was supposed to be on the B2 wing because his counselor was there. Coincidentally, I was also intended to be on B2 for the same reason. As it turned out, we were both moved to B2 and put in the same cell. MC and I were about equal contributors, but I got the bottom bunk because I had a longer sentence. Usually, when put into a cell, the setup of the space is determined by who gets the bottom bunk. When you are on the bottom bunk, the room feels more like your own because it is easier to move around and get stuff done. When I'm on the bottom bunk, I take care of all the cleaning supplies and trash for the room, making it feel more like home. Setting up the room as I wanted took about a day, and MC was okay with everything.

It had been a while since I was drug tested, and I started to think maybe they had lost interest. About that time, a new drug came onto the compound, *methamphetamines,* in the form of *ICE.* Pete, MC, and I started smoking it as soon as one of us got some. As it turned out, this was another horrible idea.

About nine days after moving in with MC, I got drug tested again and failed again—this time, they found Suboxone, amphetamines, methamphetamines, and marijuana in my system. The officer who tested me was a 28-year veteran of the prison and well-known by the inmates. I had heard that if you tell this officer there are drugs in your system (*dirty*) before he tests, he will let you go. So, I thought I would give it a try.

I told the officer I was dirty before he administered the UA. The officer responded, *"Well, let's see what you are dirty for."* The next thing I knew, we were in the bathroom together, and I was pissing in a cup. When the instant results came back, he listed the drugs found and told me the line for marijuana was so faint that he was going to omit that one. He took the cup to the Lt.'s office to send my test to the lab for verification. I had already destroyed the sample by contaminating it with bleach. I soaked my sweatpants' strings in bleach before taking the UA test. I let the string fall into the cup while urinating, contaminating the sample—another bad idea.

Third Time

For the third time, Lt. BK served me with a 100-series shot; another 112 shot, *"use of any narcotics, marijuana, drugs, alcohol, intoxicants, or related substances."* As I read the shot, I noticed a few errors, but the obvious one was my name changed to GN halfway through the report. I didn't say anything, and the guards took me to the SHU again. Luckily, this time, I was given a 2-day warning by a friendly guard and used that time to prepare. I can't say what I did for safety reasons, but let's just say I lived 'comfortably' in the SHU this time. My team placed me in a cell with GN, who had received a shot months ago but was just now sent to the SHU. Shots were not supposed to be served that late. It was starting to become clear that there was a large gap between what was *supposed* to happen and what took place; in practice, our reality is defined by how the guards feel at any given moment. If the staff feels like doing things by the book, they will, but if they don't, they won't. GN and I were on the bottom floor, in a corner cell in the SHU. GN got his shot expunged and left after six days in the SHU. Before GN left, I showed him how the report changed my last name, Hancock, to 'GN.' We agreed this shot would be easy to beat with the error. I've seen shots thrown out before, so I was not worried about it.

After GN, an old friend of mine, Sonic, from Coleman Medium, became my SHU-celly. Sonic and I chilled out in the SHU for another three weeks, and he explained why he was there. Sonic had gotten the paperwork from the SIS to drop out of a gang officially. It did not matter to me that Sonic was in a gang because he never bothered me with any of that stuff. Sonic warned me when he moved into my cell that the gang factor could come into play later; he was right about that. The head of the gang, PR, was put in the SHU on the same block. PR constantly shouted derogatory names at Sonic, saying he was a no-good traitor, etc. Eventually, PR was let out of the SHU, but Sonic opted to stay in, away from the gang and PR. Sonic is still voluntarily in the SHU as of this writing.

Sonic loved to read, and so did I. He recommended many good books, and one series stuck with me: *Shogun*. When I got out of the SHU, I asked my mom to get the Shogun book series and started reading the first book. It looks like it will be a great series, but I don't have much time to read during the week with my work schedule. I have read many book series while in prison but didn't read at all before prison. Now I find it enjoyable.

The SHU is always about deprivation and the mental strength to survive. This time was no different, except we were fed a little bit more this time; not enough to get full, but enough to survive.

My day to see the DHO finally arrived, and a guard took me to the office in the SHU. I was seated when they started reading my sanctions. No one said anything about the two names, so I politely interrupted and said, *"Excuse me, ma'am, my name isn't GN."* She said, *"What?"* I replied, *"My name isn't GN, ma'am."* For a moment, she paused to look at the shot again and finally saw what I meant. She glanced at the Lieutenant and said, *"He's right. Alright, dismissed."* I was returned to my SHU cell and released within a day or two. Once I was released for the third time, I was placed back on the B2 wing, in cell 434, where I still am as of this writing. I had no celly for the first two weeks out of the SHU, which was terrific but cannot last long. I got a celly I had met before named JS. He used to work in the warehouse in the kitchen, but JS was a sex offender. I went to my counselor, clearly upset, asking why he put a sex offender in my cell. The counselor told me JS was an excellent celly and would be a good fit. I still don't understand how he came to that conclusion, but JS has been okay. I was on the bottom bunk and organized the room to our mutual liking. Our room was in the back corner of the dorm, which was a great spot because the guards got to us last.

We had 3 or 4 fire drills while we were in this cell. The guards kicked everyone out of their cells and put us in the recreation yard so they could inspect our cells. They often use the pretense of a fire drill to raid the cells and find contraband. JS and I made it through multiple fire drills with no problems because we don't do anything in our cells except smoke cigarettes.

When I left the SHU this time, I got my kitchen job back in the same crummy line position. I asked my boss why I hadn't progressed to a better job in the kitchen even though I had been working there for almost a year. He said he doesn't trust me because I keep getting taken to the SHU, which messes up the schedule for at least a few weeks--another price for going to the SHU.

Waiting Transfer

After I finished writing this chapter, I was sent to the SHU twice more. First for smoking cigarettes, that's a 300-series shot, not a big deal. Specifically, the commanding officer charged me with shot *332: Smoking where prohibited*. Since this was only a 300-series shot, I only stayed in the SHU for about two weeks but fate did not save me from the DHO this time. Instead, the commanding officer read the following sanctions:

    -No visits with family for one month
    -No commissary purchases for one month
    -Minus 2 weeks of *good time*.

The next time was for possession of drugs, another bad 100-series shot. The DHO was pissed and gave the following sanctions:

    -Increased points to medium-security level.
    -Reduced *good time* by 6 weeks.
    -Reduced commissary
    -No computer for 6 months

I'm in the holding facility waiting to be transferred to a medium security prison. I feel so low because I DON'T KNOW HOW TO STAY CLEAN in this environment. I was fired from my kitchen job for too many absences, I'm still in the MAT program, and I'm still addicted to drugs. I know I need to find a way not to be addicted to drugs, but in this highly stressful environment, I haven't got a clue how to accomplish that feat. I have not been sober since I was 16 years old. Under the current circumstances, I do not feel optimistic about my prospects for the future; I'm scared. Will I leave prison in 12-15 years still addicted to drugs? How will I survive on the outside? Will my parents still be alive? How will I get a job? Will I understand how to use technology in 2036? Will I ever have my own family? The list goes on and on.

Prison Life for Family

The first time I visited Scott in county jail was the first time I had ever set foot inside any detention facility. There were strict rules about taking nothing back to the visitation cubes, but those were unnecessary since human contact was impossible. We were each in a small cube, separated by walls and a thick glass barrier, communicating using a phone with a cord so short it would not reach my face. There was never any physical contact, making it impossible to hug my son for *two and a half* long years. During those years, we were all scared, confused, and devastated beyond any possible words. I spent the first year and a half crying. On one hand, I was relieved Scott was in a place where he could not harm himself, or so I thought. I knew he had to be stopped, or he would overdose on fentanyl soon; of course, Scott was 29 and beyond my control. Paul and I were naïve enough to believe we could have Scott held accountable for using fentanyl by being placed in a long-term rehabilitation facility for as long as necessary. The very idea is laughable now.

First, there is no such thing as a federal long-term rehabilitation facility. Second, the defendant has no say in the charges; that is up to the prosecutor. Finally, being an addict makes that person an easy target for prosecutors who know they will be unable to defend themselves. We did not realize that our vulnerable son would be eaten alive by the system, and we held onto hope until the last minute when the gavel came down, and the judge said the sentence was 20 years. The judge shattered our hope for compassion, and our pain was worse knowing a great injustice had been done; Scott was incapable of being a dealer.

I began a letter-writing campaign to Congressmen, Senators, the Attorney General, and even the President. I received form-letter responses and campaign ads in return. At the same time, I began educating myself on all things related to DIH charges. The education took longer than expected because I had to learn new terminology to understand the legal documents and parse the laws.

In 2021, Scott was moved to FCI Coleman-Medium security prison, and those visits were *much* different than visits to the county jail. Approval for visits began with getting my name on a list. After approval, I started in-person visits. Instead of a 90-minute drive, the drive was about 6-7 hours and required an overnight stay in a hotel. The next noticeable differences were the security presence and the rules. Armed guards were everywhere, and each visitor was subject to inspection. Visitors are required to adhere to a strict dress code, including which colors are acceptable to wear. The one positive: I finally got to hug my son before and after each visit. I finally felt a little bit more complete.

I was turned away from my second visit to Coleman because I wore sandals—the whole trip and expense were wasted, and I went home without seeing Scott. I had not realized that closed-toe shoes were required year-round. It was not the last time I would be turned away from the prison. With COVID-19 in full swing, last-minute lockdowns became the norm. Notices were never posted online or communicated to families in any format; this holds for all federal BOP institutions.

While Scott was in FCI Coleman-Medium, I produced a 4-part podcast titled *The Criminalization of Addiction*. I posted it on all the major sites, such as Apple Podcasts, Google Podcasts, YouTube, etc. The *Novel Research in Sciences* journal accepted for publication a paper I wrote titled *For a Motive of Kindness…20 Years in Federal Prison*.[295] I sent the article to everyone I could think of in the criminal justice arena. Nothing seemed to generate any helpful attention or gain any traction with the people in control of our son's life. There were no responses to the podcast or the published paper.

---

[295] Hancock, G.D. (2023). For a Motive of Kindness…20 years in Federal Prison. *Novel Research in Sciences*, Vol. 13, No. 3, (February), pp. 1-12.

In January 2023, the BOP moved Scott to USP Atlanta, which cut the travel time by 1 hour. The security situation in Atlanta is the same as in Coleman, except the Atlanta facilities are not designed to accommodate visitors; there is not enough physical space in the 'check-in' room to process more than six people at a time. It has become part of my routine to visit Scott monthly and arrive early for visits. Whether it is a beautiful day or cold or rainy, the wait outside usually lasts an hour or two, depending on when the guards arrive to unlock the doors. I mindlessly go through security, removing my shoes and anything in my pockets, then wait for others to do the same. Security takes 45 minutes to an hour, depending on how many guards are available. We walk through a breezeway to an elevator, and all squeeze in to ride down three floors to the visitation area where I can hug my son and see his face, and I realize it is all worth it. His face lights up, and my heart warms for about 4 hours. Then I leave and drive home, thinking of my son and how to help him with his addiction. Those are the good visits.

Other visits do not go as smoothly. Once, my bra set off the walk-through security alarm, and a considerable hassle ensued. Another time, I visited on Mother's Day, thinking all visitors were welcome, only to be turned away to drive 6 hours back home. Rather than provide a list of heartbreaking attempts to see my son, suffice it to say that seeing him every month is close to impossible, and it is not because I do not drive to see him. So far, there has never been a whole year that I have seen him every month.

In the summer of 2023, I received an email invitation to attend the second conference of the *2023 Sentencing Reform Summit* in Washington, DC. My name was included by a drug reform advocate who had read my published paper. Paul and I flew to Washington, DC, in mid-October of 2023 to attend the Summit. The Summit attendees were prosecutors, judges, defense attorneys, and legal reform advocates, totaling about 500 people. We told our son's story to as many people as possible, and I passed out a few copies of my paper, including one to Collette Peters and another to the head of the USSC.

The most insightful conversations I had were with the federal defenders. I did not realize that they are very well educated in the ways of federal prosecutors. I asked a federal defender how he felt about having a job, knowing he would lose to the prosecutor every time. He told me his job was not about winning but getting the best deal possible from the prosecutor. That is the most realistic approach one can hope for in the federal criminal justice system.

Perhaps our most surprising interactions were with the *Aleph Alliance for Jewish Renewal members*. I have never met people with such peace and love in their hearts.

I found a contact from the Summit, 'Dave,' at the BOP, who could answer many of my questions. I told him about Scott's charge and how he was not a dealer. We spoke about the prosecutor's [mis]conduct and the evidence we had of the dealer in TG's case. Dave told me I could do nothing because the justice system did not care about Scott's guilt or innocence; we were now crystal clear on this point. Dave informed us that coming forward with an attorney would likely result in the prosecutor withdrawing Scott's plea deal. Withdrawing the plea deal would put the two additional felony charges back on the table. He told me there are many schemes to get people to spend money in hopes of freeing their loved ones from federal prison; he also told me they fail. For federal inmates, success must come through the prosecutor and the judge; no side deals or 'good' attorneys can free a federal prisoner without the prosecutor's cooperation.

Paul and I have reluctantly accepted the fact that Scott will be in prison for at least another 12 years, 15 if he loses all his good time. While I have come to terms with the reality of my son's imprisonment, I am not at peace because justice was not served. There is no justice in charging an addict with a crime he is incapable of committing.

One person cannot change the way the criminal justice system treats people with an addiction, so I have joined the many advocates calling for judicial reform. One group, **FIRST-Network**, is a group of individuals with loved ones incarcerated in federal prisons. *FIRST* stands for *Federal Inmates Requesting Sanctioned Treatment*. The FIRST-Network group collects data from inmates on various issues, such as prison conditions, to encourage the federal BOP to follow their existing rules. Although it has happened to Scott many times, I was shocked to learn that so many federal inmates define their problem as hunger. **Table 8.1.** Lists the top 10 prison conditions that cause excessive stress for inmates listed in order from 'most frequent' complaint to 'least frequent.' There were over 25 conditions listed by inmates and families as unacceptable.

Table 8.1. Federal Prison Conditions
Excessive Lockdowns
Temperature. Freezing or heat stroke
Visitation problems
Inadequate Health Care
Not enough food-hungry
Mail problems
Commanding officers do not follow rules/use extreme force/abuse of power
Building Conditions/Code Compliance-raw sewage, leaky roof, no power, mold
Case Manager-never there
Commanding officers forging names, withholding important papers, refusing to put full HWH, race-baiting, planting evidence
Source: FIRST-Network, 2024.

Recently, I visited the St. Louis Zoo with my family. We learned about the expert veterinarians from around the world who are there to care for the animals, the specialized habitats carefully constructed to resemble home, the variety of diets, and the massive budget. How is it that society cares so much about animals but can leave human beings to starve and suffer daily abuse without a thought?

Summary

Scott's stories of his time in prison show a practicing addict who has not been 'helped' by the criminal justice system. His entire story consists of obtaining drugs, using them, and being punished for them. Scott's story is not one of success; it is one of heartbreaking failure. I recently learned that fentanyl is coming into the prison system. The most likely outcome for my son, *whether in prison or not*, is death by overdose. The justice system has criminalized Scott and other addicts to *death*.

Addiction is further criminalized and punished in prison by assigning the highest level of sanctions, the same as for murder, against drug use. Under the current set of circumstances, if Scott survives, he will likely serve his entire sentence because there is no help for his addiction in prison.

The irony of prison, by Susan Zalatan

We want them to be responsible
So, we take away all responsibility

We want them to be positive and constructive
So, we degrade them and make them useless

We want them to be trustworthy
So, we put them where there is no trust
We want them to be nonviolent
So, we surround them with violence

We want them to be kind and loving
So, we subject them to cruelty and hatred.

We want them to quit being the tough guy
So, we put them where only the 'tough guy' survives

We want them to quit exploiting us
So, we put them in cages where they exploit each other

We want them to take control of their lives
So, we make them dependent on us

We want them to be part of our community
So, we separate them and lock them away

We want them to have self-worth
So, we treat them like animals and
Call it 'corrections.'

APPENDIX 8B
Prison Levels

Below is a good description of the various prion security levels, copied from the *Prison Professor's* website.[296] The number of points for male inmates is shown in parentheses.

USP High-Security Prisons (Males 24+ Points)
High-security prisons are *United States Penitentiaries* (USPs), the most violent federal prisons. Typically, federal prisoners who serve inside a USP have an extensive history of violence. Inside a USP, you will find gangs, organized crime, and a heavy concentration of psychotic people who exist without any expectation of living a normal life as law-abiding citizens. Because of sentencing laws that punish people extensively for high-dollar crimes, a relatively small percentage of people on the compound will be serving time for white-collar crimes. All prisoners in a federal penitentiary will share common areas.

Culture: Federal prisoners live by a code different from the outside world. The daily environment is filled with high levels of violence, manipulation, extortion, and altercations. Federal inmates serving time inside of USPs are militant and stubbornly resistant to authority. Many are serving life sentences and feel they have nothing else to lose. Violence is a constant in a USP.

Quarters: Federal prisoners in USPs usually share a closet-size cell with at least one other prisoner. The cells are tiny. If a man outstretches his arms in a penitentiary cell, he will touch both walls. The room will contain a metal bunk bed, a metal toilet, and a metal sink. A heavy deadbolt will lock the steel door for most of every day.

Structure of the Day: Penitentiary doors will unlock at 6:00 a.m. Inmates may then move to the chow hall for breakfast or have limited access to the recreation yard. At 7:30, the federal prisoners will either report to work, report to a program, or they will return to their cell for a lockdown period.

---

[296] This content was copied in-full from, *Prison Professors*
https://www.federalprisontime.com/federal-prison-security-levels

Because of high levels of violence in the penitentiary, prisoners confined to USPs spend a lot of time locked in their cells. Sometimes, they are on "lockdown" for weeks at a time.

Leisure Time: Strict rules and schedules restrict all movement in a USP. The environment is borderline tribal, with varying factions of federal inmates influencing activities inside. Leisure time is not a given.

Violence and Volatility: Federal inmates serving in USP will witness routine violence, including the use of inmate-created weapons, such as knives, blunt instruments, pipes, and clubs. There is a high concentration of predatory, unstable individuals living in a USP; it is the worst possible place to serve time.

FCI Medium-Security Prisons (Males 16-23 Points)

Federal Correctional Institutions (FCIs) are the designation for medium-security, low-security, and camp prison sites. The medium-security prisons confine inmates from all backgrounds and with all types of sentence lengths. Most of the people who serve time inside a medium-security FCI will have extensive criminal histories, and many will serve sentences of more than 30 years. All FCIs will include a population of offenders who serve sentences for sophisticated criminal activity.

Culture: A medium-security FCI will be less violent than a USP. They will confine between 800 and 2,000 people. Primarily, average sentence lengths will span between 10 and 30 years, although some people in medium-security FCIs will serve life sentences. The institutions will have lower levels of violence, gang activities, and volatility, though those levels will still be too high for comfort. As in the penitentiary, the atmosphere squashes hope for many.

Quarters: Prisoners in medium-security FCIs will live in housing units similar to the cells in a USP. Small cells will include metal bunk beds, a metal toilet, and a metal sink. A heavy deadbolt will lock the steel door for most of every day, but prisoners in an FCI will have more free time outside of their room than prisoners in a USP. If the room has a window, bars will cover it, and opaque glass will prevent the prisoner from being able to look outside. The windows will not open. Prisoners must keep all possessions inside a small metal locker.

Structure of the Day: Same as high-security prisons, except inmates have more time outside their cells than in high-security prisons.

Leisure Time: Like high-security prisons except the environment is less tribal.

Violence and Volatility: Prisoners in a medium-security FCI will see and hear about violence regularly, though not daily as in the USP.

FCI Low-Security Prison (Males 12-15 points)

Low-security prisons are also known as Federal Correctional Institutions. They confine federal prisoners from all backgrounds. Federal inmates in low-security FCIs do not have extensive, documented criminal histories; if they have a history of violent behavior, several years have passed since the last documented act of violence. Prison administrators are known to (often) make classification errors, leading to confining violent individuals in low-security institutions. Frequently, white-collar offenders who are well-educated are confined in low-security prisons. Federal inmates will serve time inside a low-security prison for many reasons.

Culture: A low-security prison will be less volatile than a medium- or high-security prison. Population levels will hold between 1,000 and 2,500 federal inmates. All prisoners in a low-security FCI will be within 20 years of their scheduled release date. There will be few organized disturbances, and gang activity will not likely intrude into the lives of non-gang members. Most federal inmates serving time inside a low-security FCI focus on their release date and staying out of further trouble. If a federal inmate has been convicted of a sex offense, or if the individual has a history of cooperating with authorities, the individual will face challenges from staff and inmates.

Quarters: Inmates in low-security FCIs live in open dormitories. Bathrooms are in a common area, under the "open" plan. Federal inmates live near each other, and there is minimal privacy, but there is also an absence of being locked in a cell.

Structure of the Day: Same as medium-security prisons, except inmates have higher levels of freedom within the institution's boundaries.

Leisure Time: In a low-security FCI, federal inmates can supposedly govern their lives in ways geared towards personal growth. Inmates may request access to the recreation yard and education area, participate in table games in the housing unit, or watch television in a designated area.
Violence and Volatility: Inmates in a low-security FCI face fewer instances of violence than inmates in higher-security prisons. It is unusual for prisoners in a low-security FCI to gather and riot or form an orchestrated disturbance. There are exceptions, but incidences of violence in low-security prisons are sporadic and disorganized.

FCI Camp (Males 0-11 Points)

Minimum-security camps hold federal inmates who are within ten years of their release dates, do not have documented histories of violence, and do not have any record of escape attempts. FCI camps may hold federal prisoners who started at a higher-security prison. Most white-collar offenders spend their time inside minimum-security camps. The population inside minimum-security camps generally has a higher educational level.

Culture: The focus in the camp will be on returning home; someone is released almost every day. Many inmates voluntarily surrendered to campsites, suggesting that authorities perceived them as people who could be trusted. The low level of security causes administrators to experience a significant issue with the introduction of contraband. The high levels of contraband can be extremely tempting for inmates in minimum-security camps.

Quarters: Same as low-security prisons.

Structure of the Day: In a minimum-security camp, there will not be any locked doors within the housing unit. Sometimes, the unit will remain unlocked throughout the night, allowing the inmates fresh air. Inmates have minimal restrictions on their ability to move around the camp.

Leisure Time: Same as low-security prison with more leisure time allowed.
Violence and Volatility: Prisoners in a minimum-security camp should not worry about organized violence.

www.ingramcontent.com/pod-product-compliance
Lightning Source LLC
Chambersburg PA
CBHW020456030426
42337CB00011B/129